MW00340408

GANGSTERS AND ORGANIZED CRIME IN
BUFFALO

GANGSTERS AND ORGANIZED CRIME IN
BUFFALO

HISTORY, HITS AND HEADQUARTERS

MICHAEL F. RIZZO

THE
History
PRESS

Published by The History Press
Charleston, SC 29403
www.historypress.net

Front cover: top, left to right: private collection, author's collection, *New York Daily News; bottom*:
Library of Congress.
Back cover: top: Ontario Daily Report/Inland Valley Daily Bulletin; bottom: courtesy of Sharon Manning.

First published 2012
Second printing 2012
Third printing 2012
Fourth printing 2012
Fifth printing 2012
Sixth printing 2013

ISBN 978.1.60949.564.0

Library of Congress CIP data applied for.

This book is dedicated to two Gerlandos in my life. First, my son, for missing time with me while I wrote this, and second, my grandfather, who left Sicily to escape the Mafia.

CONTENTS

CONTENTS

PREFACE

The idea for this book started sometime in the early 2000s. I vaguely recall an old girlfriend telling me that she was somehow related to Stefano Magaddino, the grand old mob boss of western New York, and that there was a book about him. So I decided to look for it. I checked the library and scoured the Internet but found nothing. Not a single book written about the Buffalo Mafia. So I decided I'd write it.

I began gathering newspaper articles from microfilm and looking through scrapbooks in the library. Along the way, I stumbled across information about all these 1920s gangsters, mainly of Polish descent, and copied those too. As life would have it, I wasn't ready to write the Mafia book. Everything went aside, and I worked on another project.

Eventually, I made my way back. In 2007, I sold my delivery business and wanted to get involved in something else. My wife and I decided we would start a tour business based on Niagara Falls mob spots, and the Mob Tours was born. Unfortunately, Niagara Falls wasn't quite ready for a bus tour of crime sights, and two years later, we added walking tours in Buffalo.

Along the way, we accumulated over three hundred Mafia books, hundreds more articles, thousands of pages of Federal Bureau of Investigation (FBI) documents and even the complete court file from the Magaddinos' 1968 arrests after traveling to New York City. We searched deed and business records, historical and library files and more, all to get the most accurate picture of this history and the people involved. At least a dozen people were contacted, including former FBI agents. Many had already passed away, but some were still alive, although I found, even in retirement, that they are not at liberty to discuss past cases.

In late 2011, I sent a proposal for this book to The History Press, and they were interested, as it was similar to other books they had done. Now all I had to do was take the thousands of pages of information and put together a book—in less than six months.

I need to thank quite a few people who were very helpful in putting this book together. Thanks go out to: Lieutenant Mike Kaska of the Buffalo Police Department, who has a great website of Buffalo police and crime history; Sharon Ippolito Manning, Jimmy Manganello and Joe DiCarlo's granddaughter for sharing family photos; the countless folks who have provided insight into the lives of some of the people found in this book; Michael Tona for his wealth of knowledge on the Buffalo Mafia; Daniel DiLandro, college archivist and Special Collections librarian at Buffalo State College; Jon Black from gangrule.com and the Cheektowaga Historical Society for use of their photos; the amazing website fultonhistory.org, a treasure-trove of newspaper articles and a huge help in searching old stories; Ron Fino for his insight and correcting some history; former *Buffalo News* reporter Anthony Cardinale for his photo; Harvey Garrett for leading me to some other photos; and Edward J. Dombkiewicz for clearing up some family history.

Also thanks to one of my oldest friends, Gilbert Neal. He is a fantastic musician, and can be found at www.gilbertneal.com.

And, as always, thank you to my wonderful wife, Michelle, and my son, who saw little of me for several months while I put this book to bed.

Many of the stories you are about to read involve violent and deadly criminal activities. Personally, I don't condone them; I am just piecing together history. Every major city in America has had its share of violent criminals, and their stories have been told, which is why I do this. It is history. I apologize if you see or read about a relative or friend, but once again, most of this was reported in newspapers, on television and in books and magazines, and a lot is on the Internet.

Finally, a woman named Meg Henderson Wade contacted me in 2009 to tell me she had dated Stefano Magaddino's grandson, also named Stefano, in Atlanta for over three years in the 1980s. When he told her his grandfather was the "Don of Buffalo," she said, "Oh, you mean his first name is Donald?" She had never heard of the *Godfather* and was quite surprised when she did some research at the Atlanta library and found out the "Don" was actually Don Stefano.

I hope you enjoy reading the book as much as I did writing it.

PROLOGUE

Never call nobody from your house! Listen here! No use a your name on the
telephone. We're in hot water.[1]
—Stefano Magaddino, November 8, 1962

G angster. Just reading the word, you probably have a picture in your
head. The typical image of a well-dressed man in a suit and hat is the
obvious thought. The definition of a gangster is simply "a criminal who is
a member of a gang. Some gangs are considered to be part of organized
crime, and gangsters are also called mobsters."[2]

From the 1920s through the 1930s, the gangster developed into a persona
that most people recognize today—John Dillinger, Al Capone and so on.
They all had monikers, either given by the police or the press: "Baby Face,"
"Pretty Boy," "Millionaire Kid." At the same time, Hollywood helped to
shape what a typical gangster would look like. The late 1920s saw several
gangster films released, and in 1930, one of the biggest, *Little Caesar*, starring
Edward G. Robinson, created a character that people recognize: the "fame,
respectability and wealth,"[3] the rise in power and eventual downfall.

In 1972, another film changed how the world perceived mobsters and
how mobsters saw themselves. *The Godfather*, with its star-studded cast, made
the life of a mobster seem glamorous and dangerous. Mafioso watched it
and started to imitate the movie. The kissing of the Godfather's ring was not
something that happened in real life prior to the movie, but mobsters and the
wannabes around them all fawned over the movie.

There are few photos of Stefano Magaddino available, and this is a rare one of the smiling Mafia leader. He looks like he could be anyone's grandpa. *Courtesy* New York Daily News.

In western New York, the pattern of gangsters and mobsters was similar to the national scene. During most of the 1920s and 1930s, criminals certainly fell into the gangster category, and although this is a "gangster guide," suffice it to say that many of the people in the book are nothing more than common criminals. Some definitely had Mafia ties, since the local boss Stefano Magaddino would never have let money slip through his hands without taking a cut.

The Mafia, as it is discussed in this book, is the crime family headed by Magaddino from 1922 until 1974, when he died. He was aware of and his family played some part in almost everything crime-related that went on in western New York during that time.

Now, you must realize that no one was actually ever convicted of being a member of the Mafia. Some were convicted of gambling, armed robbery, bank robbery, burglary, loan-sharking, narcotics dealing, murder and other nefarious crimes, but the Mafia was a clandestine organization.

Buffalo's Mafia "family," as it is called throughout this book, consisted of only about 150 members at its peak. So we can safely assume that everyone written about in this book was not necessarily a member of the Mafia. Even Magaddino was called a "reputed" mob leader for many years, although the preponderance of evidence suggests otherwise.

There are multiple different names that the Mafia is known by, and in this book, they are used interchangeably. "La Cosa Nostra" is a term that was believed to be "fabricated" by the FBI after Director J. Edgar Hoover failed to warn the public about the Mafia. Through an informant in 1961, it was originally thought to be *Causa Nostra*, translated as "Our Cause," but FBI translators opted for *Cosa Nostra*, "Our Thing" or "This Thing of Ours."[4] Television mobster Tony Soprano often spoke of "this thing of ours."

At times it was called the syndicate, Italian secret society, underworld and organized crime. It was known, but its extent was not. All the names point to the same group: the Mafia, primarily Sicilian in nature but always deadly, powerful and secretive.

There are stories and there is folklore. Over the years, there have been many people who have been thought to be tied to organized crime, but without any evidence, it is all hearsay. A former Buffalo mayor is one of them. The mayor grew up in the same West Side neighborhood as many mob members, but association by neighborhood does not mean that he was involved. There is nothing pointing to him meeting with mob guys or doing anything illegal or corrupt.

Judge Sebastian Bellomo of Buffalo often met with members of the Buffalo mob for lunch or dinner and was mentioned often in discussions that were caught on FBI wiretaps, but no wrongdoing was ever uncovered. State Assemblyman Steve Greco actually got caught up in the life. In 1984, he was arrested along with several Buffalo mobsters, including Pasquale Natarelli and his nephew John, trying to defraud New York State out of $250,000 for an AIDS research grant.[5] Former Buffalo mayor Steven Pankow had his corruption problems,[6] and there are unconfirmed rumors regarding other activities.

There is also a wealth of anecdotal stories from hospital workers, meter readers, relatives of fringe people and, of course, police officers. The following are some of those stories.

A former gas company meter reader who worked "Mafia Row" in Lewiston, where Magaddino and his three daughters lived, said he was told when he went to Magaddino's house to walk in, read the meter, not look around and get out. He said the house was full of beautiful art and statues from the old country.

In the movie *The Godfather*, there is a tense scene where Michael Corleone is at the empty hospital where his father is sick in bed. Men are coming to kill him, so Michael rolls the bed into another room and prepares for the showdown. A man was working at Niagara Falls Medical Center in the 1960s when an eerily similar incident took place.

Stefano Magaddino was in the hospital, and a man arrived and asked what room he was in. The man was seen walking around with his coat slung over his arm, like he was hiding a gun underneath it. The police were called but did not arrive quickly enough, and the man disappeared. So they moved Magaddino and swapped his body with a cadaver. Eventually, the man was cornered in a stairwell by some of Magaddino's men, and when he lifted his coat, there was no gun. It turned out he was there to pay his respects and was simply looking for the aged Don.

There are other stories about tunnels hidden under the city of Buffalo and Niagara Falls. A tunnel supposedly led from Magaddino's home in Niagara Falls under the street as an escape route. Another escape tunnel led from his Lewiston home to the LaDuca home next door or to the woods. There was also a supposed tunnel leading from the Magaddino Funeral Home, under several buildings, right to the Capitol Coffee Shop on the corner. If that was the case, the FBI would have never seen the men walking back and forth from the funeral home to the coffee shop, as they often did. An employee of the water department confirmed no knowledge of known tunnels.

Another story has been gaining steam lately about Al Capone having a stake in Buffalo's booze pipeline to Canada and the former Town Casino downtown. During the time this would have taken place, Magaddino was a very powerful mob boss, equal in standing to Capone, if not more powerful because of his Sicilian lineage. The chance that Capone came to Buffalo and either owned a part of the Town Casino or ran booze through Buffalo without Magaddino's permission would have been impossible. It is *possible* that he came here to visit a couple times maybe, as Buffalo was small potatoes compared to Chicago.

A man was looking to open a saloon in the 1950s and was having a hard time getting his liquor license. After several months, he decided to pay a visit to Don Stefano. Two weeks after the visit, he received his license. The only stipulation Magaddino made was that the man had to purchase his liquor through Magaddino's company, Power City Distributing. One hand washes the other.

A family purchased a house a block from Dana Drive in Lewiston in the late 1960s. Shortly after moving in, they noticed a car parked in front of their house several times, but no one got out. It turned out that Magaddino had the house watched to see who the new owners were and make sure they were not involved in law enforcement, as he did not want anyone too close to him. As it was, when he had private meetings at his home, the street was blocked off at both ends, and only those invited or who lived on the street were allowed in.

The biggest story out of Niagara Falls involved Magaddino's cousin and Brooklyn mob boss Joe Bonanno. In 1964, on the eve of testifying before a grand jury in New York, Bonanno disappeared. Word on the street was that he had been kidnapped by Stefano. In Niagara Falls, there are people who say he was kept in an apartment above a barbershop or at the family farm in rural Cambria, New York. You'll have to read the chapter on Bonanno to see what probably did happen.

Lastly, the family who purchased the LaDuca home said they did their due diligence to see if there was any money left behind, hidden in secret compartments or in the walls. Alas, they found none.

The final chapter in the book is really what this whole book is about. That is where all the addresses are. Hundreds of them. You can take the book, go for a drive and see where people lived or where an incident occurred.

There are dozens, if not hundreds, more stories, and on the following pages, you will find quite a few of them.

THE GANGSTER ERA

THE BLONDE BANDIT

*Just say anything you want, but before anyone else comes here to talk to me I wish
they'd give me back my lipstick.*[7]
—*Sally Joyce Richards after her arrest*

She was known as Montgomery Mabel, Mabel Paller, Sally Joyce
Richards. Her age was unknown, believed to be anywhere from sixteen
to twenty-three. Police called them the Gold Band Gang. Newspapers called
her the Blonde Bandit. They were all those things, but in the end, they were
just common criminals.

Sally, whose real name was Amelia Randaronic, snuck into the United
States from Hamilton, Ontario, in 1928 at thirteen years of age and joined
a circus. She became a moll in Buffalo gangs and is believed to have shared
in the spoils of scores of jobs.

The first sign of the girl and her gang occurred on Wednesday, November
6, 1929, when the "well-dressed and unassuming man and woman" entered
the Reliable Jewelry & Loan Company on Seneca Street. He wore a "gray
top coat and a gray cap." She was "fairly well-dressed, slender, blonde, and
right pretty."[8] They would later be identified as Peter Dombkiewicz and
Sally Joyce Richards. Dombkiewicz, twenty-one, well known to Buffalo
police, was first arrested in November 1924 on juvenile delinquency charges.

"The girl…asked that she be shown an engagement ring." The man then
asked to see a wedding ring. Store owner Max Kantrowitz bent over to
render the ring from a tray, and when he looked up, he was gazing into the

muzzle of two revolvers. The man ordered him to raise his hands, and the girl smiled. They then grabbed a tray of jewelry from the safe and ran from the store to their waiting Nash Coupe.

Their stolen car was found on Walden Avenue with bullet holes in the windshield and body, and "the seat and floor were stained with blood."[9]

All was quiet until December 28, when Dombkiewicz and Edward Samuels spent the night robbing a butcher shop, three gasoline stations, a Deco restaurant and topping off the evening at the meat market of Frank Smigiera, where the owner's son Leo pushed a shotgun through a door and blew Samuels's face off. Dombkiewicz escaped without any cash—but with his life.[10]

In 1930, Glickstein Jewelers at 1159 Broadway in Buffalo was robbed of $20,000 in jewels by Sally Joyce Richards, the Blonde Bandit. This is the location today. *Photo by author.*

The next major job they participated in was on January 20, 1930, when Dombkiewicz, Sally and Eddie Izzydorczak robbed Morris A. Katzman, owner of the Emkay Boot Shop, of seventy-five dollars and women's shoes.[11] A few days later, they robbed Anthony Kuland's furnishing store of fifteen dollars and left.[12]

The trio hit the jackpot on Monday, January 27, when they robbed the David L. Glickstein Jewelry Store on Broadway of $20,000 ($252,165 in 2010 dollars) in diamonds. "Buffalo's blonde bandit queen, the brains and motive power of a gang of jewel thieves, strikes again today, and got her biggest haul."[13]

The trio escaped in a stolen auto. On February 10, 1930, they were arrested in Montgomery, Alabama.[14] It was the "longest automobile chase the Buffalo [Police Department] has staged."[15] A total of $10,000 in gems was recovered from their baggage.

Izzydorczak pled guilty to the Glickstein robbery, and Dombkiewicz admitted to participating in sixty-four burglaries.[16] As the trial was set to start, Dombkiewicz pled guilty in hopes of saving Sally.

Dombkiewicz took the stand in her defense and said that he had forced Sally to participate. "I told her if she didn't obey me I'd shoot her like I had two fellows. And I'd have done it too."[17]

During Sally's testimony, love-struck Dombkiewicz sat brooding in the courtroom just feet away from jeweler David Glickstein. When her testimony ended, Dombkiewicz lunged at Glickstein, yelling, "That's how I treat squealers!"[18] and slashed the jeweler's throat with a razor he had hidden up his sleeve.

The next day, Sally was sentenced to twenty years to life in prison, Dombkiewicz received life and Izzydorczak, who was twenty-one years old, received fifteen years to life. After hearing her sentence, Sally asked the judge if she could speak.

"Is there any way I can marry Petey? I love him, God knows I love him. I've had two children by him already, and only lately lost a third isn't there some way I can marry him?"[19] The judge responded that she could not.

Sally didn't appreciate life in prison, so just about a month later, she attempted to escape with another prisoner. They made it as far as the prison yard before the night watchman spotted them, and they were captured before making good their escape.[20]

After the attempted escape, Sally's mother made a last-ditch effort to have her released, claiming she was not yet sixteen years old.[21] Only part of the story appears to be true. She was not released.

In December 1938, after serving nearly ten years of her sentence, Sally had her sentence commuted by New York governor Herbert Lehman. Reports say she was twenty-three at the time, but her actual age is unknown.[22]

Peter was paroled and lived in Rochester after his release. His name came up several times over the years. Peter Dombkiewicz, fifty-five, of Rochester pleaded innocent to possession of burglar's instruments after being arrested for robbing a Lockport drugstore in July 1964.[23] It is believed he died in 1976.

Information about Sally's life after prison is unknown.

THE KORNEY GANG

Well, bootlegging is not like holding up or robbing people.[24]
—*John "Korney" Kwiatkowski*

Although Italians seem to dominate the gangster headlines, back in the days of Prohibition, Buffalo's Polish community offered gangsters as bold, dangerous and trigger-happy as any gangster to ever come out of Buffalo. Possibly the most notorious were the members of the Korney Gang, led by six-foot-tall, blond-haired John Kwiatkowski Jr. He gained the nickname "Korney" and grew up on the streets of Buffalo's East Side during World War I. By the time he was old enough, he was following in his father's shoes as a baker, but unlike his father, he had much bigger aspirations.

Mug shot of John "Korney" Kwiatkowski, a ruthless Polish gangster in Buffalo. *Private collection.*

Korney was a bootlegger and holdup artist. He ran a small gang of hoods that included Stephen "Bolly" Ziolkowski, Zygmund "Ziggy" Plocharski, Joe Kornacki and Victor Chojnicki. They did the usual robberies and petty crime until Korney met Anthony Kalkiewicz, who was older by almost ten years. Kalkiewicz was street tough but not very smart.

Kalkiewicz and his gang—Lawrence Trimpa, Joseph Bartkowiak and Edward Larkman—did a lot of the same type of jobs, but Kalkiewicz was really into safe cracking, pulling off dozens of these robberies. It was about this time that the younger Korney joined him and they began pulling off jobs together.

Victor Chojnicki tipped off Korney to the Art Work Shop on Buffalo's East Side. On Wednesday, August 12, 1925, they drove to the plant. At 5:30 p.m., the plant whistle went off, signaling the end of the first shift, and the three hundred employees of the Art Work Shop began lining up for their pay.

The bandits entered the office quickly, revolvers drawn. The secretary saw the bandits and tossed the tin box full of money into the corner. Paymaster Ward Pierce reached for his revolver when Smithy, a Chicago recruit, yelled,

The Art Work Shop was the first major robbery and murder the Korney Gang committed. This is the site at 858 East Ferry Street in Buffalo today. *Photo by author.*

Korney ran a saloon at 49 Main Street in Depew during Prohibition. This is the building today. *Photo by author.*

"He's going for his gun!" Bolly turned and fired first, followed by Korney and Smithy, who hit Pierce in the abdomen and right arm.

As Pierce fell to the floor, the petrified employees stood by while the three bandits ran to the corner and scooped up as many envelopes as they could carry. They then jumped into a stolen Cadillac and sped from the scene. Korney pocketed the $1,966 ($23,956 in 2010 dollars) heist money, but they had left $8,800 ($107,224). Pierce died from his gunshot wound, and the gang was not identified. One witness came forward and implicated Edward Larkman, who was not even present. He was arrested and convicted of murder for Pierce's death.

Korney took part in other robberies. In 1926, he robbed the Loose-Wiles Biscuit Company and the Royal Linen Supply Company. He slipped up during one job and was caught robbing a store. The robbery conviction sent him to Elmira Prison for six months.

In 1927, the gang burglarized Browning Brothers Wholesale Grocers on Broadway of sixty-five tires.

The last home in Buffalo that Korney lived at was 42 Littlefield Street. This is the home today. *Photo by author.*

The tension between Kalkiewicz and Korney grew until Kalkiewicz left the gang. He did not participate in any jobs for about a year.

Their next big job was the Duffy Silk Mill in March 1928. They robbed an armored car of $24,000 ($299,029), with $2,000 ($24,919) per man, and Korney kept $14,000 ($174,433) for himself. Buffalo Police were baffled once again.

When Kalkiewicz returned to the gang, Korney was the leader. Korney seemed to like firepower and had the mysterious Smithy bring him a machine gun from Chicago, thought to be the first used in Buffalo.

In October 1928, Korney, Bolly, Kornacki, Ziggy, Smithy and an unknown friend of his planned to rob a mail car transporting registered mail. They planned the job for a Sunday night, not realizing that on Sundays there was less cash in the mail.

It would have been a clean robbery, but a motorcycle patrolman, Vincent J. Connors, happened to stumble across the robbery just as it began. The men all jumped from the Lincoln they were driving in and started showering the taxi in a hail of bullets. Charles Cavanaugh, a New York Central Railroad policeman riding in the front seat, stepped out and returned fire but was felled when a bullet struck his knee.

Before Patrolman Connors knew what was happening, Korney let loose with the machine gun, striking him at least six times. Mail clerk Ward McCartney was killed, and Pullman employee Francis Bieber was wounded. Connors lived, and the gang was not caught.

Meanwhile, Korney made amends with Kalkiewicz and rented the barn behind his house on Swede Hill in suburban Lancaster to run a brewery.

Victor Chojnicki contacted Korney and demanded money to leave town or he would spill his guts about the gang. Korney agreed to meet him at Kalkiewicz's house the next day, where he promptly killed him. Kalkiewicz and Bolly buried him in the backyard.

On April 25, 1929, the gang robbed the Fedders plant in Black Rock. They drove to the Fedders plant in a stolen car. All wore disguises and altered their appearances. They entered the plant carrying a variety of guns. Assistant treasurer Alvin J. Daigler saw them as they entered and ran into the

Anthony Kalkiewicz was the Korney Gang squealer. After his arrest, he was held at Police Precinct 5 in Buffalo. This is the site today. *Photo by author.*

The Korney Gang committed many robberies and several murders, but the one at the Fedders manufacturing plant in Buffalo finally did them in. This is the plant today. *Photo by author.*

basement vault with almost $46,000 ($580,000 in 2010 dollars). The gang grabbed two bags of cash he dropped and ran out of the building.

Outside, Bolly had gotten into a scuffle with employee John Perraton. Kalkiewicz jumped into the fray, and a gun went off, killing Perraton. The gangsters jumped into their car and sped off to change cars. Meanwhile, two witnesses followed them and one ran to a nearby police station. A Buffalo Police car rushed to the scene just as Bolly and Kalkiewicz were leaving, and a chase resulted. A running gun battle took place. Their car disabled, Bolly transferred the money to a new car, and Kalkiewicz grabbed the machine gun and started shooting the police. He injured one during the mêlée as Bolly drove away and Kalkiewicz jumped into the car.

They thought they had made another clean getaway, but they forgot that the disabled car was registered under one of Kalkiewicz's aliases and at his real address.

Korney convinced Kalkiewicz to give himself up, knowing Kalkiewicz was no squealer, and said that they would get bail money for him. He surrendered, but after hours of interrogation, he broke down and confessed all their crimes.

Bolly and Korney were arrested, and all would be tried for murder. Smithy—if he was real—disappeared. Ziggy also disappeared and would not be heard from for thirty years.

Korney was found not guilty of John Perraton's murder but was later convicted of perjury and received a twenty-year sentence. Bolly was found guilty and sentenced to death. Kalkiewicz was found guilty and also sentenced to death. He confessed that Edward Larkman was not responsible for the Art Work Shop murder, and he was released.

Korney was released in 1944 and not allowed in Buffalo, so he settled near Syracuse, where he died at fifty-nine years old on December 16, 1964. Kalkiewicz had his sentence reduced to life in prison, served thirty-five years and lived for thirteen years after leaving prison, dying in September 1977 at eighty-one years old.

Ziggy Plocharski's wife called Buffalo Police in 1964 to say he had died several months earlier and lived a clean life after the Fedders robbery.

The police never found the machine gun the Korney Gang used to terrorize the city of Buffalo. Maybe Smithy took it, or maybe it is buried in a backyard somewhere in western New York.[25]

THE BLUE RIBBON GANG

As I stand before this funny looking piece of furniture I raise my hand and swear to God Almighty that these two men you just executed were innocent.[26]
—Alex Bogdanoff

On January 1, 1928, during the New Year's revelry at the Peacock Inn, three armed men entered the establishment looking for former boxer Roger Lavin.[27] They killed the thirty-three-year-old proprietor, Michael George, and injured three others.

In July 1929, Ferdinand Fechter drove to the bank to pick up money for his "soda grill" on East Delavan Avenue, across from the Chevrolet plant, to cash the paychecks of workers at his restaurant. As Fechter pulled up to his house on July 27 with $8,396 ($105,859 in 2010 dollars), several men rushed him with loaded revolvers, fired shots at him and grabbed the money as he stepped out of the car. His family, standing on the porch, gazed on in horror. A final shot to the head clinched the murderous assault, and the four bandits fled in their stolen automobile. Fechter died an hour later.

The gangsters eluded Buffalo police. A week later, the stolen automobile was recovered with a .45-caliber revolver shell inside, and the pursuit had renewed vigor.[28]

Opposite, bottom: Another notorious Polish group was the Blue Ribbon Gang. This is where they were tear-gassed and captured by Buffalo Police in the village of Sloan. *Photo by author.*

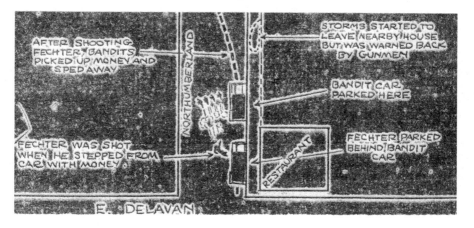

Ferdinand Fechter was ambushed and brutally killed in front of his family during an armed robbery. This diagram shows the path bandits used to perform the robbery and make their escape. *Courtesy* Buffalo Times.

The police suspected that Alexander "the Terror" Bogdanoff was responsible and trailed him through six states until he returned to Buffalo. He was seen going to Stephen and Edward Grzechowiak's home, so the house was put under surveillance for a month. The gang learned that the police knew something, so they moved to a home in neighboring Sloan. The police hid a dictaphone in the house to listen to their conversations.[29]

Buffalo Police decided they needed to move in before another deadly robbery took place. On Sunday morning, September 8, police gathered outside the Sloan home and, at 6:30 a.m., filled the home with tear gas. Two women and two children staggered out, choking back tears. Another round of tear gas filled the home, but the gangsters never emerged.

Gas-masked police entered and searched the home and found three members of the gang coughing in a bedroom and their leader hiding in the attic. The four arrested were Alex Bogdanoff, the leader, as well as Stephen Pilarski, Max Gorney and Stephen Grzechowiak. Gorney and Pilarski lived at the address. A fifth member, Stephen's brother Edward, was captured two hours later leaving St. Stanislaus Church, and the final bandit, Max "the Goose" Rybarczyk, was captured on his way to pick up a suit at the cleaners.[30]

While searching the house, police found pieces of blue ribbon hanging in the bedrooms, so the men became known as the Blue Ribbon Gang.

Bogdanoff admitted that the only reason he was back in Buffalo was to kill "Ziggy" Plocharski of the Korney Gang for reneging on "some loot." He admitted to fifty-four holdups over a ten-year period, receiving over $250,000 (almost $3.2 million in 2010 dollars).[31]

The men were all found guilty of killing Ferdinand Fechter. Three of the men were sentenced to death in the electric chair at Sing Sing Prison.[32] They appealed their death sentences, but just after 11:00 p.m. on July 17, 1930, after a two-week stay, Grzechowiak and Rybarczyk were electrocuted. Last was Bogdanoff, who said the other two were innocent, and then he was killed.

What happened to the rest of the gang is unknown. To this day, the executions of Rybarczyk and Grzechowiak are cited as examples of wrongful convictions and executions.

BUFFALO'S MOLLS

I heard Buffalo was a fast town so I came here to have a good time.[33]
—*Stella Mackowska, aka Vera LaMont*

The 1920s will forever go down as a time of change in America. From the passing of the Eighteenth Amendment and onset of Prohibition in 1920 right through the stock market crash of 1929, every ethnic group, men, women and even children found crime to be a way to make a living.

High-profile female criminals are not a common occurrence, but during the '20s, Buffalo was full of them and their dastardly deeds. What prompted so many women to get involved in crime, sometimes with dangerous or even deadly outcomes?

Several factors possibly play into this. First, the legalization of women's right to vote empowered many women across the country. As World War I ended in late 1918, many women felt they had a contributed to the effort and were no longer going to sit idly by while men ran everything. They started cutting their hair shorter, in what was called a "bob." Their hemlines also got shorter. Couple this with Prohibition, and women would never be relegated to the back seat again.

According to author Ellen Poulsen, the phrase "gun moll" came into being during Prohibition. "Moll" originally meant a "female pickpocket"[34] and evolved to mean "a woman companion of a professional criminal."[35] There have been some well-known ones, such as Bonnie Parker of Bonnie and Clyde fame and Al Capone's wife, Mae.

Let's start with one of the biggest ones. Carmela Magaddino, wife of Cosa Nostra boss Stefano, was a typical Sicilian housewife. She always wore black, as if she was forever in mourning. A neighbor said that she was a very nice lady, although even by the 1970s, she still spoke very little English. As wife of the leading Mafia figure in western New York for over fifty years, she could not have been blind, having seen her share of meetings taking place at their Lewiston home, as well as the bombing of her sister-in-law when they lived next door in 1936.

Minnie "Jew Minnie" Clark was thought to be Joe DiCarlo Jr.'s wife in the 1920s. As proprietor of the Auto Rest Inn in suburban Williamsville, she led her own life of excitement. On March 16, 1924, fifty hooded Ku Klux Klan members entered her full saloon and demanded she stop selling alcohol or they would close it down.[36] DiCarlo later married Elsie Pieri, sister of Salvatore J. Pieri, who seemed to be incarcerated more than not. Elsie was born into the Mafia life and ended it there.

The Blue Ribbon Gang's Stephen Grzechowiak was married to a girl named Blanche. On Sundays, the two would go to a farm near Marilla, New York, and target practice with other members of the gang. Blanche did her part by chatting with local precinct police, who didn't suspect her, as she tried to see what the police knew about the gang.

Richard Reese "Candy Kid" Whittemore's wife, Margaret, was nicknamed the "Tiger Girl" by the press after she passed two loaded pistols to her male companions and took aim herself at detectives attempting to arrest her husband in 1925.[37] Margaret was identified as a gun-toting holdup artist as early as 1924.[38] The gang, including Margaret, was arrested in March 1926. Richard offered to confess to a string of crimes if Tiger Girl was released.[39] She was eventually released and Richard tried. He was acquitted in Buffalo only to be sent to Baltimore, where he was convicted of murder and hanged.

The tale of the Bobbed-Haired Bandit brings two gun molls together. First there was Stella Mackowska, eighteen years old. She was part of a trio that robbed the Hoyler Jewelry store and killed clerk Rufus Eller. The three were all arrested and charged with murder, but young Stella testified against her partners and escaped the death penalty.

One of the largest robberies to occur in Buffalo took place in 1929. Known as the Carson Robbery, a daring home invasion during a society engagement party netted nearly $250,000 ($3.1 million in 2010 dollars) in jewels for the thieves. The gang was eventually identified, and Red Duke and his girlfriend, Bernice Frank, were among those arrested. Another suspect, Billy Seiner, claimed to have been at his girlfriend Helen Groblewski's[40] house during the robbery. Her brother William was an alibi witness for Stephen "Bolly" Ziolkowski of the Korney Gang. When the Carson robbers were found guilty, Helen "screamed, fainted and swore. 'He's innocent and I know it.'"[41] Stanley "Million Dollar Kid" Przybyl, the suspected leader, was arrested later. His girlfriend, Ethel Mason, was at his side as they were arrested in a rented Miami apartment.[42] Mason, who was still married but separated, testified on his behalf, but the Kid was sentenced to life in prison.[43] Ethel's outcome is unknown.

Anthony Kalkiewicz of the Korney Gang met a woman named Clara Mackowiak, whom he fell for. When Kalkiewicz decided to call a life of crime quits, he moved to suburban Lancaster, New York with Clara and rented a big house with a barn in the rear. Unfortunately, his past caught up with him, and he was dragged into one last robbery with the Korney Gang. No word on Clara was ever heard again. She may have kept in touch with him for a while but probably moved on, never forgetting her exciting time with the Korney Gang and her love for Tony.

APARTMENT 821

"Are you Pretty Boy Floyd?" FBI Agent Melvin Purvis asked.
"I'm Charles Arthur Floyd," was Floyd's response.[44]

The 1930s were a violent time in America. Prohibition lingered on, the Great Depression began and criminals got more violent and dangerous. One of the most infamous was Charles Arthur "Pretty Boy" Floyd.

On June 17, 1933, Floyd and Adam Richetti became the primary suspects in the Kansas City Massacre, which occurred when four law enforcement officers were killed while gangster Frank Nash was being transported.[45] Floyd denied involvement and met up with Juanita and Rose Baird in late September 1933 in Toledo, Ohio. The four left Ohio and headed to Buffalo, where they rented apartment 821 at the Amiantus Apartments, on Buffalo's predominantly Italian West Side.[46]

Rose said they "barely got along and did not have any extra money, staying in the apartment practically all the time." The men remained in the apartment except for a few trips. They would leave at night and stay away for days or weeks, but what they did or where they went is unknown. They read the newspaper and listened to the radio.

In October 1934, Floyd gave the girls $350 to buy a car, and a few days later, they packed up and left Buffalo. Floyd sat in the backseat with a machine gun. On the drive, they crashed into a telephone pole and had the girls tow the car into town for repairs. While there, Floyd and Richetti

"Pretty Boy" Floyd, Adam Richetti and their gals hid out in the Amiantus Apartments at Eighteenth and Rhode Island Streets in Buffalo for a year after the Kansas City Massacre. The building has been demolished, and a park now stands in its place. *Photo by author.*

apparently were spotted by police, so the girls left without them. Richetti was captured during a gun fight.

Floyd escaped and hitched a ride on October 22, 1934. He was spotted by lawmen who tracked him to a farmhouse, where an estimated fifty rounds were fired at him as he tried to escape through the woods. A mere three bullets struck him, and he died fifteen minutes later.

Richetti was subsequently tried for the Kansas City Massacre, sentenced to death and executed on October 7, 1938.[47]

THE $93,000 QUESTION

Believe me, I'm not going to burn alone for this job.[48]
—*Richard Reese Whittemore*

One of the most interesting tales to come from the gangster era involved one of the East Coast's biggest names. But he was the last one to be accused of the crime, and doubts still linger as to whether he was the actual bandit.

On June 1, 1925, five bandits entered the Levy jewelry store on Main Street in Buffalo. They handcuffed the employees and customers to fixtures in the rear of the store and escaped with $50,000 ($616,500 in 2010 dollars) worth of jewels.[49] No one was apprehended for the heist.

Just eight days later, on June 9, a car with the treasurer of the Wire Wheel Corporation was trailed from the Manufacturers and Traders Trust Company branch at Main and Swan Streets in Buffalo. At Nottingham Terrace and Elmwood Avenue, the car was forced from the road and robbed of its $6,000 payroll.[50]

One of Detroit's most notorious gangsters, Harry Harris, and one of his pals, Louis Stone, were arrested in Detroit on October 7, 1925, and believed to be responsible for multiple robberies in Buffalo and Niagara Falls, as well as other cities.[51]

Harris jumped bail on October 21 and escaped.[52] A mere nine days later, a sensational armed robbery took place in Buffalo, and Harris was immediately the prime suspect. That day, Marion Gould, his suspected wife, also jumped bail.[53]

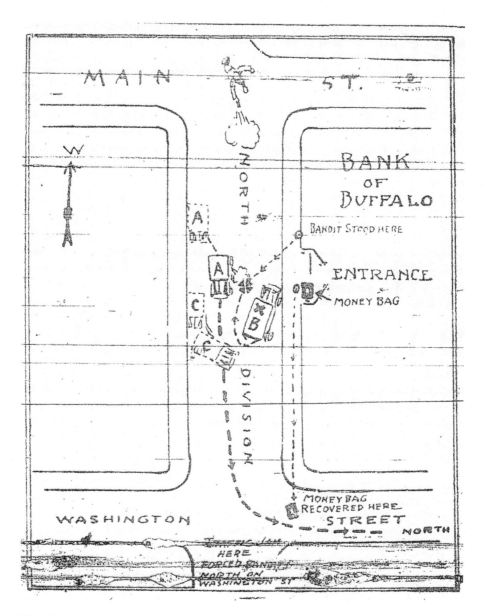

The $93,000 Bank of Buffalo robbery in 1925 had police chasing after multiple gangs until they settled on Richard Reese Whittemore. This diagram shows how the gang was able to corner the bank car and make their getaway. *Courtesy* Buffalo Evening News.

A Federal Reserve Bank armored car pulled up to the Bank of Buffalo branch at Main and North Division Streets at 9:15 a.m. As the guard exited the truck to make a cash delivery, multiple things transpired at once. A bandit was standing by the door and a car with bandits pulled next to the truck, and all began shooting. The driver of the armored car was struck and killed. The messenger carrying the bank bags was injured, and another guard was also shot, dying later. "The bank employes [*sic*] never had a chance."[54]

The bandits grabbed the money bags containing $93,000 (almost $1.2 million in 2010 dollars) and escaped in their car. Harris was immediately chosen from a rogues' gallery of photos, as were Mike Sperazzi, Joe "Polack Joe" Kobierny[55] and George "Dutch" Anderson, other well-known gangsters.[56] It was a sensational robbery that made national headlines.

Buffalo Police were searching for Harris when Philip Kozak was arrested in Detroit and took credit for the robbery. It was reported that "the confession absolves Harry Harris and his gang."[57] After traveling to Detroit to interview Kozak, Buffalo Police determined that his confession was fabricated.[58]

Finally, on March 20, 1926, Baltimore prison escapee Richard Reese Whittemore, twenty-eight, known as the "Candy Kid," was picked up in New York City with his wife, Margaret, and six members of his gang.[59] Police say they admitted to six robberies but denied involvement in the Buffalo robbery.

Buffalo Police maintained that Whittemore and his gang were the Bank of Buffalo crooks. Witnesses picked them out of lineups,[60] and the Erie County district attorney pressed to let Buffalo try him first.[61]

The trial for Whittemore began on April 19, 1926. He was positively identified by prosecution witnesses, while defense witnesses positively stated that he was not one of the bandits. Others said that Whittemore was in Philadelphia and could not have made it to Buffalo in time for the robbery.[62]

The case was given to the jury on April 27, 1926. At 10:30 p.m., they were still deliberating, but by 11:00 p.m., they told the judge that they were unable to reach a decision. The crowd in the courtroom cheered as the judge discharged the jury.

Richard Reese Whittemore was sent to Baltimore to stand trial for the 1925 prison escape and guard murder. There, he was found guilty and hanged in August 1926.

Harry Harris was killed in Jacksonville, Florida, during a gun fight with police on August 4, 1926,[63] so who really pulled off the Bank of Buffalo robbery will probably never be known.

THE MILLIONAIRE KID

Auburn is one of the finest clubs in the country. They'll never keep me there.[64]
—*Stanley Przybyl discussing Auburn Prison*

In Buffalo during the late 1920s, a number of Polish gangsters proved to be dangerous, good-looking and smart. Stanley "the Millionaire Kid" Przybyl was considered, at least by the press, "the east side's flashiest and most colorful criminal."[65] He gained his nickname "by his flair for excellent and well-tailored clothes, sporty cars, the bright lights and gay ladies."[66]

On November 14, 1929, wealthy Buffalo businessman John L. Carson held a lavish dinner party for eighteen prominent society members in his large suburban Snyder home to announce the engagement of his daughter. When the maids did not return with the desserts, the guests began to wonder what the delay was. Suddenly, seven armed bandits entered the room. Their faces were covered by handkerchiefs, they wore long coats and hats and they carried "revolvers, automatics and sawed-off shotguns."[67] Led by Clinton "Red" Duke, twenty-eight, who directed Stanley Przybyl; his brother Edward; Theodore Rogacki; William Seiner, twenty-four; and two others they robbed the guests of money, jewels and furs totaling $250,000 ($3.15 million in 2010 dollars). The biggest item was a $200,000 pearl necklace.[68]

On Thanksgiving Day, November 29, Duke, Rogacki, Duke's girlfriend Elizabeth Frank, Edward Przybyl and Seiner were arrested. Stanley Przybyl was also wanted but eluded the police. Duke was captured without incident at the Markeen Hotel.[69] None of the stolen gems was recovered during the arrests.

Police traced the gang to a hideout on Best Street, where they discovered "a key, keyring…and three artificial pearls" in the ashes of a stove.[70] The rest of the jewelry was believed to have been taken to New York City the day after the robbery by Duke and sold.

A January 1930 trial found all guilty of participation in the robbery. Duke was given thirty years to life, Rogacki twenty-five years to life, Edward Przybyl twenty years to life and Seiner life in prison.[71]

Just two days later, Stanley Przybyl, twenty-seven, was arrested in Miami Beach with his married girlfriend, Ethel Mason, as they were entering their apartment.[72] Przybyl stated, "There must be some mistake gentlemen."[73]

They were returned to Buffalo, where a speedy February trial took place. It took jurors just an hour to find Przybyl guilty. Sentenced the same day as the Blonde Bandit and "her pal," Przybyl received life in prison because of past offenses.[74] His appeal was denied.

Most of the jewels were never recovered.

BOBBED-HAIRED BEAUTY

Bad booze and bad women; that is the combination that put me in this mess. [75]
—*Frank Minnick*

The female gangster was not a common occurrence, especially in Buffalo. But when early 1924 arrived, so did she. Fortunately for the city of Buffalo, her reign was short and her punishment quick. Unlike 1929's Blonde Bandit, this girl was quiet, not cocky, and the crime was much more severe.

According to a drunk twenty-eight-year-old Frank Minnick, "[George] Bittle told me he was going out to grab some easy money. I was so drunk...I agreed to go with him." [76]

Estelle Mackowska, eighteen, had come to Buffalo from her home in Ohio in January because "I had heard about this city and became curious about it." [77] She met Minnick on Tuesday, May 7, the same day she moved into a rooming house on South Division Street. He knew her as Vera Lamont.

About nine o'clock on the night of Saturday, May 11, 1924, the three walked to the August H. Hoyler jewelry store on Genesee Street. "When the jeweler pulled out two trays a shot was fired," [78] Minnick said. The shot struck clerk Rufus Eller, who was killed. [79]

When Minnick awoke from his drunken stupor the following morning in Pfang's Hotel in suburban Hamburg, Lamont was asleep next to him. He took a taxi back to Buffalo and stopped to get a newspaper. That was when he saw the headlines and vaguely remembered what had transpired the previous night.

He was arrested and fingered Bittle as an accomplice; Bittle was also arrested as he entered his house. Lamont was the last arrested, found hiding in the room at the hotel.

Minnick's trial came first, commencing on May 19. It took the jury twenty-three minutes to find him guilty of murdering Rufus Eller.[80] His sentence was death in the electric chair. His wife, angry and upset, said, "I hope and pray…[they] will send the girl to the chair, too."[81]

Bittle's trial was next, and the state planned on using Stella/Vera as a witness against him. His trial commenced on May 24. No one positively identified him, but Minnick's statement was used against him and Stella testified against him. The jury deadlocked, and a mistrial was declared.

The Bobbed-Haired Bandit, aka Vera Lamont, robbed Hoyler Jewelers in 1924. A clerk in the store was killed, and one of Lamont's partners went to the electric chair. This is the location today. *Photo by author.*

During Stella's trial, she claimed she had been duped into the crime and the two men took advantage of her. Her jury also deadlocked, so she pled guilty to first-degree manslaughter to avoid a second trial and was sentenced to five years in prison.[82]

Bittle and Mackowska both spent the better part of a year in jail awaiting new trials. Minnick, twenty-six, who actually pulled the deadly trigger,[83] died in the electric chair at Sing Sing Prison on March 12, 1925.

After Bittle's second trial, he was convicted of murder and sentenced to death.[84] His wife, Helen, fought for his freedom, and Stella eventually spoke out on his behalf. New York governor Alfred Smith agreed that he deserved a new trial, sparing him the electric chair.[85] In December 1938, Bittle was pardoned by New York governor Herbert Lehman and released on parole for life.[86]

The whereabouts of Stella and George after prison life are unknown.

THE MAFIA, PART I

THE BARREL MURDER

They'll get me some day, and when they do they will do a good job. I know it. When they are sure they can escape they will fill me full of lead. It will come—some day.[87]
—*Lieutenant Joseph Petrosino*

B enedetto Madonia said he was a stonemason living in Buffalo but he "was a man unused to manual labor."[88] His brother-in-law Giuseppe DiPriemo was tied into "a group of Sicilians" in New York City.[89] Madonia, according to his wife, Lucy, had done work for these Sicilians, "shuttling by rail from Pittsburgh to Chicago and Buffalo," a route the Secret Service had determined was used by counterfeiters, of which Madonia had a previous conviction back in Sicily.

Around early March 1903, DiPriemo wrote his sister to say he was in trouble and needed $1,000, which Madonia raised. He sent the money to an acquaintance in New York City with instructions to help DiPriemo. With Madonia hundreds of miles away, he instead kept the money. Madonia sent letters and threats, but they fell on deaf ears. Finally, Madonia decided to travel to New York to secure the return of his money.

He arrived in New York City around April 3, 1903, and over the next week, he tried to retrieve his money from Giuseppe "Clutch" Morello, a leader of the Italian secret society.

On the night of April 14, Madonia was eating in a small restaurant on Prince Street[90] when Morello and several of his men entered. Within moments,

One of New York City's great Italian detectives was Joe Petrosino. He helped solve Benedetto Madonia's murder and went on to work on other Italian crimes. This is a copy of his diary showing his visit to Buffalo while investigating the murder. *Courtesy Jon Black, gangrule.com.*

Madonia was restrained and dragged to a sink, where a fourteen-inch stiletto dagger was plunged into his throat. His throat was slashed and the blood poured into the sink; there was little mess. The killers wrapped fabric around his neck, and his body was stuffed into a waiting barrel. The barrel was then left on East 11th Street, where it was discovered the following morning.

It was a baffling case for New York detectives until Sergeant Joseph Petrosino, New York's "expert on Italian crimes,"[91] joined the case. Petrosino was able to ascertain who the probable killers were, and they were arrested.[92] More evidence poured in that finally identified the body as that of Madonia.

Petrosino tracked the story to Madonia's brother-in-law, DiPriemo, who was in Sing Sing Prison, and questioned him. When DiPriemo saw Madonia's photo, he identified him and said, "Yes I know that man,"[93] and told Petrosino about him but refused to give any information on Morello. Petrosino then traveled to Buffalo to meet Madonia's widow and explain her husband's fate.

Petrosino took the little knowledge he gathered in Buffalo and headed back to New York, where seven men—including Giuseppe Morello— were charged with Madonia's murder. It was believed that he was "killed for demands to the Morello gang."[94]

The trial turned into a fiasco, as members of Morello's gang filled the courtroom to intimidate witnesses. Madonia's widow was unable to identify her husband's watch, which was found on the body. Her brother also denied that Morello or any of his men played a part in the murder. The main suspect, Tomasso Petto, was released, and the case remained unsolved.[95]

Joseph Petrosino went on to head an Italian Squad that investigated murders, bombings and black hand extortions.[96] In 1909, Lieutenant Petrosino set sail to Sicily to conduct an investigation. It was to be a secret visit, but it turned out that many people knew of his visit, including the Mafia. On March 13, 1909, Petrosino was murdered in Sicily, and Morello was the main suspect.

Joe "The Boss" Masseria designated Morello as "Boss of All Bosses"[97] until August 15, 1930, when he was gunned down in his office.[98]

EARLY MAFIA FAMILIES

You can no longer tell a mobster by his fedora hat.
—*Ron Fino, former Local 210 business manager and FBI informant*

From the earliest days of the twentieth century, several different men emerged as potential or possible Mafia leaders. Even as early as the 1920s, Buffalo Police believed there was an Italian "secret society," but the vow of silence, later known as Omerta, was always present. Rarely did witnesses even come forward for fear of reprisal.

To the uninitiated, a brief outline of how a Mafia family, or La Cosa Nostra (LCN), operates is necessary. At the top is the boss, who usually reigns supreme. Generally next in command is the underboss, but the consigliere is often higher than the underboss and is the voice of reason for the boss. Sometimes the consigliere is a lawyer or an elderly Mafioso. Under the underboss are the caporegime, or capos or captains, who run a crew of soldiers. These are the people who are out on the streets doing all the work, making the money. All of these people—in the old days, primarily Sicilian—were "made" men, and official members of La Cosa Nostra. At the very bottom are the associates, people who are not official made members of the mob but are out doing the dirty work, sometimes trying to become made members and other times on the outside just sending a cut of their crimes to the capo in their area.

One of the earliest references claims that Angelo Puma, from the same city as later leaders Angelo B. Palmeri and Stefano Magaddino, was a "Mafia leader."[99] He supposedly was involved in "blackmail, extortion, and

Salvatore "Sam" Pieri was a member of the Buffalo Mafia. He was listed on a 1963 FBI chart as a former underboss. This is his former home on Jersey Street today. *Photo by author.*

gambling enterprises." Buffalo's Little Italy, located in what was left of the Erie Canal district on Buffalo's waterfront, was where a "suspected" criminal organization was operating, "controlling the gambling and vice enjoyed by the longshoremen and sailors."[100]

On April 26, 1929, a tremendous explosion ripped through the former Frontier Hotel owned by Puma, who had been associated with Philip Mazzara, Philip Mannor and Joseph DiBenedetto. The powerful explosion blew out windows in buildings across the street. Puma was the target, but he was not home that night and survived the murder attempt.[101]

There were two men who are generally acknowledged as the first leaders of Buffalo's Mafia: Giuseppe "Don Pietro" or "Joe" DiCarlo and Angelo "Buffalo Bill" Palmeri. Most historians believe that DiCarlo was the first real boss and

Palmeri "a top lieutenant."[102] The two men were also related, as Palmeri married a cousin of DiCarlo's wife.[103] Palmeri owned a saloon on Court Street, and DiCarlo owned Buffalo Italian Importing Co., just a few blocks down.[104]

DiCarlo was called "overlord of Buffalo's Italian Colony"[105] by the local press and was considered a powerful crime boss. Originally settling in Brooklyn, he moved to Buffalo in 1908. By 1920, he was proprietor of a saloon on Front Avenue. As time went on, he acquired other saloons, including one on Dante Place, which was on Buffalo's Erie Canal and was previously known as Canal Street before the large influx of Italians in the early twentieth century.

According to news reports, DiCarlo "built up powerful connections"[106] with other Italians around the country. Fellow countrymen sought him out for help, and he became the "big boss" of Buffalo. There are claims that DiCarlo controlled the docks, but no proof of that has surfaced.

Palmeri hailed from Castellammare del Golfo, Sicily, and was called "Buffalo Bill" by the police because he wore "five-gallon hats and carried a pistol in a holster in full view of any who cared to look."[107] He was an old school "mustache Pete," as they were called, who extorted money from "groceries, push cart vendors, and Italian food vendors"[108] and was possibly involved in Black Hand activities. The Black Hand was a mysterious extortion racket where the victim received a letter demanding money or a threat of violence would result. It was often signed with the picture of a black hand.

Joe DiCarlo Jr. was named Buffalo's Public Enemy No. 1 by the Buffalo Police. He was involved in gambling, narcotics and other crimes. This is a rare family photo. *Courtesy Joe DiCarlo's granddaughter.*

About 1919, Palmeri moved to Niagara Falls, about twenty miles north of Buffalo, leaving Buffalo to the more powerful DiCarlo.

DiCarlo had a son named Joe Jr. who took after his old man. He was "a born gangster."[109] When his father died on July 9, 1922, Junior may have assumed that he would take over the family business, but "he was never able to fill Don Pietro's shoes."[110] "He's just a punk," one Buffalo detective declared.

It is believed that Palmeri contacted Magaddino in Brooklyn and asked if he was interested in running the rackets in Buffalo. Not long after, Magaddino arrived in Buffalo, worked in a produce market for about a month and then moved to Niagara Falls, where he would settle. Palmeri then began an advisory role as Magaddino ascended the underworld ladder.

In November 1922, Junior was involved in a cocaine ring after persuading a "friend," "Busy" Joe Pattitucci, to purchase from him at a higher price.[111] When federal agents raided Pattitucci's Stella Restaurant, they flipped Pattitucci, convincing him to submit information about his associates.

In August 1923, DiCarlo was arrested along with Peter "Pete the Slash" Giallelli. On January 1, 1924, Pattitucci was shot outside Frank Lumia's restaurant, but he was not killed. A police officer was able to get the license plate of the escape vehicle, owned by Joseph Ruffino. DiCarlo, Ruffino, Gaetano Capodicaso and Giallelli were subsequently arrested for the shooting. The case was prosecuted by Colonel William J. Donovan, a Buffalonian and federal attorney.

When the jury returned the verdicts, only Capodicaso was acquitted. DiCarlo received six years in Atlanta Prison and was fined $5,000.[112]

DiCarlo and Ruffino appealed their convictions and did not begin serving their sentences until April 1925.[113] Just a month later, Angelo Palmeri and Capodicaso were arrested for illegally obtaining pistol permits. The result is not known.[114]

DiCarlo was transferred to a reformatory in Ohio after serving a "portion of his sentence."[115] His stay there was apparently pretty cushy. A story he never denied said that the warden let DiCarlo borrow his car and leave the prison. He was released in 1929 and, with his brother Sam and cohorts John "Peanuts" Tronolone, Salvatore and Joseph Pieri, controlled most of the gambling in Buffalo, paying tribute to Boss Magaddino.[116]

On December 21, 1932, Palmeri died of a heart attack while sitting in his automobile in front of his home.[117] He was only fifty-two. His death was a blow to many who were experiencing the crush of the Great Depression. Palmeri had become a good Samaritan over the years, and many came to rely on him for food or a small gift of cash.

Dewey's Diner was a gangster hangout behind the Roanoke Hotel on Elmwood Avenue and West Chippewa Street in Buffalo. The FBI decided the best way to watch the diner was to rent a room in the hotel. This is the former hotel today. *Photo by author.*

DiCarlo's growing gambling business had gained so much attention that the Buffalo Police Department named him its first Public Enemy No. 1. Between 1930 and 1945, he accumulated over twenty arrests and was constantly harassed by the police. His associates Joseph Ruffino and Anthony Perna were arrested on charges of passing a counterfeit bill in February 1933.[118] Ruffino was convicted in April 1933.[119]

On July 27, 1936, DiCarlo and Tronolone were arrested for assaulting a bookmaker at the Cheektowaga dog racetrack. Both were acquitted the following March.[120]

DiCarlo's bad luck continued in April 1938, when he was sentenced to one year for coercion related to a cigarette vending business.[121] A Buffalo Police captain was suspended and fired in May 1938 for "soliciting business for Joe DiCarlo" when he was caught trying to get a DiCarlo vending machine into the Little Harlem restaurant in Buffalo.[122] DiCarlo was again indicted in September 1939 on conspiracy charges related to vending machines after the testimony by former police captain Daniel G. Regan,[123] who retired after his brush with DiCarlo and the law. The charges were part of an investigation into municipal corruption.[124]

DiCarlo went into hiding for nine months, finally appearing in late May 1940. He was charged, along with Regan and two others, with "obtain[ing] control of and dominat[ing] activities of bookmakers, gamblers, dealers, and users of slot, digger and vending machines, pin and ski ball games, and musical instruments."[125] The grand jury charged former Buffalo police commissioner James W. Higgins, Democratic state committee man Julius Caputo, Frank A. "Tony" DeFusto, two police lieutenants, Erie County Democratic chairman Frank J. Carr and three others with conspiracy to obstruct enforcement of gambling laws.[126] It was believed that "big-time gambler" Tony DeFusto built a house in the Adirondacks for the police commissioner in exchange for allowing gambling in Buffalo.[127] Higgins and six others were still cleared of the charges, but Caputo, thirty-nine, pleaded guilty to two charges, one of which involved police protection for gamblers, and received a two-year prison sentence and a $1,000 fine. Caputo had run a bookmaking operation from a Niagara Street building for at least five years and was friendly with Herman Weinstein.[128]

By November 1944, a special grand jury indicted DiCarlo and Tronolone on gambling charges. It was believed that the underworld controlled "millions" in bookmaking,[129] and Buffalo Police under his control were "transferred and broken, on orders from racketeers and gamblers."[130]

The grand jury arose from a "one-man crusade against alleged gambling and vice"[131] started by Edward J. Pospichal, a suburban gas station proprietor. Pospichal complained to then New York governor Herbert Lehman about corruption in Buffalo and suburban Cheektowaga and Sloan as far back as early 1941.[132] In November 1944, Pospichal accused Buffalo Police of "covering up for Joe DiCarlo."[133] He found out the hard way the price of crossing the gangsters of Buffalo. Case after case brought before Buffalo's courts ended with small fines, some as low as twenty-five dollars, and the release of suspected gamblers. On January 28, 1945, the "bullet-torn" body of Edward Pospichal was found frozen and tossed in a dirty snowbank along an isolated stretch of River Road. An autopsy showed he had been beaten "about the head" and shot five times in the head and neck.[134]

One man questioned during Pospichal's murder trial was William E. "Willie the Whale" Castellani, a "dapper gambling figure."[135] Castellani had "hurriedly" left the Elmwood Avenue apartment of his girlfriend the day Pospichal was killed, leading police to suspect that he was involved in the murder. Pospichal had demanded police investigate an "alleged gambling establishment"[136] on Michigan Avenue that Castellani had been linked to.

Despite all his misdeeds, Castellani decided to reconcile with his wife, and they planned to be remarried. On March 16, 1945, just hours before the ceremony, Castellani was found by his wife with one bullet in his head from an apparent suicide. She conveniently removed the gun from his hand. The coroner agreed that it was suicide and did not perform an autopsy. Whether Castellani was killed by a rival, his wife or his own hand may never be known.

Pospichal's murder case eventually went cold, but in 1956, during the construction of the New York State Thruway a .32-caliber pistol was found in the vicinity of where Pospichal's body was found.[137] After testing, it was determined that it was not the murder weapon.

After a trial in April 1945, DiCarlo and Tronolone were both found guilty of conspiracy to violate gambling laws. Police captain Thomas F. O'Neill, forty, whose billy club was found near Pospichal's body, was convicted of willful neglect and omission of duty for failing to suppress gambling.[138] O'Neill received a six-month sentence, while DiCarlo and Tronolone received eighteen months. All were fined $500, and all three appealed their sentences. Only O'Neill was granted a new trial.[139] In February 1946, he was exonerated, returned to active duty[140] and received $2,800 in back pay.

After this last prison stint, DiCarlo and his gang relocated to Youngstown, Ohio, realizing that the constant surveillance and police pressure in Buffalo would not allow him to profitably run his operations any longer.[141] DiCarlo found Youngstown politicians and city officials tolerant of his activities until a racket-busting mayor was elected in 1947, making his life miserable.

With the heat on, DiCarlo decided to try other cons to get by. In 1948, he bet $16,000 on the World Series, lost and "welshed" on the bet.[142] During this time, he was "desperate for a big killing."[143] He got mixed up in fixing a boxing match between middleweight boxer Jake LaMotta and Tony Janiro in June 1947.

In 1951, the U.S. Senate linked DiCarlo with Chicago and New York City mobsters during the Kefauver Crime hearings.[144] On January 19, 1951, he was a witness before the committee and refused to "answer pertinent questions."[145] DiCarlo was subsequently charged with contempt, but in 1952, the charges were dropped.

After being forced to the Youngstown suburbs, DiCarlo and his gang left town and moved to Miami Beach, Florida. When he threw a lavish $35,000 wedding reception for his daughter in February 1955—supposedly paid for by his pal Michael "Trigger Mike" Coppola of New York City—federal officials decided it was time for Joe to finish paying the remaining $4,000 fine he still owed the government.[146]

DiCarlo's Miami interests were not as good as he thought, and he eventually moved back to Buffalo. In August 1961, he was questioned by police after Anthony Palestine, twenty-one, and Vincent Santangelo, twenty-two, were found killed gangland style in a field in the Buffalo suburb of Lancaster.[147]

In January 1966, DiCarlo's wife, Elsie, died. The funeral arrangements were handled by the Magaddino Memorial Chapel.

In 1973, an FBI affidavit called him a "syndicate lieutenant" tied to local gambling and loan-sharking activities. He was seventy-three years old at the time.

DiCarlo died on October 10, 1980, at the Hamlin Terrace Nursing Home after a "lengthy illness,"[148] ending the life of one of Buffalo's original gangsters.

John Tronolone never moved back to Buffalo as his stature in the Cosa Nostra grew over the years. According to one account, he was "made" in Cleveland in the 1940s.[149] He made Miami his home after he and the DiCarlo gang moved there in the mid-'40s.

Tronolone became consigliere of the Cleveland family under boss Jack Licavoli and underboss Angelo Lonardo.[150] He would become a figurehead boss in 1983 after Lonardo became a government witness. The Genovese Family represented Cleveland on the Mafia Commission, and they had to go through Tronolone any time they wanted to contact Tony Salerno, head of the Genovese Family.

Tronolone was convicted in 1975 of operating a bookmaking operation that grossed over $1 million per week. He was fined $2,000 and sentenced to two years in prison.[151]

In 1981, Tronolone and fourteen other mobsters were indicted on federal racketeering charges, including twenty-nine counts of conspiracy to murder, labor racketeering, illegal gambling, bid rigging for local food and construction industries and conspiracy to defraud the Teamsters Union through election fraud. In 1985, after Tronolone's acquittal on racketeering charges and the death of Licavoli, Tronolone became the permanent boss of the Cleveland family.[152]

By 1989, Tronolone was an old man, and apparently he let his guard down. He made a deal with an ex–Hells Angel to help fence some stolen diamonds. Instead of sending an underling to do his dirty work, he made the deal himself. The ex–Hells Angel was in actuality an undercover police officer, and Tronolone was arrested and subsequently convicted.[153]

On May 29, 1991, at age eighty, Tronolone died while awaiting an appeal of his prison sentence.

THE MAGADDINO FAMILY

I don't think it will hurt him. All we're going to do is hold his hand. [154]
*—FBI Agent Neil J. Welch explaining to Magaddino's attorney that he would
need to be fingerprinted*

The western New York Mafia was controlled by the Magaddino Family, specifically Stefano "the Old Man, Don Stefano, the Undertaker, Big Steve" Magaddino, from 1922 until his death in 1974. There were four prominent members of his family: Antonino "Nino," his brother; Peter A., Stefano's son; Peter J., Nino's son; and Peter J., Nino and Stefano's cousin.

Magaddino was one of the most elusive Mafia dons in American Mafia history. He never gave an interview, never posed for photos and was a respected businessman in Niagara

Stefano Magaddino was a grand Mafia boss steeped in the traditions of the old country. He was able to stay active for fifty years. This photo appears to have been taken in the 1950s. *Courtesy Anthony Cardinale.*

Falls. His family was active in civic affairs like Easter Seals, but their dark side was always close to the surface. "He's a man who liked peace, not war. But if he had to use violence, he would." [155]

The Magaddino and Bonanno clans came from the Sicilian town of Castellammare del Golfo. It is a beautiful city known as a fishing and resort area. *Photo by author.*

As someone close to them noted, "These people had a hand in everything. They had people in the DA's office. They had people in police departments. They had judges, lawyers, just about everybody was working for them."[156]

Stefano never used the telephone to transmit messages, preferring word of mouth. He had a "high-pitched voice" and often dominated conversations that were usually in his native Sicilian.[157] When disputes arose, he would have meetings, sometimes in his home, where they would "get together and talk it over and the Old Man would quiet it down."[158]

"He didn't gamble, he didn't drink, he didn't smoke and he didn't cheat on his wife."[159] He was an anomaly in mob circles. For many years, Magaddino commanded by "the power of respect,"[160] with some fear thrown in.

Stefano was born on October 10, 1891 in Castellammare del Golfo, Sicily. He was five feet eight inches tall, 175 pounds with brown eyes and gray hair by the 1960s. He arrived in the United States on February 7, 1909, aboard the SS *San Giorgio*. He settled in Brooklyn from 1909 to 1922 and lived on Roebling Street. He married Carmela Caroddo on October 19, 1913, in

Brooklyn. She was born on February 1, 1894, in Castellammare del Golfo and arrived in the United States on November 15, 1909.

Magaddino was involved in a family feud that had killed his brother Pietro in Sicily, as well as members of the Buccellato clan. When he arrived in America, the feud continued. Camillo Caiozzo was the suspected killer of his brother, so when he arrived in America, Magaddino was waiting for him.

Magaddino and Gaspar Milazzo, also from Castellammare del Golfo, ran an influential gang in Brooklyn that became known as the Good Killers in the 1910s. They forced Bartolo Fontano to kill his friend Caiozzo, but the murder ate away at Fontano.

In 1921, the organization of "Bonventure and Magaddino families" and their allies[161] made national headlines after the body of Caiozzo was discovered in New Jersey. Fontano confessed to New York City police detective sergeant Michael Fiaschetti, saying his friend's ghost haunted him.

Magaddino, thought to be the leader of this criminal syndicate,[162] was lured to Grand Central Station in New York City by Fontano under the guise of needing money to escape. When they met, Magaddino told him to take a train to Buffalo, where the "chief" would take care of him. Magaddino was then

arrested. It was August 16, 1921, and his first recorded American arrest. Angered by the deception, he attacked Fontano in the police station, and during the altercation, Magaddino was struck by a police nightstick.

The press went wild with the stories, and nationwide coverage of a string of murders grew. Some cities tried to close cold cases and linked them to the Good Killers. Magaddino and five others were held on suspicion of murder. When extradition papers were finally filed for the men, only three were included, and Magaddino was released after thirty days.

When a bomb exploded at Magaddino's sister Arcangela's house on Whitney Avenue in 1936, it also damaged Stefano's home next door. This is his home today. *Photo by author.*

Shortly after, Magaddino and Gaspar Milazzo were ambushed and shot at as they walked out of a Brooklyn store. It was believed that the murder attempt was from members of the Buccellato family. Magaddino and Milazzo were suspects in Buccellato retaliation shootings and thought it was an opportune time to leave Brooklyn. Milazzo landed in Detroit, and Magaddino headed to Buffalo.

An FBI informant acquainted with Stefano said that from 1916 to 1921, Magaddino "used to travel from city to city selling cheap [olive] oil and scaring people into purchasing oil from him."[163] After arriving in western New York, Magaddino became involved in bootlegging. He said, "We, me and [his cousin Joe] Bonanno had about forty trucks on the road. Buffalo and Niagara Falls, I accumulated about forty trucks, cars, salesman, cars and every [obscene] thing."[164] This was the only reference found to Bonanno participating in his bootlegging operation, which was before Bonanno became a Mafia boss.

Magaddino's first known western New York arrest was on April 22, 1924, by Niagara Falls Police when he was charged with cruelty to animals. Disposition was never known.

Stefano claimed to be a "salesman for a wholesale fruit and grocery firm" from about 1925 to 1930.[165] He later "bragged" that at the same time he was making $10,000 a day (about $120,000 in 2010 dollars) through illegal gambling.[166] In 1927, Stefano was "interested in" the Falls Bottling Works Co. with Peter Certo and Mrs. Catherine Certo.[167]

On May 31, 1930, Gaspar Milazzo was gunned down in Detroit in what some historians believe was the primary catalyst of the Castellammarese War, which broke out in New York City. The principals behind the war were Salvatore Maranzano, who had taken over the Brooklyn Castellammarese family with Magaddino's blessing,[168] and Joe "The Boss" Masseria, said to be Mafia boss of bosses.[169] Magaddino aligned with his fellow countryman Maranzano. It has been widely stated that Magaddino sent $5,000 a week to Maranzano, but that information comes from mob turncoat Joe Valachi's memory and is unverifiable. The war came to an end on April 15, 1931, when Masseria was killed. Maranzano now wanted to eliminate those who had opposed him during the war. Even Magaddino "refused to contribute $10,000 asked of him for Marazano's private fund."[170] Maranzano was murdered six months later on September 10 in his Park Avenue office.

What has become known as the Mafia Commission was formed at this time, and by the first meeting, Magaddino was a member of the seven-man committee.

The Magaddinos had four children, three daughters and son Peter A. "Big Pete" Magaddino, born on February 25, 1917, in Brooklyn, New York.

Stefano's son Peter A. was being groomed to take over as boss of the Magaddino Family. He was a licensed mortician and about thirty years old when this photo was taken. *Courtesy* Niagara Falls Gazette.

Peter attended Georgetown University for two years and also enrolled in law school at University at Buffalo.[171] One source said he received a bachelor's of law degree from Georgetown University. Peter married Frances Montana, niece of John C. Montana, and they had two sons.

In 1933, Stefano formed Power City Distributing Company, of which he was the president. This legitimate beer distributor opened immediately after Prohibition ended and was located in Niagara Falls. The company carried Utica Club, O'Keefe's, Pfeiffer's and Budweiser.[172] Magaddino had an office there "but never spent a great deal of time around the office."[173] In 1934, the New York State Liquor Authority had a "suspicion that Magaddino was at the time interested in the business of smuggling aliens into the United States."[174]

On January 23, 1947, gun permit 2450 was issued to Magaddino by the Niagara County Clerk. It was renewed in 1949 and was still active in 1958.[175]

The Magaddino Funeral Home was the next big enterprise the family got involved in. Originally started by Paul Palmeri and Alfred Panepinto, the business operated from 1925 to 1935. Palmeri was Angelo Palmeri's

Peter A. Magaddino

*Cordially extends a standing
invitation to visit our
beautiful funeral home.*

MAGADDINO MEMORIAL CHAPEL INC.

1338 NIAGARA ST. At PORTAGE RD.   DIAL 8221

★ *6 Spacious Beautifully Appointed Parlors*

★ *Catering to All Faiths*

★ *Air-Conditioned Throughout*

★ *Private Selection Rooms*

★ *Ample Off the Street Parking*

Many years of planning and designing have been devoted to giving the
utmost in comfort and convenience keeping always in mind.
"The cost must be within the means of all"

Peter A. Magaddino

In 1955, the Magaddino Funeral home expanded and built a new facility at Niagara Street and Portage Road in Niagara Falls. It could now handle up to six funerals simultaneously but usually only handled about fifty a year. *Courtesy* Niagara Falls Gazette.

younger brother. In 1935, Palmeri and Peter Spallino began a partnership that lasted until 1939 or 1940, but Palmeri was not listed as an undertaker in any city directories. It is believed that Nino Magaddino became Palmeri's partner around 1940. The business was chartered on July 3, 1940, with

$10,000 capital stock.[176] Palmeri decided to leave town and relocated in New Jersey.

On February 13, 1942, the Magaddinos took over the business, and the name was changed to Magaddino Funeral Home, Inc. Peter A. was president and became the licensed embalmer in 1948 after graduating from mortuary school,[177] and his sister Angeline LaDuca was secretary. Business sales averaged $40,000 annually, and a new building was erected in 1955 on Niagara Street that cost over $100,000. On April 20, 1955, the business was renamed Magaddino Memorial Chapel, Inc. An FBI informant believed that it held only forty to fifty funerals a year, not nearly enough to cover the overhead of the new building. Throughout the years, Nino worked nearly every funeral,[178] and by 1957, he was vice-president and treasurer.

Antonino "Nino, Antonio, Tony" Magaddino was born on June 18, 1897, in Castellammare del Golfo, Sicily. He was five feet eleven inches tall and 185 pounds. INS records report Nino's arrival in New York City aboard the SS *Patria* on November 1, 1923,[179] after being summoned by his brother Stefano.

He was married on February 2, 1922, in Italy to Vincenza (Vincinent) Vitale, who was born on May 11, 1895, in Castellammare del Golfo. Their daughter Giuseppina (Josephine) Magaddino was born on May 30, 1924, in Italy, and Pietro (Peter J.) was born on January 12, 1923, in Italy. Both children were admitted to the United States from Canada on September 1, 1950, having lived there since 1948. Peter also worked at the funeral home for many years.

Nino was arrested in 1916 in Trapani, Italy, for double murder and received six months clandestine expatriation, which was common in Italy prior to 1935. He was acquitted and pardoned in 1930. The same year, he was also arrested for clandestine activities (held for one month) and homicide (held for nearly a year and then released for insufficient evidence).[180]

He was arrested by U.S. Immigration and Naturalization Service on February 21, 1935, and charged with illegally entering the country. John C. Montana, president of Van Dyke Taxi, appeared as a character witness at his hearing and said Nino was "upright, honest and sober." Nino was granted citizenship on June 21, 1948, and Niagara Falls attorney Anthony Scalzo was a witness.

In 1940, the United States Treasury received word from a representative in Milan, Italy, that the "Grand Council of the Sicilian Underworld" was composed of nine individuals, including "Stefano Magardino," and that these men "pass on and direct all of the affairs carried on by this gang throughout the United States and Europe."[181] Of course, they were unable to find such a person in Niagara Falls, since "Stefano Magardino" was not a listed person in Niagara Falls. In 1951, the book *Mafia* listed "Stephano Margardino" as a leader in organized crime in America.

Niagara Falls in those days was known as a "honky-tonk border city, where prostitutes outnumbered salesgirls and bookies blared out race results to passersby in the streets."[182] It was known for its chemical plants, hydroelectric power and "red light districts."[183] During World War II, the U.S. Army forced Niagara Falls to clean up its act.

Nino and Stefano had another brother, Gaspare, who came to America. He initially immigrated to Brooklyn before 1910 and married Pietrina Corrado, who was the sister of Stefano's wife Carmela. According to his Petition for Naturalization and Ellis Island record, Gaspare arrived in the United States with his wife at the port of New York aboard the SS *Normandie* on September 2, 1935. His son Giovanni "John" was born in Brooklyn in 1913. While in Brooklyn, Gaspare worked as a baker in the bakery owned by relatives Vito and Salvatore Bonventure. Immigration records reveal that Gaspare arrived in the United States again in 1935

Gaspare Magaddino was the older brother of Nino and Stefano. When he arrived in Niagara Falls, he opened a bakery at Eighteenth and Ferry Streets. This is the building today. *Photo by author.*

from Tunisia, Africa, and moved to Niagara Falls with his wife and son John. While in Niagara Falls, Gaspare operated his own bakery and became a well-known resident of the city. Although no criminal records were found for Gaspare in Niagara Falls, speculation has surfaced that he had some power in the Buffalo crime family headed by his brother Stefano.[184] Locals tend to believe that Gaspare was the crime boss until his death, but most historians believe Stefano was always boss.

Gaspare died on August 16, 1950. More than one thousand people attended his funeral, which was held at the Magaddino Funeral Home and then St. Joseph's Church. There were 350 automobiles in the funeral procession that stretched eight blocks and tied up traffic on Pine Avenue for more than an hour. Burial was in St. Joseph's Cemetery.[185]

Stefano purchased a home on Lower Mountain Road in Cambria, New York, in 1944 and sold it in 1972. The property had forty-seven acres of land, several acres of grapes and was used as a summer retreat until about 1958, when the family moved into their new home in suburban Lewiston, New York.

Stefano Magaddino purchased a large farmhouse in 1942 in rural Cambria, New York. Some of the land was rented to a farmer, but Magaddino grew grapes and used the home as a summer retreat for about ten years. This is the house today. *Photo by author.*

In 1946, Nino's FBI file said he was living with Stefano on Whitney Avenue in Niagara Falls, but he later purchased a home across the street.[186]

The former superintendent of police in Niagara Falls, Martin T. Considine, said in 1949 that Nino and another man offered to shut down all the gambling joints during a police chief convention.[187] It is not believed that the offer was accepted.

Niagara County undersheriff Arthur Muisiner said in 1952 that Stefano and his son Peter had great criminal influence in the Niagara Falls area. After bootlegging, gambling was the main source of income for the Magaddino Family.

By 1957, it is strongly believed that Stefano was the chairman of the Mafia Commission. With several issues going on in the Cosa Nostra, he was asked to call a meeting of the commission, which he planned for November 1957 in Apalachin, New York. (See "November 14, 1957")

FBI agent Joseph Griffin was assigned to the Buffalo office in 1964, joining three other agents. He often teamed up with Bill Roselli during the "early years."[188] Griffin said, "During my first two years in Buffalo, we conducted an average of three raids per week against Arm [slang for Buffalo] bookmakers."[189] Combined with the intelligence they were receiving, they felt they were making an impact against the Magaddino Family.

Niagara Falls, known as the Honeymoon Capital, once "ill-famed for prostitution and vice," was considered "clean" by 1958.[190]

On July 25, 1958, revocation proceedings started against Power City Distributing by the New York State Liquor Authority to revoke its license due to sixteen infractions. Magaddino's son-in-law Charles Montana, secretary of the corporation, filed a petition for voluntary bankruptcy on July 22, 1958. On August 23, 1958, Power City was found guilty of eighteen charges and ordered to surrender its liquor license, with an auction held September 4, 1958, to sell all the assets.[191] For the first time since Prohibition, Magaddino was out of the beer business.

Magaddino was served a subpoena in early November 1958 to testify before the New York State Investigating Commission, but it was postponed. The following week, he was sent a warning when a grenade was tossed through his kitchen window. When he saw the grenade, he threw it back out the window,[192] but it turned out to be a dummy. No one was injured, but it has been said that all his windows were replaced with bulletproof glass after that episode.

Stefano finally testified before the state crime commission on January 14, 1959, and "refused 37 times" to answer questions.[193] "He even refused to say whether or not he could write English."[194] He did say he was a "$100 a week

In 1958, Magaddino had four houses built in Lewiston, New York, for himself and his three daughters. The jockey in front was there in 1968. This is Magaddino's home on Dana Drive today. *Photo by author.*

salesman" for Camellia Linen Supply Co., which was formed by Charles Montana after purchasing the Community Laundry in Buffalo. Stefano's wife was also a partner after investing $10,000. They had a Niagara Falls distribution site on Market Street, as well as an outlet on Haberle Avenue.[195] The business catered to restaurants and barbershops. They would offer to undercut the current supplier by a few cents and, once they were the supplier, raise the prices back to where they were, or higher. Few dared complain.[196]

During this time, Nino claimed to be employed as a chef at Andy's Restaurant in Buffalo. Employment records show he was employed from April 3, 1954, until December 7, 1957, when he "quit." He made ninety dollars per week, plus meal allowance; however, there was "no indication that he actually worked" there.[197]

As Stefano's sibling, Nino enjoyed the "prestige" of being the boss's brother. He dressed in fine clothes, kept a gumar (girlfriend) and would often spend time in the nightclubs and gambling joints in Buffalo and Niagara Falls. Nino often carried Stefano's messages to his troops. "Whatever he said, it was like the Old Man talking," a local mobster explained in 1974.[198]

When the Magaddino family first settled in Niagara Falls, they lived on Whitney Avenue. This was where Nino lived until his death in 1971. This is the house today. *Photo by author.*

Stefano appeared to be the buttoned-up opposite of his brother. He dressed conservatively and kept a very low profile. Even in death he has a simple headstone, no mausoleum or large family plot like John Montana has.

The differences between Stefano and Nino were obvious in June 1963, when Stefano said that Nino spent "all of his money…on women and he [Stefano]… had to support" Nino's family. He said that Nino was a playboy and he hated that. In October 1963, Stefano again complained about Nino having led a "loose life." In February 1964, Stefano said that Nino was "boastful, a liar, immoral" and had apparently threatened to be a stool pigeon. Stefano told Nino he would not have lived if he was anyone else and he was not grateful for the help he was given while Nino was hiding out after Apalachin.[199]

The Magaddinos watched with interest as mob turncoat Joe Valachi testified on live television in October 1963, naming Magaddino as a Mafia leader. A *Niagara Falls Gazette* reporter visited Magaddino's home in Lewiston looking for a comment and was greeted by his wife. "He doesn't want to make any comment. He is a very, very sick man. Please do not bother him," she said. When asked if she wanted to make a comment, Mrs. Magaddino replied, "What do you want from me, I am a very sick woman. Do you want to kill me?"[200]

Magaddino was heard on a wiretap saying, "We passed laws that this guy has got to die." He generally deemed Valachi's stories as "fairy tales," knowing, in fact, that much of them were quite accurate.

The stress probably did have an impact on his ability to run his crime family, as well as his health. During a wiretapped conversation between Vincent Scro and attorney Al Pacini, Scro describes his father-in-law's temperament in 1963. "He's been awful nervous lately. He was out to dinner at some restaurant the other night and some big fat woman was sitting at another table and she was talking about the Cosa Nostra and Magaddino and all that [obscenity] and they could hear her. Dad was pretty upset."[201]

Pietrina Magaddino, Gaspare's wife, died on June 17, 1964. Services were held at the Magaddino Memorial Chapel. The FBI hid in "a concealed position" to photograph attendees to the funeral home on June 19, 1964. Peter A., Peter J., Stefano, Sam Rangatore and others were seen.[202] Up until 4:10 p.m., Stefano was still present, but later that night he was hospitalized after suffering another heart attack. His first known heart attack was on February 28, 1960. That same month, tax liens against Magaddino and other family members had been filed in U.S. tax court.

Magaddino's paranoia started to really show on November 27, 1964, when he "began accusing former friends as being spies and operating against him." He discussed how his cousin Joseph Bonanno was talking with others in Montreal who were working against him.[203] On December 9, 1964, he was heard again talking about Bonanno with an unidentified man, accusing Bonanno of being a "sick man" and "sbirro" (police spy). He said that during Bonanno's early years in America he helped him financially, sending him "1500 or 1600" (probably dollars) and paying his expenses.

On January 21, 1965, Magaddino met with two unknown subjects and detailed the growth of La Cosa Nostra in the United States, starting when he was seventeen years old (around 1910).[204]

Stefano was to face another grand jury, this time investigating Bonanno's disappearance, on May 5, 1965, but he was suddenly taken to Niagara Falls Memorial Hospital. He was treated by "private and court-appointed physicians" for a heart ailment and was conveniently released on May 24, after the grand jury was no longer in session, thus missing his opportunity to testify.[205]

On July 12, 1965, the U.S. Department of Justice ordered the FBI to "terminate all of our microphones," according to FBI agent Griffin.[206]

In August 1968, Magaddino was called as a witness in *Joseph Cerrito v. Time, Inc.* Stefano claimed to be too ill to testify. The court was willing to convene in his home or a hospital room so he could testify, but his lawyer, Joseph P. Runfola, insisted that doctors be consulted to state that any testimony, even in the comfort of his bed, would be too much. He never did testify.

One of Niagara Falls' biggest gamblers was Benjamin Nicoletti Sr. Born in Valguarnera, Italy, on January 28, 1911, he was one of the top bookmakers in Niagara Falls and operated craps games in various local towns. First arrested in 1930 on a robbery charge, in 1939 he began his gambling arrest record.[207] According to Special Agent Griffin of the FBI, an informant told him "that Benjamin Nicoletti, Sr.…was supervising a bookmaking operation for Stefano Magaddino."

He "deals directly through his son, Benjamin Nicoletti, Jr.," who "employs Patsy Passero, Gino Monaco, Louis Tavano, Sam Puglese, Augie Rizzo, and Mike Farella as bookmakers."[208]

"Once a week, normally on Tuesday, Benjamin Nicoletti, Jr. meets with his father to balance their books, with the son passing on to the father the percentage of the profits due to the father and the percentage of profits due Stefano Magaddino. Nicoletti, Sr. [then] settles up with Stefano Magaddino."[209]

FBI agents began to notice a pattern by at least April 1968 in which Nicoletti Sr. and Peter A. would meet at a local restaurant, talk business for a short time and then depart separately. In April

Benjamin Nicoletti Sr. (right) was a top bookmaker and gambler in Niagara Falls and Tonawanda. His reign took a nosedive in November 1968, when he was arrested along with the Magaddinos. This is after his arrest. *Courtesy Buffalo State College Archives,* Courier-Express *Collection.*

da—1968—196

Commissioner's
Warrant of Arrest

Form No. 90 (Rev. 7-26-50)

United States District Court

FOR THE

WESTERN DISTRICT OF NEW YORK

Commissioner's Docket No. *68*

Case No. *111*

UNITED STATES OF AMERICA

v

STEFANO MAGADDINO

WARRANT OF ARREST

To any authorized Agent of the Federal Bureau of Investigation:

You are hereby commanded to arrest STEFANO MAGADDINO , and bring him
here insert name of defendant or description

forthwith before the nearest available United States Commissioner to answer to a complaint charging him

with being engaged in the business of gambling and bookmaking in violation
here describe offense charged in complaint
of the laws of the State of New York, and knowingly conspiring to use and
using and causing to be used telephone facilities in foreign commerce with
intent to promote, manage, establish, carry on and facilitate the pro-
motion, management, establishment and carrying on of said gambling and
bookmaking business.
in violation of U.S.C. Title, 18, Sections 1952, 2, and 371.

Date   November 26 , 1968 .

_____
United States Commissioner.

1. Here insert designation of officer to whom warrant is issued.

RETURN

Received *November 26, 1968* at *Buffalo, N.Y.* and executed by arrest of. *Stefano*
Magaddino   at *Lewiston, N.Y.*   on *November 29, 1968.*

_____
Name.
Special Agent in Charge — FBI
Title.
Western District of New York.

Date *November 29, 1968*   By_____, Deputy

#23-a

This is the warrant of arrest used by the FBI to arrest Stefano Magaddino in November
1968. When they pulled him over on Ferry Avenue in Niagara Falls, his brother Nino was
driving and Stefano was munching on a bag of peanuts. *Author's collection.*

and May, they were observed in the K-Mart cafeteria on Military Road in
Niagara Falls. Some conversations indicated that Peter would assume control
as head of the family.[210]

FBI agents covertly watched as Peter A. met with Nicoletti Sr. on four Tuesdays, starting on October 1, 1968, at Round-the-Clock Restaurant in Niagara Falls. On October 8, 1968, they met at Your Host Restaurant on Niagara Falls Boulevard in Tonawanda, New York, sitting in the last booth. Peter was overheard by an FBI agent sitting in an adjacent booth talking about "himself as taking over when" his father stepped down. As he got ready to leave, he was handed a rolled-up piece of paper, possibly the payment. They both then left about five minutes apart.[211]

For the next couple meetings—October 29 and November 12—they again met at Your Host. Nicoletti was "observed handing something…under the table to Magaddino," who also reached under the table and "then placed his hand in his left pocket."[212]

On Tuesday, November 26, 1968, arrest and search warrants were executed for members of the Magaddino crime family after Peter and Nicoletti had their last fateful meeting at Round-the-Clock Restaurant. Both were apprehended outside the restaurant. Police officers searched Nicoletti's 1965 Cadillac after arresting him and found a purchase order for a brand-new black 1969 Cadillac and miscellaneous paperwork but nothing incriminating.

Simultaneously, New York State Police and FBI agents arrested Gino Frank Monaco, Sam Joseph Puglese, Michael Farella, Augustine Rizzo, Patsy Passero and Louis Tavano. But Benjamin Nicoletti Jr. was not found.

Aware of Stefano's weak heart and avoidance of any testimony in recent years, the FBI decided to take it easy on the old man. At 3:40 p.m., he was pulled over in a car driven by his brother Nino on Ferry Avenue. FBI agent Joseph Griffin walked up to the car as Stefano was munching on a bag of peanuts[213] and handed him a warrant for his arrest, telling him he needed to report to federal court in Buffalo by the next morning. Magaddino proceeded straight home and apparently went to bed and did not appear in court as authorized. He was put under twenty-four-hour watch with four federal marshals stationed outside his home.

Stefano's home was not searched that day, but the other homes were. A minute bit of evidence was found. At Nicoletti Sr.'s home they found, among other items, a few decks of cards, a few hundred dollars, a pair of dice, a football pool ticket and an address book. In Nicoletti Jr.'s house they found correspondence to Canadian addresses, a few hundred dollars and some miscellaneous items.[214]

In Patsy Passero's 1965 Dodge they found $1,565, while in his home they recovered four telephones, dice, playing cards, racing forms and other

The Magaddino Memorial Chapel was the base of operations for the crime family from about 1958 through Magaddino's "retirement" in 1972. There was a rumor that they invented a coffin with a hidden space to stuff an extra body. *Photo by author.*

miscellaneous items. In Sam Puglese's home they found some flash paper, about $150 and some racing forms. At Niagara Sundry, where Michael Farella was working, agents found racing forms, a telephone, "21 pieces of white paper" and some pens and a pencil.[215]

So far, this hardly exposed a clandestine organization and vast gambling empire. It looked like either the raids may have been premature or the Magaddino Family was not nearly as powerful as was suspected by the authorities.

The search of Augustine Rizzo's home in nearby North Tonawanda turned up a somewhat better cache than they had found in the other homes: racing forms, playing cards, dice, a Bay State single-barrel sawed-off shotgun and a H&R .32-caliber revolver.

When authorities searched the Magaddino Memorial Chapel, everything began to look brighter. Inside Peter A.'s office they found $1,235 in the lower left desk drawer; $1,740 in the top drawer of a file cabinet; a "brown vinyl briefcase" in the third drawer of the file cabinet containing four envelopes with four bundles of money: $4,371 in a white envelope, $11,000 wrapped

When FBI agents searched Peter Magaddino's home in November 1968, they found more than they imagined. A trunk was stuffed full of money, over $2 million in today's dollars, which led to dissent and revolt in the crime family. This is the home today. *Photo by author.*

in yellow lined paper, $3,600 in a white envelope and $8,045 in a small white envelope, totaling $27,016; and, finally, $8,000 wrapped in aluminum foil in a locked metal box in the bottom drawer of the file cabinet, for a grand total of $37,991 (or over $235,000 in 2010 dollars). The search concluded at 6:50 p.m.[216] Peter would later claim this was money that he had not yet deposited from funerals, but the authorities did not buy it.

The turning point really came when the FBI searched Peter's personal residence. Unlike the others, it looked like Peter and his father Stefano had been hiding something from the family.

At 3:40 p.m., FBI agents found a suitcase, the location of which is still debatable. Some accounts say in the attic and some say hidden in the bedroom. Regardless of where it was found, inside they discovered $473,134 in cash. That is over $2.9 million in 2010 dollars. Add the two findings and you have over $3.1 million in money that was hidden from the Magaddino crime family by its boss and heir apparent.

According to a story in *Time* magazine, Peter's wife, Frances, unaware of the suitcase and its vast sums of money, was upset by the finding.

She swore and said, "He told me we didn't have enough money to go to Florida this year."[217]

They also found a loaded semiautomatic pistol and a list of names, addresses and figures. Included on that list were Gaspar DiGregorio of the Bonanno family; Joe Falcone of Utica, New York; Anthony DiStefano of Fulton, New York; Fred and Victor Randaccio; and a few others, most members of the mob. Probably more important than anything found during the searches was the money and these names tying Magaddino to other suspected Mafia members.

The reason this was such a blow to the family started prior to the finding of the money. Peter Magaddino was preparing to become the next family boss. He went to his capos in 1967 and explained that it was a slow year so they wouldn't be giving out any Christmas bonuses.[218] Although the capos were unhappy, there was little they could do.

When the $473,000 was discovered in Peter's house the following year, the family assumed that Peter and Stefano had been holding out on them for years, and all hell broke out. The fear and intimidation that Stefano had manifested for years slowly started to disintegrate. They knew Peter wasn't as strong as his father, and Stefano was just an old man.

The family broke apart into several factions, each vying for control of the family. War was a concern. Peter, of course, stayed loyal to his father, but the arrest changed him. No longer was he all over town. Surveillance found him leaving home in the morning, going to the funeral chapel and then heading back home in the evening.[219]

The Rochester, New York Mafia family had been under Magaddino's control for years. After the money was discovered, its members suddenly declared that they were going to break free. Some of Magaddino's closest men were now against him, and his life could have been in danger.

Due to Magaddino's position on the Mafia Commission, he was allowed to retain 15 percent of Rochester's gambling operation until his supposed retirement in June 1972.[220]

On November 29, 1968, U.S. commissioner Edmund F. Maxwell traveled to the Lewiston home of Stefano and arraigned him on international racketeering and conspiracy charges while he lay in his bed wearing "lime-colored pajamas."[221]

While Magaddino was being arraigned, Neil J. Welch, special agent in charge of the FBI, conducted searches of the homes of Magaddino and his three sons-in-law, Vincent Scro, Charles Montana and James LaDuca, all on Dana Drive (also spelled Danna) in Lewiston, better known as the

This photo shows FBI agents searching Stefano's Lewiston home in November 1968, after they arraigned him in his bed. *Courtesy Buffalo State College Archives,* Courier-Express *Collection.*

"Magaddino Compound." The searches found very little of substance to use in the prosecution of the Magaddino Family. At Charles Montana's house, they found a .38 Colt Special and three reels of film. At Vincent Scro's home, they found canceled checks, a couple betting slips and some "lined white paper containing names, addresses, and some figures." Very damning. But at James LaDuca's home, they hit the jackpot: five loose decks of "Bee" playing cards and three boxes of "#92 Special 'Bee' playing cards."[222]

At Magaddino's home, they were able to find a Smith & Wesson revolver, some miscellaneous items and "one black metal box containing papers." They also found a large, empty safe in the basement.

A federal grand jury indicted the group on December 4, 1968, charging them with using facilities in interstate commerce to promote gambling and conspiracy to do the same. On December 12, 1968, federal judge John O. Henderson, U.S. attorney Andrew F. Phelan, a court reporter and attorney

After Stefano Magaddino was handed his arrest warrant, he headed home and to bed. Two weeks later, Federal Judge John Henderson (in hat) headed to Magaddino's Lewiston home to arraign him in his bed. *Courtesy Buffalo State College Archives,* Courier-Express *Collection.*

Joseph P. Runfola all met in the bedroom of Stefano Magaddino for his arraignment. Magaddino was once again tucked in his bed.

Judge Henderson: Mr. Magaddino, can you hear me?
Magaddino: Yes. [Supposedly spoken weakly.]

The judge explained the reason for convening in his bedroom.

Judge: Do you understand?
Magaddino: Yes.

A plea of not guilty was entered by his attorney. The judge then asked Magaddino if he had any questions. Attorney Runfola said he had explained it to Magaddino and he understood the charges. Magaddino had no questions, and a mug shot was taken of him.

Stefano's daughter Josephine died in March 1969. During the fall of 1969, Nino was diagnosed with terminal lung cancer and given six months to live. He had one cancerous lung removed in October 1969. By March 1970, he rarely left home, had lost considerable weight and had difficulty walking. All his activity stopped. Nino's wife died on January 19, 1970, and the funeral was held on January 22. According to reports, Stefano did not attend the funeral, which had about twenty cars in the procession.[223]

Stefano was admitted to Buffalo General Hospital in March 1970 for five days of court-authorized examinations. A total of nine physicians all concluded that if Magaddino were to testify, or even be a defendant in a courtroom, it could be "hazardous to life to subject."[224]

On May 26, 1970, Judge Henderson questioned Dr. Howard G. Bruenn, who was consulted by the Department of Justice, on how ill Magaddino really was.

> *The Court: If he came into this courtroom and faced trial, what do you think his life expectancy is, improved or lessened?*
> *The Witness: Lessened.*
> *The Court: You recommend that he not be tried, regardless of the merits?*
> *The Witness: Yes, sir.*
> *The Court: Because he might die in this room?*
> *The Witness: Yes, sir.*

The IRS placed a tax levy against Peter A. on May 20, 1970, in the amount of $1,055,979.72 ($5.8 million in 2010 dollars), effectively freezing any assets he owned.

Stefano entered Mount St. Mary's Hospital in Lewiston on May 13, 1970. On May 28, his personal physician, Dr. Pellicano, testified before Judge Henderson as to the state of his heart.

> *The Court: Doctor, is there anything the Government could do to create a condition whereby we could bring Mr. Magaddino into the courtroom without subjecting him to death?*
> *The Witness: I don't believe so.*

In November 1970, Peter A. was hospitalized for what was thought to be cancer and had chest surgery to remove a non-malignant tumor.[225]

Nino died on April 13, 1971, at seventy-three years old. He had been hospitalized for about a week when cancer finally ravaged his body. His funeral was on April 15, with burial next to his wife in St. Joseph's Cemetery.[226] A funeral procession of twenty-five cars was escorted by motorcycle police.[227] FBI agents did not see Stefano at the funeral home during the funeral.

Peter A. assumed full control of the funeral home after Nino's death.

On an almost daily basis in 1971, Stefano visited the Camellia Linen Supply Company in Buffalo.[228]

A motion to sever Stefano Magaddino's case due to his declining health was submitted by his attorney. Judge Henderson said that "a very great and persuasive burden of proof"[229] was needed for him to do so. Even the U.S. attorney indicated that it would be "hazardous to Magaddino to subject him to the emotional rigors of court."[230]

After listening to evidence from doctors and the U.S. attorney, Judge Henderson wrote in his decision, "This court has no choice but to order that Stefano Magaddino's trial be severed."[231] The case against him was dropped. Rumor has it that Magaddino was dancing with his grandchildren in the yard that day. So much for the bum heart.

On June 28, 1971, hearings were begun to determine if the government had illegally seized evidence by utilizing wiretaps. Deputy superintendent of Niagara Falls police Albert J. Lynch testified about how they learned some of the names of people they "considered organized crime."[232]

Judge Henderson asked Lynch, "Was it a matter of how your name ends, in a vowel or otherwise?"

Lynch responded, "No, sir, we had different nationalities."

Later, Niagara Falls detective lieutenant James E. Gray testified about organized crime, and Judge Henderson was somewhat perplexed. "The term has intrigued me, a term I never used in my life in the courtroom as a prosecutor, and the last witness talked about the Mafia, a term I never

In 1958, the Magaddino family moved together, forming the second "Mafia Row" on Dana Drive in Lewiston. This is the former home of Vincent and Arcangela (Magaddino) Scro. *Photo by author.*

This is the former home of James and Angeline (Magaddino) LaDuca on Dana Drive in Lewiston as it looks today. *Photo by author.*

Charles and Josephine (Magaddino) Montana lived in this home on Dana Drive in Lewiston. *Photo by author.*

used privately or in the courtroom before the mandate of the Attorney General came down. I don't understand what this term is. Is it a bugaboo, what is it?"[233]

A few minutes later, during questioning by Harold J. Boreanaz, attorney for the Nicolettis (and related to actor David Boreanaz), the judge again broke in and said that he did not understand what organized crime was.

"To the best of my knowledge," Lynch said, "organized crime is—it is a corporation of people, the higher-ups and the workers, and they share in the wealth."

Later that day, Judge Henderson said, "You know, gentlemen, I can't help feel after listening all day to the $25 fines in the City of Niagara Falls…what a thing for the Federal Court to be sitting here on basically a gambling case, except by gimmick they laid off across state lines and it is a federal case. These gamblers make tons of money. Think about it, why should a Federal Court be concerned with the city of Niagara Falls."[234] The judge was not happy to be spending time on what he thought was a trivial local matter, "in light of more important cases."[235]

On July 30, 1971, Agent Griffin testified for a second day in federal court. Under questioning by attorney Boreanaz, Griffin was asked, "Stefano Magaddino was a principal source of investigative endeavor, wasn't he?"

"He was," Griffin responded.

"He was *reputed* to be a leader of some organization, wasn't he?"

"He *is*," Griffin replied.[236]

By November 1971, it was clear to the FBI that Peter did not "have sufficient influence or backing from other crime elements to rise to his father's position of power," although it was believed that he had some backing in Toronto and Syracuse.[237] He would be passed over.

Sam Rangatore was born in Niagara Falls on November 18, 1908, and was thought to be Stefano's chauffeur or bodyguard at times. He operated Rangatore Vending Machine Company and died on December 29, 1971.[238]

On May 17, 1973, Judge Henderson ordered the government to supply the defendants with "the reports, files, and memoranda compiled from the tapes and logs of illegal electronic surveillance" the FBI had conducted. The judge also ordered the "disclosure of the identity of a confidential informant" used to secure the twenty-two search and arrest warrants.[239]

The government declined to do so, and the indictments were immediately dismissed against the remaining nine defendants, but the government immediately appealed the decision. It was not argued until January 9, 1974, and decided on May 2, 1974.

On appeal, Patsy Passero and Augie Rizzo had the order reversed, since they did not prove their phones "were tapped or their conversations intercepted," but the court upheld the decision of Judge Henderson to dismiss the other indictments.[240]

On July 19, 1974, Stefano Magaddino was rushed to Mount St. Mary's Hospital at 3:00 p.m. after suffering another heart attack. At 7:20 p.m.,[241] the eighty-two-year-old "Mafia chieftain" was dead. His funeral was a somber, private affair. Reporters were told to leave. A "cluster of onlookers" stood outside St. Joseph's Church to view the funeral,[242] with the crowd estimated to number two hundred by the time the funeral Mass ended. No

The FBI struck pay dirt when they found over $3 million (in current value) in Peter Magaddino's home and the Magaddino funeral home. This is Buffalo SAC Neil J. Welch of the FBI on the right posing with the confiscated money, guns and a few bookie items. *Courtesy Buffalo State College Archives,* Courier-Express *Collection.*

other Mafia family bosses attended his funeral. Several reasons are possible. Some claimed they did not want the FBI photographing them. Another credible reason is that all of Magaddino's contemporaries were dead, leaving those younger and less steeped in the traditions, who saw Magaddino as one more person out of their way.

After Stefano's death, Joe Salardino of Denver told an informant that if Peter "gets out of line," the Pieri faction would kill him.

In September 1975, the IRS considered canceling the lien and returning the $500,000 found in the November 1968 raid, which they finally did in 1976. Peter agreed to pay $173,753 plus $77,000 interest payment for back taxes.

On November 19, 1975, Federal Judge John T. Curtin, who took over the case after Judge Henderson died, signed an Order of Dismissal that

Stefano Magaddino died in 1974, and the funeral was a somber, private affair. This is the funeral cortege as it travels along the streets of Niagara Falls. *Courtesy Buffalo State College Archives,* Courier-Express *Collection.*

had been filed by U.S. attorney Richard J. Arcara for Patsy Passero and Augustine Rizzo, stating, "It would be an impossible task to segregate out from the 75,000 pages of wiretap transcript," as well as the unavailability of government witnesses, the case against just these two men. This essentially ended the case against the Magaddino Family.[243]

What started as a racketeering case against the Magaddino Family, with much fanfare and press, ended up crushing the spirit of the Magaddinos, allowing others to take control of the western New York Mafia. The case was dismissed, with no charges against those originally charged.

In mid-February 1976, Peter A. Magaddino entered Roswell Park Memorial Institute for a serious throat ailment and underwent several weeks of treatment for lung cancer. He was given three months to live.[244] He entered Mount St. Mary's Hospital in June 1976 in poor health and subsequently was returned to Roswell Park Memorial Institute, where he died on August 16, 1976, at fifty-nine years old. He was buried on

August 19 in St. Joseph's Cemetery, next to his father.[245] His mother died in August 1986.

This was, in effect, the end of the Magaddino crime family. One could argue about the power of Stefano, his overall influence in the national Mafia and the commission or whether he was the longest-tenured mob boss, but one cannot argue that he was a dominant figure in western New York, Brooklyn, southern Ontario and other locations for many years. No other children or grandchildren aspired to take his place; in fact, many moved out of the area. Peter was the last vestige of the old crime family, and after his arrest in 1968, he pretty much gave up that dream. Things had been too easy for the Magaddino Family, and that really rocked their boat. Peter's death signified the end of an era, and the changing tide in Buffalo and Niagara Falls would go on for years.

THE MAGADDINO RELATIVES

Another degenerate, coomba. Those guys are not people, they're animals.
They're degenerates.[246]
—*Vincent Scro talking to Charles Montana, James LaDuca and Father Art*
LaDuca about drug dealers

Stefano Magaddino was the father of two families. In his blood family, he had three daughters and one son. Arcangela married Vincent Scro (born July 28, 1924, in Auburn); Angeline (born June 5, 1921) married James V. LaDuca (born October 19, 1912, in Buffalo); Josephine (born January 11, 1919, in Philadelphia) married Charles A. Montana (born November 6, 1912, in Buffalo); and Peter married Frances Montana.[247]

One of Stefano's sisters married Gaspar DiGregorio of Brooklyn, a member of the Bonanno crime family, and another, Arcangela, married Nick Longo, also of Brooklyn, but they settled next door to Magaddino in Niagara Falls.

Longo was said to be a "top lieutenant" for Magaddino and involved in bookmaking operations. It was intimated that a Buffalo/Niagara Falls bookmaking syndicate was pressuring thirty-eight-year-old Frank LoTempio of Batavia to pay tribute to Magaddino, to which he apparently fought back.

In the early morning hours of May 19, 1936, a bomb was secretly placed outside the door of Longo's home in Niagara Falls. Arcangela, forty-two, heard a noise and went to investigate, only to have the bomb explode, tearing

Nick Longo was in New York City in May 1936 when a bomb killed his wife and injured their three daughters. The home had a hole blown in the side, but it was repaired. This is the home today. *Photo by author.*

a hole in the wall, killing her and injuring their three daughters, Rosa, Lena and Josephine, who all survived.

It is believed that the bomb was intended for Nick, but the killers did not know that he was in New York City at the time. Stefano's home to the left and the home to the right were also damaged by the blast.

Just weeks later, on June 27, 1936, LoTempio attended a wedding at Holy Cross Church in Buffalo and was gunned down in the middle of the street.

LoTempio's sister was married to Niagara Falls undertaker Alfred Panepinto. Panepinto and his family moved back to Batavia from Niagara Falls, and he was killed while playing cards at Frank's brother Russell LoTempio's poolroom on Saturday, August 15, 1937.[248]

Samuel Izzo (aka Yates), also of Batavia, was felled by four bullets on August 26, 1936, after attending a wake in Buffalo.[249] Police did not

When Stefano Magaddino's sister was killed in 1936, it was suspected that Frank LoTempio of Batavia was behind it. He was killed leaving a wedding at Holy Cross Church in June 1936. This is the church today. *Photo by author.*

believe there was any connection between the killings. None of the killers was ever found.

Pallbearers for Arcangela Longo's funeral were all men close to Stefano: John Montana, Salvatore Lagattuta and Angelo Acquisto of Buffalo; Salvatore Falcone of Utica; and Augustus Scalia and Sam Rangatore Jr. of Niagara Falls.[250]

Nick Longo was, according to one source, banished to New York City by Magaddino, and Stefano took in his nieces. Longo died in Brooklyn on May 10, 1959, at sixty-six years old.[251]

In 1946, LaDuca moved into the former Longo house after marrying Magaddino's daughter Angeline in June. He worked for Power City Distributing, and his wife worked for the Magaddino Funeral Home. In 1951, LaDuca was secretary-treasurer of the funeral business and his wife was working for Charles Distribution Corp., owned by brother-in-law Charles Montana.[252]

In 1947, Scro was a director of Buffalo Beverage Corporation, as was Peter J. Magaddino; it is unclear which Peter.[253]

In 1958, Stefano, his wife and their three daughters and sons-in-law all moved to Dana Drive in suburban Lewiston. Magaddino had four ranch-style houses built in a row for his family by LaDuca's brothers. The houses have been called "sumptuous," and the street became known as "Mafia Row." The development was also known as Rumsey Ridge.

By the 1960s, the FBI believed that Scro was the family consigliere as well as accountant.[254]

Magaddino's daughter Josephine died in March 1969, and the funeral was held on March 18, 1969, at the Magaddino Memorial Chapel.[255] Montana sold his house on Dana Drive and eventually moved out of Niagara Falls, remarried and settled in Cheektowaga.

One of Arcangela and Nick Longo's daughters, Rose Mary, died on July 26, 2011. Daughter Josephine married Albert Certo of Niagara Falls, and daughter Arcangela married James DiGregorio of Brooklyn.[256]

Montana and LaDuca both found legitimate factory work after the fall of the Magaddino Family. LaDuca retired after twenty-five years with

When Stefano Magaddino's sister Arcangela Longo was killed by a bomb in 1936, it is believed that he avenged her death. This is the family plot in St. Joseph Cemetery in Niagara Falls. *Photo by author.*

Kaufman's Bakery in Buffalo and died on September 25, 1993. His wife, Angeline, died on February 26, 1993.[257]

Nino's son Peter died in 1990 at sixty-seven years old.

The Scros outlived all the family except Peter's wife, Frances. The Scros sold their Dana Drive home in 1980 and were living in Florida and Virginia. Vincent died on July 22, 2009, at eighty-four years old.[258] It is believed that Frances Magaddino and Arcangela Scro are still alive at the time of this writing.

THE CRIME FAMILY

They know everybody's name. They know who's boss. They know who is on the commission. They know Amico Nostro *(Our Friend, the password).*[259]
—*Stefano Magaddino*

Organized crime? Who ever heard about organized crime and its extended families during the '40s and '50s?"[260] That's what most people thought before the Apalachin meeting in 1957. Buffalo and Niagara Falls were ripe with crime for years, but no one ever thought there was a national "syndicate" connecting it all together.

Daniel "Boots" Sansanese Sr. was serving time in prison in the early 1950s. "While in prison, a close friendship was made with his cellmate, Joseph Fino. Through the years after their release, these two men became known as the 'arm' or 'muscle' for the organization." Buffalo then was known as the Arm.[261] Sansanese was born on May 27, 1908, and had been questioned as a suspect in "practically every gangland murder in Buffalo–Niagara Falls area."[262] His only known employment was as a strong-arm man for Fred Randaccio and Stefano.

Herman Weinstein was a non-Sicilian family associate. Born on January 1, 1896, in Austria, he ran the Peace Bridge Motel and Bowling Alleys in Buffalo. Weinstein was described as an "old time hoodlum" who was connected with Joe DiCarlo and Julius Caputo in the 1930s. Known as "the original Mr. Fixit," he was involved in black market gas ration coupons during World War II.[263] Arrested numerous times, his first

Daniel Sansanese was a capo in the Magaddino Family. This was one of the homes he lived in over the years on Porter Avenue in Buffalo as it looks today. *Photo by author.*

conviction was in 1950 for bribery, which was reversed and dismissed on appeal.

The Magaddino Family had a penchant for making people disappear. It would be hard to put an exact number on it. One of Stefano's supposed top hit men was John "Johnny Keys" Simone, who was rumored to have killed at least ten people during his time in Buffalo.

George A. Meranto was arrested with Ben Nicoletti in 1930 for robbery.[264] In 1934, Simone, Sam Grana, Angelo Ciambrone and Meranto were arrested in Tonawanda while trashing a house with two women home.[265] Why they were there was never ascertained.

It is believed that Meranto, a known gambler and supposed "shakedown artist," "slapped a man named Magaddino"[266] around early December 1943. It was a terrible mistake, the kind for which there was no apology. Meranto was killed on December 19, 1943, and Simone was said to be the shooter. His body was found the next day in the Erie Canal in suburban Amherst, with multiple bullets to the head and neck, taken at close range.[267] In the usual twist of fate in Niagara Falls, the Magaddino Funeral Home made his final arrangements.[268]

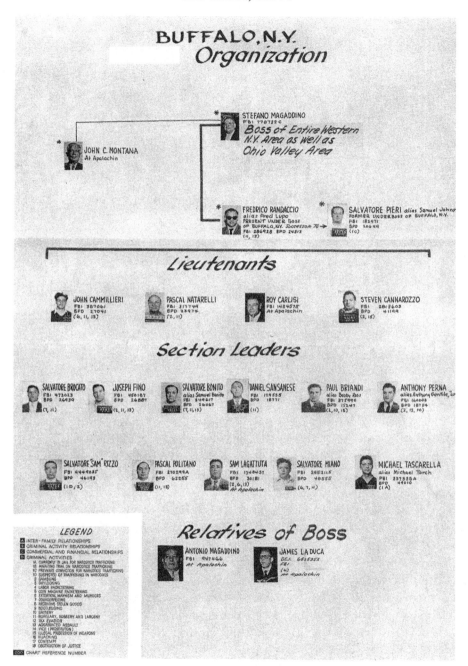

In 1963, the government and Mafia informant Joe Valachi put together a chart of the Magaddino Crime Family. This chart shows what the FBI felt was the family hierarchy, which was somewhat accurate. *Author's collection.*

Steve Cannarozzo worked at Madison Cab on Rhode Island Street in Buffalo. He was friends with Fred Randaccio, and Mafia meetings were said to take place in the office. This photo is taken outside the building looking across the street. *Courtesy Jim Manganello.*

Dominick D'Agostino was one of Stefano's longtime associates, often heard on wiretaps in the early 1960s. In 1927, D'Agostino owned the Laurel Hotel, which burned to the ground two years later,[269] and he ran American Dry Cleaners in 1942; both businesses were in Niagara Falls.

Anthony "Lucky" Perna ran the Perna Funeral Home in Buffalo with his son and was associated with Roy "the Clam Man" Carlisi, Sam Lagattuta and Stefano. Perna was involved in loan sharking and had a long arrest record, including rape, kidnapping, assault and counterfeiting. He was arrested in 1931 on an extortion charge along with Joseph San Filippo[270] and in 1933 on suspicion of murder in the Callea brothers' deaths. The extortion charges were dropped after the complainant changed his story.[271]

Another violent Buffalo mobster was Salvatore P. "Sam" Rizzo, born on August 14, 1913. He was arrested on various charges over the years, including gambling and rape, and was an associate of Salvatore Pieri.

One member of the Buffalo Mafia whose stature was uncertain is Steve "Flattop" Cannarozzo, born on May 26, 1921. Cannarozzo was listed on a 1963 FBI family chart of the Magaddino Family. He is best known as the manager of Madison Taxi Company in Buffalo, owned by his father, Victor.

James V. Delmont was born in Buffalo in 1916. He was a hot-tempered "small-time hoodlum"[272] arrested on various charges, including robbery, bookmaking and burglary, but until 1939, he had not served time in prison. After a stint for robbery in Pennsylvania, he was given a small bookie operation in Buffalo. Arrested several more times, he worked odd jobs to supplement his income.

His "principal occupation," he claimed, was armed robbery, working with Charles "Limey" Miller, Fred and Frank Aquino and Richard Battaglia. They would beat their victims and then rob them. A fatal mistake was made when they robbed some Mafia members. Miller, the Aquinos and Battaglia were all killed, but for some reason, Delmont was spared and given a job as a driver at Madison Taxi.

On June 18, 1959, Delmont "had a violent argument with Steven Cannarozzo,"[273] went home, returned to the taxi company and fired a gun "some four or five times"[274] at Cannarozzo, striking him and dispatcher Rosario Moscato, but neither was killed.

Delmont left Buffalo five days later, telling his wife he was headed for California. Instead, he traveled to Miami to see former Buffalonian and Cleveland mobster John Tronolone, godfather to one of his children. He asked Tronolone to intercede on his behalf, but Tronolone declined and told him to go to Vancouver, Canada, to wait it out.

Delmont went to California and ended up taking refuge in a monastery in Sacramento, where the Mafia would not kill him. While there, he confided in one of the men, saying, "The Mafia is stronger than the FBI. They're going to kill me at night."[275]

By October 1959, his fighting with other members of the monastery had grown to the point that he was asked to leave. He made his way to a Catholic convent in San Francisco and resided there until May 24, 1960, when he was again asked to leave. From there, Delmont took a bus to Los Angeles and called a former prison buddy, who picked him up and let him stay at his house.

On June 3, 1960, law enforcement officials in Buffalo said they noticed a lot of activity at the Magaddino Memorial Chapel, with six mob leaders arriving at 11:00 a.m. for a meeting and phone call to Los Angeles.[276] That night, Delmont went out and did not return. The following morning, fifty miles away in Ontario, California, a man's body was found in an open field seventy-five feet from the road. He had been beaten, and "at least 12 blows from a blackjack or a club shattered the top of his skull."[277] It took four days to identify him, but the Mafia had finally tracked down Delmont.

Salvatore "George Raft" Bonito was born on March 30, 1914 in Buffalo. His main dealings were in bookmaking and shylocking, better known as loan

James Delmont was a mob associate who worked as a taxi driver for Madison Cab. After shooting Steve Cannarozzo, he was a wanted man. A year later, they tracked him down in California and killed him. *Courtesy* Ontario Daily Report/Inland Valley Daily Bulletin.

sharking. Stefano often referred to him a "messenger boy" because he dealt with other bookmakers and thieves in Canada.[278]

Edward V. Scillia was born in Buffalo on June 23, 1908, and was an associate of Randaccio, Fino and Natarelli. Scillia was into bookmaking and policy rackets and was often seen traveling with the above men.[279]

Dominic B. Mantell, owner of Mantell's Carrousel of Flowers in Niagara Falls, was born on January 13, 1918, in Niagara Falls. He was a known gambler and operated horse books and craps games, His florist shop was next door to the Magaddino Memorial Chapel, and he was often seen out with Nino.[280]

Pine Bowl Bowling Alleys in Niagara Falls was a popular hangout for the Magaddinos during the 1960s. It was managed by Samuel J. Kaufman, aka Peter Mack, who was close enough to the family that he was heard on the funeral home wiretaps numerous times.

On May 2, 1967, a confidential FBI informant told Agent Joe Griffin that there would be a big party at Panaro's Lounge in Buffalo.[281] The bar, known as Snowball's, was run by Michael Panaro. Another informant said it would be billed as a stag party for Joe Todaro Jr. but in essence it was to honor Todaro's status as a newly made man in La Cosa Nostra. Prior to the party, there would be a dice game to raise money for Todaro.

The FBI discussed the party with Captain Kenneth P. Kennedy of the Buffalo Police Gambling Squad. Although they had little else to go on, they contacted the State Liquor Authority with the intention of raiding the location. They planned to arrest anyone with a criminal record on charges of consorting with criminals. Griffin said, "These charges would probably eventually be thrown out, but it would give us an opportunity to again display to the community evidence that organized crime did in fact exist."[282]

The FBI set up surveillance at seven o'clock on the night of May 8, 1967, and determined that most of the Magaddino Family members were, in fact, in attendance. At 10:10 p.m., a Buffalo Police truck pulled to the rear door, and FBI, state and Buffalo Police conducted a Liquor Authority inspection.

An estimated three hundred people were in the restaurant, including "several local judges and businessmen," and all said they were there for the stag party.[283] The lawyers in attendance told the attendees not to give their names, so only those men known by sight were arrested.

In the basement, they found some mobsters gambling, but the initial search did not find the top mobsters they had seen enter the building. Almost two hours later, they saw a padlocked wine cellar and forced Panaro to open it. Inside were seven of Magaddino's top men: Dan Sansanese Sr., James LaDuca, Fred Randaccio, Victor Randaccio, Roy Carlisi, Pat Natarelli and Nick Rizzo. Rizzo was drunk and took a swing at an officer. He had to be subdued and had an additional charge tacked on.[284]

Along with those men, also arrested were Joe Sciales, Joe DiCarlo, Sam Frangiamore, John Cammilleri, Fred Saia (who would later become a government informant), Joe Todaro, Albert Billiteri, Benny Spano, Joe and Nick Fino, William Sciolino, Steve "The Whale" Cino, Salvatore Rizzo, Matt Billiteri, John Sacco, Louis Sicurella, Lawrence Panaro, Augustine Territo, Sam Rangatore, Steve Cannarozzo and Frank Valenti of Rochester.[285] Of all those in attendance, only thirty-six men were actually arrested. As Griffin suspected, the next morning, Buffalo City Court judge James B. Kane Jr. dropped all the charges after lawyers argued that there was no "intent to breach the peace." Even Buffalo Police admitted that it appeared to be just a social gathering.[286]

The infamous site of what Buffalo Police called the "Little Apalachin" raid in 1967. Panaro's was a frequent mob hangout on Hampshire Street and hosted a stag party in 1967 that was broken up by the FBI and Buffalo Police. *Courtesy Niagara Falls Gazette.*

The event was dubbed "Little Apalachin" by the police due to the number of LCN members they found in one location. According to insiders, Magaddino was angry at LaDuca and Fred Randaccio for getting arrested and drawing attention to the family. He also blamed Randaccio for the pressure the family was receiving from the FBI and instructed them to use their political connections to have legitimate Italian American groups file a lawsuit against the Buffalo Police for harassment.[287]

Joe Todaro did just that and filed a civil lawsuit against twenty-four police officers, saying he suffered financial losses and was subjected to "public scorn, ridicule and humiliation."[288] The real reason for his arrest, his lawyer argued, was consorting "with well known Italians,"[289] which, in itself, is not illegal.

Buffalo Police submitted a report to the State Liquor Authority after the raid. With the negative publicity, legitimate customers stopped visiting Snowball's, and Panaro lost his liquor license.

William "Billy the Kid" Sciolino got his start working with Buffalo burglar Tom Gascoyne.[290] Others in the crew included Ronald Carlisle, Gregory Parness, Frank D'Angelo, Russell DeCicco, Dennis Borden and Stanley Seneca.

After Stefano's arrest in 1968 and the splintering of the family into different factions, it is believed that Sciolino was talking with the Rochester faction about making a deal. The Frangiamore faction believed that he became an informant after being arrested on a couple felonies.[291] Sciolino, forty, was brutally murdered in a daring daylight hit on March 7, 1980, while sitting in a construction trailer on Main Street during construction of Buffalo's rapid transit system. When John Sacco became a government informer, he said that Leonard Falzone told him, "We clipped him because he was a rat for the FBI."[292]

The crew would suffer additional losses when Seneca and D'Angelo were also murdered and Parness's brother became a government informant.

By early 1969, Stefano was vulnerable, and with Fred Randaccio in prison, there was a void in Buffalo. It was at this time that the Arm decided to split from Magaddino. Secret meetings were held in Fort Erie, Ontario; Rochester, New York; and several homes in Buffalo.[293] After the series of meetings, the men agreed to stop paying tribute to Magaddino and to attempt to take over the family. Joe Fino was chosen to lead the defecting faction, Dan Sansanese Sr. would be underboss and Sam "the Farmer" Frangiamore would be the consigliere.[294]

Police believed that Salvatore Pieri, fifty-nine at the time, took over as boss for Magaddino until he was arrested in September 1969 by the FBI on a $300,000 stolen jewelry charge. He was indicted, tried and convicted for trying to bribe several jurors during the trial, ending his chance at boss.[295] Police believed an informant within the Magaddino faction may have tipped them off.[296]

After the Magaddino arrests in November 1968, the FBI went after other enterprises. One of the "very lucrative, illegal source(s) of income for the Mob" was loan-sharking, and the biggest fish was Albert Mario "Babe" Billiteri Sr.[297] Billiteri was born on July 17, 1926. He was a made man and considered a capo for many years.

Special Agent Griffin put together enough evidence to get a microphone approved for inside Billiteri's home, but there was always someone at home so he was unable to install it. Finally, on July 4, 1969, a "black-bag job" took place in broad daylight. Billiteri was going to a picnic, so the FBI set up a fake street repair crew in front of his house and slipped inside the house to install the microphone.[298] According to Agent Griffin, the inside of Billiteri's house "was furnished like a palace," with expensive paintings, imported furniture and a "walk-in closet with hundreds of suits, shirts, and fancy shoes."[299]

One of his regular visitors was Samuel "Toto" Lagattuta Jr. Born on August 28, 1933, by 1969, he was five feet six inches tall and 310 pounds. Lagattuta, Pasquale J. "Patty Naples" Napoli and Matthew "Steamboat" Billiteri were collectors, or "strong arm men or enforcers,"[300] for Billiteri. Napoli was born on March 31, 1935, and was five feet eight inches and 220 pounds.

Billiteri never suspected anything and spoke freely in his home, identifying victims and giving instructions to beat those who did not pay. On Saturday,

The FBI placed a wiretap in Albert Billiteri's Buffalo home, which led to a raid. Police believe this book was used to keep track of loan shark payments. *Courtesy Buffalo State College Archives*, Courier-Express *Collection.*

November 21, 1969, FBI agents arrested Billiteri's crew—his brother Matthew, Sam Lagattuta, Albino Principe, Napoli and Billiteri's son Frank T.—on loan-sharking charges. The FBI believed this was the "largest and most vicious loan shark ring" in Buffalo.[301] Billiteri turned himself in on November 28, 1969.[302]

Napoli and Billiteri were indicted by a federal grand jury on December 9, 1970.[303] The case was eventually turned over to local authorities when no witnesses would testify that they "had been injured or threatened with injuries."[304]

102

Billiteri and Napoli decided that the evidence was overwhelming, and both pled guilty in July 1972. They were fined $10,000, and Billiteri was sentenced to five years while Napoli received three years.[305]

"Acting Buffalo La Cosa Nostra (LCN) boss, Joe Fino proclaimed an edict that no one can be beaten to collect a loan shark debt without his personal permission."[306]

Roy Carlisi took over Billiteri's business. One of his lieutenants collected and sent a percentage to Billiteri's wife while he was imprisoned.[307] Albert Billiteri died on May 16, 1998, at seventy-one years old.[308] Sam Frangiamore was made boss, with Joseph Todaro Sr. his underboss and Joseph Pieri Sr. consigliere.[309]

By March 1974, it is believed that capo Roy Carlisi was "possibly the most powerful Mafia figure in the Buffalo area,"[310] and although he was not the official family boss, he wielded plenty of power. Born on January 10, 1909, in Chicago, his brother Sam went on to be boss of the Chicago family.

Carlisi was thought to be one of the wealthiest mobsters in Buffalo, said to have close to $1 million. He was high in the hierarchy of the Magaddino Family. He was associated with Joseph "Chicago Joe" Sciales, Charles Cassaro and Andy Sciandra of Andy's Cafe.[311]

Daniel Sansanese Sr. died while in prison.[312] Daniel J. Sansanese Jr. died on June 16, 2003, at sixty-eight years old. Ben Nicoletti Sr. died on May 2, 1982, in Lewiston.[313]

APALACHIN

NOVEMBER 14, 1957

[They] *dashed into the woods, throwing away guns and wads of money.*[314]
—*Albert S. Kurek,* The Troopers Are Coming

The story of Thursday, November 14, 1957, has been told in countless books, so we won't rehash the entire tale here. At the time of the meeting, Stefano was one of the leaders of the Mafia Commission and was believed to have approved the meeting and the location of Apalachin, New York. The host of the meeting was Joseph Barbara Sr., a native of Magaddino's home in Sicily and believed to be Magaddino's man in the Endicott, New York area.

According to testimony from New York State trooper Edgar Croswell, he stumbled across the entire meeting by accident. Joseph Barbara Jr. booked three rooms at a Vestal, New York motel for a "convention" of Canada Dry men (his father owned the local distributor). Croswell found out and visited Barbara's house that evening, where he saw a car registered to James V. LaDuca of Niagara Falls.

The next day, Croswell and several others decided to see if Barbara Sr. was "having another meeting"[315] and pulled into the driveway. "As we came in here," Croswell testified, "a lot of men ran from around the barbeque pit…some ran for the house, and some came out of the house and ran the other way." The police then parked out on the town road, the only way out, and set up a road block.[316]

As they were setting up, they saw "10 or 12 men running from the direction of Barbara's house into the pine woods. There was no place that

Joseph Barbara hosted a meeting at his Apalachin estate in November 1957 that would go down in Mafia history. He was a sick man and died the following year. *Author's collection.*

these people could go," so eventually they were all rounded up, sixty of them. "We were picking them up as they came out of the woods, one or two at a time."[317]

Those in attendance from the Magaddino Family were Carlisi, D'Agostino, LaDuca, Lagattuta, Nino, John Montana and Costenze and Frank Valenti.

When they questioned LaDuca, they found matches from the Parkway Motel in his pocket and a hotel bill in the wastebasket at the motel in his name. That Sunday, LaDuca's car was spotted in the barn at Barbara's house, and police officers claim that Stefano's clothes were in the trunk, even though he was never seen.

In early 1961, FBI director J. Edgar Hoover finally relented and started the Top Hoodlum Program.[318] He directed field offices in ten cities to set up squads of agents to specifically tackle organized crime, but Buffalo and Niagara Falls were not on the list.[319] Agents were instructed to locate "the meeting places of these organized crime leaders."[320] Hidden microphones were installed across the country, informants were developed and physical surveillance became the norm. The earliest known microphone installed in western New York was in the Magaddino Memorial Chapel in 1959. In Albany, New York, a watchdog committee of the state legislature subpoenaed witnesses to explain the purpose of the meeting and a federal grand jury investigated the western New York ties to the meeting.[321]

On Saturday, December 14, 1957, "witnesses" from Buffalo testified in Albany. Nino feigned that he had no knowledge of the English language, demanded an interpreter and pleaded the Fifth Amendment twenty-four times. D'Agostino took the Fifth seventeen times. LaDuca refused to answer every question, including his age or telephone number, and Carlisi refused forty questions.[322]

In December 1957, Samuel Lagattuta and James LaDuca went into hiding. In February 1958, a federal grand jury investigating the event brought more witnesses into a Buffalo courtroom. Peter A. was before the grand jury just two minutes, as he failed to bring the records he was subpoenaed for and had to return on April 2 and 10.[323]

LaDuca's brothers Joseph and Albert were questioned regarding the homes on Dana Drive in Lewiston they built for suspected Mafia homeowners.

Sam "Toto" Lagattuta was a strong-arm man for Albert Billiteri in Buffalo. He was questioned after the 1957 Apalachin meeting. *Courtesy Buffalo State College Archives,* Courier-Express *Collection.*

Tioga County also held a grand jury and subpoenaed all the attendees to testify. Dominick D'Agostino was offered immunity for his testimony but instead refused to talk and was arrested on contempt charges.[324] Carlisi and Lagattuta joined D'Agostino with contempt charges.

The U.S. Senate Select Committee on Improper Activities in the Labor or Management Field held hearings June 30 through July 3, 1958. James LaDuca and John Montana were two of the witnesses called to testify. LaDuca stated his name and address and then refused to answer any other questions, invoking the Fifth Amendment seventy-seven times.

Because of the Apalachin meeting, New York governor Averill Harriman "established a fifty-man criminal intelligence unit" within the state police to investigate organized crime on October 28, 1958.[325]

The fallout from the Apalachin meeting was considerable. LaDuca was accused of accepting $10,000 from the Richford Hotel in Buffalo while acting as secretary-treasurer of Local 66, the Hotel and Restaurant Employees Union representing its employees,[326] and lost that position. Montana's complete dominance of Buffalo taxi service was broken. The Magaddino brothers were exposed to all of western New York. Stefano avoided being caught at the meeting, angering many, including Chicago mob boss Sam Giancana, who had told Magaddino to have the meeting in Chicago, where he controlled everything. "It never would've happened in your place," Magaddino was overheard saying during a telephone conversation with Giancana.[327]

D'Agostino was stripped of his citizenship in 1964 and died on August 18, 1970. He was seventy-nine years old.[328] Lagattuta died on September 11, 1964, after suffering a heart attack. He was sixty-seven years old.[329]

KIDNAPPING COUSINS

Buffalo is but a small town compared with Chicago and New York. And yet,
Stefano had a seat on the Commission.[330]
—Joe Bonanno

The Magaddino Family was allied with the Bonanno clan in their
homeland of Sicily, and Stefano Magaddino was first cousins with
Joseph "Joe Bananas" Bonanno, born on January 18, 1905, who would
go on to run the Brooklyn Mafia family that bears his name. According to
Bonanno, "the Bonanno house was preeminent" in Sicily.[331]

A feud between the Buccellatos and Bonannos resulted in many deaths,
including that of Stefano's brother Pietro in 1920. When Bonanno's
father went to America, the elder Magaddino took over the clan, which
resulted in the Buccellatos casting their grudge against the Magaddinos.
Another cousin, Peter J. Magaddino, was close friends with Bonanno
in Sicily.

When Bonanno was nineteen, he came to the United States with his
cousin Peter. Neither had a visa to enter the country legally, so they made
their way to Havana, Cuba, and then to Florida, eventually catching a train
to Jacksonville.[332] While in Jacksonville, Bonanno and Peter were arrested
by immigration officials. Upon hearing of his cousins' "plight," Magaddino
sent two of his men, including Willie Moretti, down to Florida to get
them released.[333] Bonanno said that Stefano was one of the most powerful
Castellammarese in America at the time.[334]

This is a great surveillance photo of Magaddino (left). It is unknown where the photo was taken. *Courtesy Buffalo State College Archives,* Courier-Express *Collection.*

Peter settled in Niagara Falls and became a member of the Magaddino Family. Born on October 26, 1906, in Castellammare del Golfo, he was the brother of Gaspare of Brooklyn, a reputed killer. When Bonanno was married in November 1931, his best man was Stefano's brother-in-law, Gaspar DiGregorio.[335]

Over the ensuing years, the cousins were aligned with the conservative faction of the Mafia Commission, generally opposing the narcotics trade and prostitution, but their relationship would continue to deteriorate.

In 1956, Bonanno's son Salvatore "Bill" was married with a reception for three thousand guests in the Grand Ballroom of the Astor Hotel in New York City.[336] Stefano "was given an honored table in front of the dais"[337] and, according to one source, said to a man at his table, "Look at this crowd, who the hell's going to be able to talk to my cousin now? This will go to his head."[338] And maybe it did; Joe elevated Bill to the number three position in his family, bypassing DiGregorio, which also upset Stefano.[339]

For a number of years, Peter J. served as vice-president of Power City Distributing, and Stefano claimed he was robbing the business blind. "Tell me something," Stefano asked him. "Tell me how you have been stealing the money. You degenerate." He went on to say that Peter drained the bank account of $30,000 and stole $80,000 and, "like a miserable miser, I was getting $57 a week."[340] Peter would play with the business's money, doing things like buying $300 steaks. When the company folded in 1958, Peter lost his job and operated a malt and hop shop in Niagara Falls.[341]

In 1962, there was strife in New York City. Stefano, with his position on the Mafia Commission, was aligned with Carlo Gambino and Tommy Lucchese and became more estranged from his cousin Joe. Bill was later implicated in a plan with his father to eliminate Gambino, Lucchese and Magaddino.[342] He said it was a "false and damaging rumor."

The Bonanno Family had ties to Montreal for many years, and Stefano had ties to Toronto and southern Ontario, Canada. In April 1964, Bonanno traveled to Montreal and was "invited" to "invest"[343] in a cheese company. While in Canada, he applied for citizenship but was jailed on unrelated charges.

During a vote in New York for the consigliere position in the Bonanno Family, DiGregorio lost to Bill Bonanno and, angered by the outcome, complained to Stefano, creating a wider rift between the cousins.[344]

It is believed that during Bonanno's absence while in the Canadian jail, Stefano convinced DiGregorio to take over the Bonanno Family.[345] Bonanno was released from jail in August 1964 and returned to the United States. Magaddino tried to have him brought before the Mafia Commission to discuss his actions, but Bonanno declared that he longer recognized the commission since it "never formally agreed to extend the five-year term beyond 1961."[346]

Magaddino sent word to Bill that he wanted to see his father. "Everybody wants your father," Magaddino said, "but I want him worse than anybody else."[347] He said that Bill made excuses for his father.

Bonanno went into exile, spending time in his Arizona home while plotting to set up Bill as boss of the Los Angeles family and continuing to defy the commission. Stefano was heard saying that Bonanno was out of line for working without commission approval. "Not even the Holy Ghost could come into my territory without authorization," Stefano declared.[348]

In September 1964, Bonanno called a family meeting, but DiGregorio refused to attend. Stefano then declared DiGregorio boss of the family[349] and sent his cousin Peter J. to assist DiGregorio. It was during this time that Peter was either "ousted" from the Magaddino Family or decided it was time to leave Niagara Falls. He never returned to the Magaddino Family, instead becoming Joe Bonanno's bodyguard.

On September 18, 1964, Bonanno was called before the Mafia Commission but skipped the meeting. In October 1964, Bonanno was subpoenaed to appear before a federal grand jury in New York. On October 14, Stefano met with two of his men. Part of the conversation was caught on a wiretap, probably in the Magaddino Memorial Chapel. "New York...the lawyer... we got the car" was all the FBI heard.[350]

On October 20, the night before his testimony, Bonanno met with his lawyer for dinner and then headed to the lawyer's home to spend the night before testifying. This is where the truth will never be known, as multiple versions of the story exist. According to Bonanno, a little after midnight they arrived at the lawyer's apartment. As Bonanno exited the taxi, two men "stepped up and forced Bonanno into a car at gunpoint."[351] A warning shot was fired at the lawyer. Bonanno said, "They shoved me down on the floor of the car. We drove for hours. We were in the country somewhere, a farm."[352]

That same day, FBI agents observed men at the Magaddino Funeral Home and heard them drink "several toasts for some unspecified reason and a spirit of festivity prevailed."[353] Were they toasting Bonanno's disappearance?

Bonanno said he was brought inside and sat waiting, with someone guarding him. "Many hours later...in walked my cousin Steve Magaddino."[354] He said Peter and Nino were responsible for his kidnapping. Some accounts say he was taken to the Catskills,[355] while others say he was taken to Niagara Falls and held in an apartment above a barbershop and then later moved to the Magaddino farmhouse in Cambria, New York.

But the FBI said there was no way Stefano or Peter could have been involved in the kidnapping, as they were under constant surveillance. The farmhouse was also checked by state police, and no signs of life were present.

According to one source, on the night that Bonanno was supposedly kidnapped, the source was bowling with Nino in Niagara Falls.

According to Bill Bonanno, his father was not held captive and was free to leave at any time but chose to stay as a "respite."[356] Supposedly, the cousins talked "for six weeks."[357] Stefano told Joe, "You take up too much space in the air.[358] You've always been like this, even with [Salvatore] Maranzano. Why do you try to be such a big shot?"[359]

Most historians seem to agree that Bonanno staged the whole kidnapping to avoid testifying before the grand jury and appearing before the Mafia Commission and blamed his cousin.

Bonanno said that Stefano wanted him to retire to Arizona, so he agreed and was released in December 1964, only to emerge two years later. In the end, Bonanno did retire, but he outlived his cousin by many years. Joe

Bonanno died on May 11, 2002, at ninety-seven years old. He had outlived almost everyone from the "old days."

Bill Bonanno died at age seventy-five in January 2008.

Peter J. Magaddino's brother Gaspare, sixty-two, was killed on April 21, 1970, in New York City. He had been sought by authorities in connection with murders and bombings in the United States and Sicily.[360] Peter died on January 14, 1998, in Tucson, Arizona. He was ninety-two.[361]

THE MONTANA AFFAIR

That is one thing I would never do. I would as soon die than take the fifth amendment, because I have not done anything in my life that I am ashamed of.[362]
—John C. Montana

John C. Montana went to his grave protesting his involvement in La Cosa Nostra. He was a politician and businessman and was well-liked in Buffalo. After being caught at the Big Barbecue in Apalachin, New York, his stature in Buffalo declined, and many questions were left unanswered. He always insisted that he was innocent and he did not have so much as a parking ticket on his record. But was he as innocent as he alleged?

Montana was born in Montedoro, Italy, on June 30, 1893. His family line appears to intersect with other men from the city of Montedoro, some of whom would go on to become American Mafioso. Andrea, or Andy, Sciandra and his family came from the same town as Montana and also settled in Buffalo.[363]

Montana arrived in the United States in 1907 at thirteen years old. His early career included being a messenger and operating a popcorn cart. In 1922, he formed the Buffalo Taxi Service & Sightseeing Co., Inc. His biggest competitor at the time was Van Dyke Black & White Taxi Corp., which was started in 1917 by Frederick Van Dyke. By 1930, Montana was vice-president of Van Dyke, and not long after, he took full control.

His rise in power included two stints as Niagara District councilman in Buffalo in 1927 and 1929. During his tenure, the Buffalo Airport, New York Central passenger train terminal and Buffalo City Hall all began construction. With his influence, he was able to secure exclusive rights for his taxis at the airport and train terminal, as well as the Statler Hotel in downtown Buffalo. One source claims that Montana even used his influence to stop a trolley connecting downtown with the train station from being constructed so he would have complete control.[364] Many small taxi operators were angered by these deals, but Montana was a powerful businessman, and few opposed him.

In May 1931, the first Mafia "National Conference" was scheduled for Chicago.[365] The train from New York City included many of the top American mobsters, including Joe Bonanno, Charlie Luciano, Meyer Lansky and Salvatore

John C. Montana was a businessman, former councilman and secret member of the Magaddino Family who was caught at the Apalachin meeting in 1957. Here he is testifying in 1958 at a hearing before the Senate Labor Rackets Committee. *Author's collection.*

Maranzano. When it arrived in Buffalo, Maranzano disembarked to make a telephone call, which took longer than expected. The train was ready to depart.[366] The Buffalo contingent—Stefano, his cousin Peter J. and Montana—were on board when Montana found out that Maranzano would be left behind. He was able to use his influence to hold the train until Maranzano returned.[367] Stefano "beamed with pride" and said, "See what kind of men I have under me? John can stop trains."[368] Bonanno declared many years later that John Montana was Magaddino's number-three man during this time, behind Stefano's brother Nino, who was generally thought to have little power.

In 1933, Montana was a director of Empire State Brewing Corp., a beer distributor based in Olean, New York.[369] During this time, he first met Joseph

Barbara Sr. Power City Distributing was also a distributor of the beer. The company was shut down in 1940. Around the same time, Montana became involved in Buffalo Beverage Corp., which was a Budweiser distributor, with James LaDuca, Charles Montana and Peter J. Magaddino. According to Montana, they went out of business about 1947.[370]

In 1939, Montana's nephew Charles A. married Stefano's daughter Josephine, with a grand reception held at Buffalo's Statler Hotel. It was attended by "thugs from all over the country."

Montana continued in various civic roles in the city, but his Mafia connections were kept well hidden. In 1956, he received the Man of the Year award from the Erie Club of Buffalo, a police organization.[371]

Accounts vary as to when Montana became involved in Mafia affairs, but he is believed to have been Magaddino's underboss from 1922 to 1953 or 1957. If 1953 is accurate, then Angelo Acquisto took over from him until he was caught "siphoning profits."[372] Instead of killing Acquisto, Magaddino "ostracized him" and cut him off from the Mafia. The disgrace finally forced Acquisto to kill himself in his home in 1956.[373]

In February 1957, Montana took over as director of Frontier Liquor Corp. of Buffalo.

On the morning of November 14, 1957, Montana left Buffalo with Nino Magaddino, driving his new Cadillac, supposedly on his way to Pittston, Pennsylvania, and then to a meeting in New York City the following morning. Shortly after leaving Buffalo, he said he experienced a problem with his windshield wiper. About "10 miles this side of—you people call it Apalachin, I call it Endicott"[374]—he had brake failure. This was during a rainstorm, and he claimed he did not know how to fix wet brakes, so he drove to Joe Barbara's home to see if "he would get a mechanic and take care of the car."[375]

Unbeknownst to Montana, Barbara was hosting a party when he arrived. He parked in the driveway and left Nino in the car "to wait."[376] Montana sat down for a cup of tea with Mrs. Barbara.

"Then Joe said there was a roadblock," Montana said. "When I saw the commotion, I wanted no part of it," so he got Nino and started to "walk away from it" through the woods.

Most other accounts dispute Montana's description of the events. State police claim he was caught running through the woods with Nino and was only apprehended because his cashmere coat got snagged on a fence. He swore he was not running. After their capture, Montana and Nino were placed in a car, and Montana spoke to Edgar Croswell, the officer in charge. Croswell

The most substantial home John Montana owned was located on Starin Avenue in Buffalo. He was living there when he was caught at the Apalachin meeting in 1957. This is the home today. *Photo by author.*

said that Montana offered to help him if he was let go, which Montana later vehemently denied. After being held a short time, Montana took a train back to Buffalo and sent mechanics to pick up his car a few days later.

The picnic at Barbara's house was organized by Stefano Magaddino, so it would have been nearly impossible for Montana to be driving with Nino and not know about the picnic. Even Barbara's maid had a conflicting story. She said she "heard Montana apologize for being late, saying that his car had broken down."[377]

All those who were captured at the Barbara estate were subpoenaed to testify before a grand jury in February 1958. Montana met the grand jury for a total of eight minutes with his attorney, Frank Raichle.[378] When he testified before a Senate committee in 1958, Senator Irving Ives of New York said, "The story doesn't make too much sense, Mr. Montana, I am sorry to tell you."[379]

Montana was the only person to testify who did not invoke the Fifth Amendment against self-incrimination.

Montana and others from Apalachin were arrested in late May 1959 by federal authorities for obstructing justice. He posted $40,000 bail and was released. The charges were later dropped, but the continued public scrutiny took its toll on his taxi business, once the second largest in the state. He lost prime spots at local hotels and the airport.[380] The fallout from Apalachin went far and wide. The New York State Liquor Authority (SLA) began investigating Frontier Liquor Corp. and Power City Distributing.[381]

Just when it appeared that everything was over, Montana's name again surfaced during the testimony of mob informant Joseph Valachi in 1963. Valachi revealed that Montana was a lieutenant in the Magaddino Family and after Apalachin, he asked Stefano to be demoted, an unheard-of practice.

"He felt," Valachi said, "he did not want the boys to contact him anymore. He didn't want to be mixing with them because he was arrested at Apalachin."[382] He then went on to say that Magaddino told Montana not to worry: "From now on you will be a plain soldier."

Montana, once the darling of the Buffalo Italian community, died on March 18, 1964, after suffering a heart attack. Funeral arrangements were handled by the Magaddino Memorial Chapel. He left an estate valued at $839,581 ($5.8 million in 2010 dollars).[383]

BOOKIES AND GAMBLERS

THE MAJOR PLAYERS

[An Italian Secret Society] *of ruthless gangsters that depends for income on rackets ranging from bookmaking to shakedowns and kidnappings.*[384]
—Buffalo Police Detective Chief John J. Whalen

To properly understand how the Mafia in western New York ran and made their enormous profits, we have to study gambling throughout the area. According to former undercover FBI agent Joe Pistone, better known as Donnie Brasco, "Gambling is probably the most important source of income for the Mafia. Every Mafia member was involved in gambling and used profits from it to sustain his other activities. It is the blood that pumps through the veins of the system 365 days a year."[385]

Long before off-track betting, state-run lotteries or legalized casinos, the Mafia supplied most of the gambling to those who needed a fix. From full-blown casinos and high-stakes dice and card games to sports betting, the mob survived by the funds made from gambling. One of the earliest forms of mob-controlled gambling was the Italian lottery, also known as the numbers or policy rackets.[386] Gambling was by far the most lucrative business they were involved in and a significant part of organized crime activity in western New York.

That easy money was what brought the powerful Magaddino Family to its knees in 1968. "Niagara Falls was regarded by many as a wide-open town in the Prohibition and depression eras…Bookmaking emporiums were equipped with tote boards, loudspeaker systems…and direct wires connecting them with the race tracks."[387] It is believed that Stefano took over running the wire services in Buffalo and Niagara Falls.

Police were in constant search of vice, especially during Prohibition. In February 1932, Niagara Falls Police raided two locations a week apart. The first on Main Street was said to be one of the ritziest places of its kind in western New York.[388] The next week, the Rover's Social and Athletic Club was raided, and seventeen men were arrested. Leonard Welch operated the club where the men were playing "blackjack and other card games."

By 1943, an anti-gambling drive had been ordered by Niagara Falls Police superintendent Martin T. Considine.[389] During a raid, Robert G. Dunn was arrested and pled guilty to maintaining a place for gambling on Main Street in Niagara Falls. Boards to list horse race results and "alleged" horse race betting sheets, several tables and "decrepit wooden chairs" were confiscated, dealing what authorities thought was a blow to the powerful gambling syndicate.

A year later, another "new" gambling squad was empowered and began visiting "fourteen suspected gambling and bookmaking establishments"[390] and other vice-related properties. Two raids were made, with a grand total of two arrests.

During World War II, business was very good, with thousands of military servicemen and factory workers in the area pumping money into the gambling coffers. But in Niagara Falls, "the armed services demanded in 1945 that the city clean up the then-famous 11th Street area, which, from Buffalo Avenue to East Falls Street, was the prostitution center."[391]

Over the ensuing years raid after raid would be conducted. Sometimes no evidence of gambling would be found, and other times, dozens of people would be arrested. But it never stopped the flow of gambling money.

One of the top gamblers in Niagara Falls was Norman "Nemo" Joseph, first arrested in 1937.[392] In March 1946, North Tonawanda Police battered down the doors of his establishment and arrested forty-eight men and seized $8,000 during a late afternoon raid.[393] They found craps tables, horse racing sheets and telephones and loudspeaker system used to broadcast the race results. In June 1946, forty men, including Joseph, were arrested in five Niagara Falls raids.[394]

In 1954, Niagara Falls Police were tipped off about a home located in Colonial Village. They tapped the telephone lines and found they were "receiving and laying off bets."[395] In March, Joseph was arrested for operating a "betting center whose operations extended to many cities in this country and Canada."

The Alexander Motel near Hamilton, Ontario, was raided around 1959, and Joseph was arrested. Police said they were doing an "average daily volume of $22,900 in bets."[396]

Just when they thought they had cleaned up vice, the IRS conducted raids in multiple cities in May 1959, and Joseph was arrested at his Lewiston home with $8,150 in cash on him. He was still running a long-distance operation out of the Bridge Coffee Shop and Zacaria's Barber Shop in Niagara Falls.[397] Even after his arrest, director of Public Safety Charles Gorman stated, "The person arrested we do not consider to be any Mr. Big or anything like it."[398] Buffalo Police claimed that "Niagara Falls bookmakers were doing $30,000 a day in bet-making business" in the late 1940s.[399]

The Four Corners Club in North Tonawanda was a popular gambling joint and was raided in March 1949, but "not so much as a morning newspaper was found in the place,"[400] indicating that they had been tipped off to the upcoming raid. That same day, Niagara Falls Police raided two locations, arrested twenty-eight men and seized six dollars in cash.

The club was raided again on June 10, 1950, when police smashed their way in and surprised the forty members in attendance at the "plush" club.[401] Police carted off eight busloads of men and $40,000 worth of gambling equipment. The club was run by Anthony Marinelli and Jack Sullivan, who pled guilty to "keeping a room for gambling," but Salvatore Pieri of Buffalo and five other "big shots"[402] "shared the profits." Daniel Sansanese Sr. was also arrested, but by sentencing, he was serving time in Attica Prison on unrelated charges. Most of the others arrested pled guilty to common gambling.[403]

On April 10, 1951, Manuel Morinello left a suicide note in his truck stating that he had "lost considerable money gambling" at an establishment in Niagara Falls. As a result, Albert F. "One-Arm Blackie" Previte was arrested on charges that he was "maintaining a room for gambling."[404] At his trial in June, "poor memory" of witnesses led to "considerable comment at the time."[405]

Forty-four-year-old Previte disappeared in May 1953. In 1956, an anonymous tip said that he was buried in the basement of a Linwood Avenue home in North Tonawanda. The police and a contractor examined the site and determined it was not possible.[406]

Jack H. "Sharkey" Ehrenreich, a suspected Buffalo bookmaker, was caught running his own betting window at Buffalo Raceway in 1954 and "banished" from the track.[407] He was called "Buffalo's betting commissioner." In 1959, Ehrenreich told the state crime commission that "his weekly gross averaged $14,000 per week,"[408] but it was "cut in half after the raids. I never paid anybody and I never got any OK."

In March 1958, the *Niagara Falls Gazette* ran a series of articles on crime and vice in the city. In one article, it claimed that local gamblers no longer

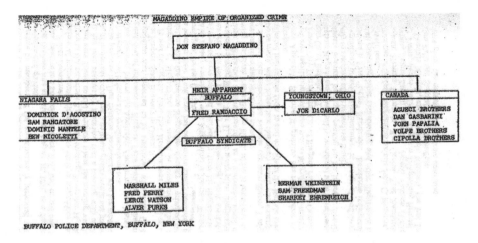

This 1963 chart shows the reach Stefano Magaddino had and his connections in those cities. *U.S. Senate exhibit.*

used "batteries of telephones." One bookie said all the "big money goes to Buffalo or Cleveland or, sometimes, Erie."[409] "Police believe they have rid the city of nearly all dice and card games."

In early 1958, an investigation into bookmaking during work hours at the Bell Aircraft plant in Niagara Falls took place. Twenty people were identified as being involved, including Angelo Bonito aka "Charlie Hy." Bonito was born on December 18, 1905, and was close to Fred Aquino, meeting him at the Allentown Grill nightly during this time.[410]

At 9:00 p.m. on February 8, 1959, Niagara Falls Police used a wrecking bar to enter the rear room of Pasttime Poolroom, where they found men gambling around a pool table. Forty-six men were arrested, including Jerry Critelli, who was "charged with maintaining an establishment for gambling purposes."[411] Through their attorney, James LiBrize, forty-four of the men pled guilty and were fined a measly fifty dollars each.[412] LiBrize himself would be brutally murdered in 1969.

Less than two months later, "raiders led by Niagara Falls Assistant District Attorney William Hunt, Jr., confiscated cards, dice, pornographic literature, a slot machine and an estimated $10,000 in cash at Nick Rizzo's Cataract Barber Shop on April 4, 1959."[413] In Rizzo's upstairs apartment, police found seventeen men, and two eluded police for ninety minutes by hiding in a closet. "Money was found in half a dozen places, including a garbage can." Telephone calls from potential bettors were taken during the raid by police.[414] Rizzo received one of the stiffest fines "in the history of City Court" at the time, $1,250, and was charged with "maintaining a gambling establishment."[415]

The Oh Boy's Social and Athletic Club was raided in late June 1959, and twenty-five men were arrested, including Gino Monaco, Anthony Volpe, James Romano and Frank Fantauzzo. The location had previously been raided when it was known as the Algonquin Club.[416]

The Oliver Street Social Club was raided on October 16, 1964, netting forty-one arrests, including Nicoletti Sr. and Jr.; James Vona, the reputed owner; Frank Fantauzzo; and Anthony Volpe. Police also found $12,740 in cash.[417] In April 1971, Nicoletti pleaded guilty to the charges. Junior served three months in Niagara County Jail for the charge, and the others received probation for their part.[418]

On Saturday, August 22, 1959, Niagara Falls Police raided fourteen suspected gambling establishments across the city in what they called "Operation Bookie."[419] A total of sixteen were arrested during the raids, and at least one of the locations had been on the police's watch list for months.[420]

Raids were continued by New York State Police in October 1959. Most local police agencies were not even told of the raids until ten minutes beforehand to avoid communication leaks.[421] Twenty-seven different locations were raided in Buffalo and one in Niagara Falls. The raids prompted New York to conduct a series of crime hearings, with many suspected bookies and gamblers subpoenaed to testify. Buffalo bookmaker Nicholas "Sonny" Mauro claimed that he had ceased his operations on June 8, 1960, and said he operated "from many different locations from rented apartments, railroad and bus terminals and other convenient locations." He claimed to net "about $7,000 in 1959," with thirty "agents" working for him.[422]

FBI agent Joe Griffin said that they considered Mauro "the principal sports bookmaker in western New York"[423] and, therefore, their primary target. Informants said Mauro worked for Sansanese Sr. and was laying off bets (for example, using other bookmakers to try to cover for heavy bets against one team or horse). On September 15, 1964, the FBI raided Mauro's "heavily barricaded" bookmaking office in Buffalo.[424] He was convicted in 1966 and sentenced to one year in Erie County Jail.

After his release from prison in early 1967, he went right back to work, but at that time he was making interstate phone calls, which was in violation of federal statutes. The FBI began surveillance at his location on Cherry Street in Buffalo and raided it in February 1967. They found a secret staircase leading from the second floor to the basement, as well as another secret compartment on the second floor, where they found Mauro and two associates hiding. The raid uncovered a $100,000-a-day operation. After making bond, Mauro was back on the street and back to his usual habits. FBI agent Griffin said he "personally raided and arrested Mauro five times."[425]

A rookie Buffalo Police officer was able to gain undercover entry to what he believed was a high-stakes dice game at the Fall Mark Sportsman's Club in Buffalo in November 1968.[426] Mauro and five others were later arrested at the club. Two years later, they were all acquitted.

Police "smashed" their way in and found "a bookmaking center" run by Mauro on Elmwood Avenue in Buffalo in December 1969. After the arrests, the local press corps was called by the police, and Mauro and others were held until the photographers arrived at the apartment. Mauro's attorney, Harold P. Fahringer, later claimed that the $75,000-a-week operation was a figment of the police's imagination. Mauro was called "Buffalo's No. 1 suspected gambler."[427]

It was revealed during the state crime hearings that Buffalo and Niagara Falls' crime ties were bigger than was previously known.[428] About fifty bookmaking operations were thought to be operating in Buffalo at the time, and a Buffalo Police lieutenant abruptly resigned during the probe after being questioned about his role in Buffalo bookmaking. Commission Agent Daniel Moynihan stated, "Buffalo bookies grossed 100 million dollars [in 1959] and netted 10 million dollars."[429]

Nicoletti Jr. followed in his father's footsteps and became involved in Niagara Falls' gambling operations. During a 1966 federal grand jury investigation, Junior and Louis Tavano were both offered immunity if they testified. When asked about his father's relation to Stefano, Junior claimed ignorance.[430]

The authorities continued harassing and raiding locations in Erie and Niagara Counties. A major bust came in May 1961, when U.S. Treasury agents arrested six men as part of a "$5,000-a-day horse race and baseball betting establishment" in Buffalo.[431] A tip led them to place surveillance on the location on Allen Street, said to be one of the largest in the city. The operation was run from an upstairs apartment and included four telephones and "at least 38 runners."[432] The raid was set up by IRS agents, who did not notify Buffalo Police until shortly before the raid. Two members of the anti-gambling squad accompanied the agents, who smashed a rear door to gain entrance to the apartment.

The location was said to be controlled by mobster Joe Fino, who was often seen there. Four men were arrested as they took bets by phone; one was Fino's brother Anthony. The owner of the building, Louis Viale, fifty, was arrested at his men's shop on the first floor. One of the phone lines was connected to

The apartment above 19 Allen Street held a profitable bookmaking operation said to be controlled by Joe Fino. In May 1961, Treasury and IRS agents raided the location and took over one hundred phone bets in thirty minutes. This is the building today. *Photo by author.*

a phone in Viale's basement down the street. The phones were so busy that two **IRS** agents started taking calls and recorded over one hundred calls in thirty minutes. One caller did not place a bet but simply said, "Close up." It was obvious that word had gotten out that a raid was inevitable.

Three men were arrested in October 1963 for running a "bookie setup" that handled more than $450,000 a year in the Elmwood-Utica area of Buffalo. One of those arrested was Salvatore Bonito who had been named a "Cosa Nostra section leader" the previous week by a Senate subcommittee.[433] Also arrested were Thomas Callea and Michael Celio. Buffalo Police Assistant Detective Chief Kenneth P. Kennedy said the three "had been under surveillance for two months."

On November 18, 1964, Peter A. Magaddino met with an unknown subject who proceeded to count out $14,169 as the proceeds from the "skin game," known as *ziginette.*[434] *Ziginette* is the biggest money card game in Italy (according to John Scarne, author of *Scarne's Encyclopedia of Card Games*), played with a forty-card deck. The object is to bet that the dealer's or another player's card will be matched before your card. The skin game is played with a fifty-two-card deck.

An FBI informant told authorities that Fred Randaccio, Pat Natarelli and Benedetto "Benny" Spano ran the Blue Banner Social Club in Buffalo. The FBI developed evidence against the club several times, but apparently Buffalo Police would not raid the location. In late September 1966, they were able to obtain a "shake up in Buffalo Police Department anti gambling and vice squad" and obtain officers who were "reliable and cooperative" with the FBI.[435] The club was finally raided by Buffalo Police and supervised by the FBI on October 7, 1966. They felt the raid was the first "successful local disruption of Cosa Nostra gambling operations in Buffalo."[436]

The club was located in a rear building "fronting as a garage" and "consisted of plush paneled rooms with bar and dining facilities. Full security measures used by gamblers consisting of three entrance doors all wired with

The Blue Banner Social Club was located in a rear garage apartment on Prospect Avenue. During the 1960s, this was a popular location for gambling in Buffalo, and a veritable who's who of the Buffalo mob could be spotted coming and going. This is the home today. *Photo by author.*

red lights and buzzers in the back gaming rooms."[437] Eighteen men were on the first floor playing cards, nine were playing dice on the second floor and one escaped to the roof but was captured when he reached the ground. Twenty-seven men were arrested, and police seized a "great quantity of gambling equipment the like of which they have not seen in years."[438] The FBI estimated the club handled $25,000 daily, and $5,500 in cash was seized from the tables.

Those arrested included Sansanese Sr., Albert Billiteri, Natarelli, Spano and Nick Fino, but Nicholas Rizzo, known as the banker in Buffalo, was conspicuously missing. As officers were leaving, one of the FBI agents noticed that the second-floor room was slightly smaller than the first floor and proceeded to investigate. The paneling "protruded" from the wall, and agents found a hidden door in the bathroom. They called for Buffalo Police to bring axes in and started to smash the walls. It did not take long for Rizzo to start screaming that he was in the wall, and out he came, with an additional $3,000 in "house" money and additional gambling equipment.[439]

Although he was not caught at the club during the raid, Fred Randaccio was seen "in the vicinity" about thirty minutes later. Several weeks later, the club was once again operating.

The Turner Social and Athletic Association was the scene of a large raid in December 1967. Two officers scaled ladders to "observe gamblers from the roof for a half hour" before the raid commenced.[440] Using axes and sledgehammers, state police, FBI agents and Buffalo Police "battered down three doors" and found forty-five men in the upstairs social club, which was once a firehouse. Over $11,000 was found, and several present were "identified with the organized criminal element." Three had recently been arrested at the Oliver Street Social Club. Among those arrested were Anthony Volpe, Nicoletti Jr., Nick Fino, Salvatore Bonito, Sansanese Sr., John Cammilleri and Frank Fantauzzo.

The biggest gambling raid in western New York would come in November 1968 when mob boss Stefano, the Nicolettis and others were arrested. After the Magaddino arrests, police increased their attempts to rid the area of gambling.

In August 1969, a major law enforcement operation was unleashed. Twenty-three persons were arrested, and homes and businesses were searched across the area. The major players arrested included Nicoletti Jr., Samuel Puglese, Augustine Rizzo and Anthony Volpe, all charged with racketeering and promoting and carrying on gambling between the United States and Canada.[441] The Delmar Grill, Coffee Joe's, a music store and a cigar shop, all in Niagara Falls, were searched. Nicoletti tried to evade the long arm of the law by climbing onto the second-story roof of the house he was in. Unfortunately, he could not get down, and a fire truck was required to get him off the roof.[442]

One of the first cases FBI agent Joe Griffin was able to use court-authorized wiretaps in was against Joseph Lombardo and Frank Stasio in the fall of 1970. Both were alleged bookmakers and operated from a rented apartment in suburban Cheektowaga. The bookmaking office was wiretapped, and on December 12, 1970, the FBI raided a total of five locations, including a Las Vegas location from where they were receiving their betting lines.[443] A total of $25,000 in cash was found, and a safe deposit box at a bank in the Riverside section of Buffalo yielded another $96,700. Stasio and Lombardo were both arrested in a phone booth outside the Twin Fair Department Store in Tonawanda.[444] They were indicted, but there was a mistrial due to a hung jury, and they walked away after not receiving a speedy trial.[445]

Another popular location was Nairy's Social Club in Buffalo, which was believed to have been started by John Cammilleri, Charles Cassaro, Joe Fino and Joe Moses in the spring of 1974.[446] Informant Joseph Galioto and undercover FBI agent Richard A. Genova infiltrated the club.[447] Genova went undercover after Cammilleri's murder in May 1974 and operated until they "decided to break his cover" for safety reasons.[448]

The main game played at the club was *ziginette*, and bets averaged "in excess of $20 a card" and went as high as $800 per card.[449] According to FBI reports, after each hand was over, a 5 percent "house" cut was taken from the pot. It was believed they made at least $1,000 per day.[450] Gaetano Miceli, Mike Bona and Frank Fantauzzo were the "supervisors" of the game. Law enforcement also believed the "majority" of the money being bet was from "burglaries, robberies and assorted thefts and frauds" in the Buffalo area.[451]

Nick Rinaldo supposedly received permission from Sam Frangiamore and Joe DiCarlo to start a competing *ziginette* game. His game ran at Connecticut Hall, on the second floor. This operation had William Sciolino, known for his debt-collecting skills, as a special operator.[452]

During the investigation, Frank "Poochie" Chimento, a known loan shark, relayed a story told to him by Daniel Sansanese Sr., who said to never "beat up a loan shark victim…kill him instead."[453]

By January 1975, informant Galioto had reported that Joe Fino mentioned there was talk to merge the two clubs and force Mike Bona out.

In late January, Buffalo Police entered the clubs for voluntary inspections, which led to appearance tickets for inadequate building permits.[454] FBI search

Connecticut Hall on Connecticut Street was where the card game *ziginette* was played and thousands of dollars changed hands. The club was located upstairs, and Angie's Place diner was downstairs, where many of the local mob hung out. *Courtesy Buffalo State College Archives,* Courier-Express *Collection.*

warrants led to the seizure of "approximately $7,800 in cash, numerous gambling records and a number of handguns" on February 7.[455]

In April 1975, a Buffalo city court judge dropped the inadequate building permits charges against Nairy's Social Club and its sergeant-at-arms, Joseph A. Moses, but new charges were drawn up.[456]

After revelations came to light that Salvatore Pieri was involved with the clubs, Pieri, who was out on parole for a 1970 jury tampering charge, was sent back to prison to complete his sentence. He was released on June 11, 1976.[457]

The police continued raids on suspected gambling and bookmaking operations through the 1970s. In March 1977, FBI agents busted

Nairy's Social Club was another big gambling location on West Ferry Street. When John Cammilleri was killed in 1974, his stake in the club was taken over by others. *Courtesy Buffalo State College Archives,* Courier-Express *Collection.*

Connecticut Hall and Nairy's Social Club, after another undercover agent infiltrated the clubs.[458] Those arrested included some of the usual suspects: Salvatore Pieri, William Sciolino, Rinaldo and Joe Fino. All were charged with "conspiracy and operating a gambling business." Cassaro, Gaetano "Tommy Chooch" Miceli and Moses were also sought.[459]

It was not until March 24, 1977, that the gambling case against Pieri, Joe Fino, Nick Rinaldo, Bill Sciolino, Michael Bona, Gaetano Miceli, Joseph Moses and Charles Cassaro finally came to fruition. They were all charged with various gambling counts.[460] During the February 1978 gambling trial for the social clubs, Pieri's attorney, Harold Boreanaz, argued that the FBI did not have any incriminating evidence against Pieri simply because he was not involved.[461] A federal jury eventually found Pieri innocent but convicted Sciolino and Rinaldo. Both clubs were shut down, and gambling activities simply moved to new locations.[462]

Amherst, state police and Erie County sheriffs raided two upstairs apartments at the Little White House restaurant in suburban Williamsville, New York, in April 1977. The restaurant's owner and manager, Robert G. Hanny, was arrested, along with thirty-six others. None of the usual suspects was in attendance, but relatives of several were. It was the typical haul, with playing cards, dice and a measly $1,050 seized.[463]

The next day, another series of raids was completed across the area, nabbing Nicoletti Jr., Mauro, Angelo Bonito and nine others. It was believed they were all part of a "sophisticated telephone network for relaying coded betting information," handling about $100,000 weekly.[464]

Bookies and Gamblers

The late 1970s saw major raids on suspected gambling operations, but as one story noted, people like Mauro had been arrested at least thirty times by then but only served a total of four days in jail.[465]

It would be impossible to cover every arrest, every raid and every search, so some of the patterns have been highlighted, as well as some of the perennial gamblers and bookies, to give you an idea of the enormity of the business and why the mob always wanted a piece of that gambling pie.

THE WHIRLPOOL CLUB

May I preface my remarks by saying that I feel Buffalo is one of the least crime-ridden cities in the country.[466]
—*Lieutenant Michael A. Amico, Buffalo Police Department*

One of Niagara Falls' "big-time gambling establishments"[467] was the Whirlpool Club on Twenty-fourth Street. The club was chartered in 1924 to gather "persons interested in the development and perfection of radio and wireless telephony."[468] The so-called social club was under constant surveillance by local police, since club meetings usually involved gambling and not telephony. It was said to be a plush club with a variety of gambling choices, and it was usually quite busy.

In January 1955, Niagara Falls Police were making checks at several local clubs every thirty minutes to find evidence of gambling "but were not able to find any." It was a daunting task trying to outsmart the gangsters.

At 1:00 a.m. on April 16, 1955, the Whirlpool Club was the target of a police raid as "a flying squad of police"[469] descended on the club. A *Niagara Falls Gazette* reporter had been called to witness the raid by District Attorney Bill Earl. When the raiding team, led by Police Chief Charles J. Gorman, knocked on the door and did not receive a response, crowbars were used to pry open the wood door. Inside, twenty-eight men were gathered around a pool table, and another fifty-eight men were in an upstairs apartment.[470]

During the interrogation, the guests of the club said they were there because a 1:00 a.m. club meeting had been called. Of those in attendance,

The Whirlpool Club was a plush gambling location in Niagara Falls on Twenty-fourth Street. After it became a target for the police, it was raided several times and dozens of men were arrested. This is the building today. *Photo by author.*

fifty-nine were from Buffalo and nineteen were from Niagara Falls. Only ten men were actually arrested, including Nicoletti Sr., his son-in-law Dominic Mantell and Nick Rizzo. Some gambling paraphernalia was confiscated.[471]

In September 1955, a judge issued an order "vacating and annulling the charter" of the club after no one appeared on its behalf. This did not stop the club from operating, though, because effective October 27, 1954, the charter for the Oh Boy's Social and Athletic Club had been reinstated, its charter dating to 1919. The members of this club used the Whirlpool Club building as their new headquarters.[472]

The club would continue to operate on and off until July 1962, when another major raid took place. After breaking through two doors, police found men "scattering in every direction." Twenty-nine men were arrested, including Nicoletti Sr. and Matthew "Whitey" Sciera, who was found hiding on the roof.[473] A snooker table and $12,730 were found in various places throughout the two floors, "the largest haul since" the 1955 Whirlpool raid.

The club was operating on Monday and Friday nights and Sunday afternoons. The gamblers met at the Imperial Hotel, where they were screened and probably checked for weapons and cash. They were then driven to the club. About 12:30 a.m., they would be driven back to the hotel before the taverns closed so they would blend in with the crowds.[474]

No further raids are known to have taken place at the club, which probably shut down sometime after this last raid.

THE MAFIA, PART II

THE BUSINESS OF FUNERALS

Don't forget my house in Deal if you are down on the shore. You are invited.[475]
—Willie Moretti testifying at 1951 crime hearing

Paul Palmeri appeared to be a simple undertaker in Niagara Falls. Sam DiCarlo was the younger brother of Joe DiCarlo Jr. and son of Buffalo's former crime boss. Willie Moretti was known as Willie Moore during his time in Niagara Falls. As this story unfolds, they were all leading secret lives.

Palmeri was the younger brother of Angelo Palmeri. He had a clean record and ran the Panepinto and Palmeri Funeral Home in Niagara Falls. His choice of friends, though, was questionable.

In 1931, Niagara Falls Police received word of a secret meeting in a hotel room of "an alleged group of Capone gangsters."[476] Police investigated the claim, but the group was gone by the time they arrived. Rumors also persisted that Capone was behind "gangland murders" in Niagara Falls.

In November 1931, Palmeri was visiting Chicago for unknown reasons when he was arrested as part of a kidnapping ring suspected of one hundred kidnappings during 1930 alone.[477] Rumors that the ring was centered in Niagara Falls and the kidnappings were planned and carried out from there were not confirmed, but they were also never completely cleared.

The charges were eventually dropped, but Palmeri had more legal trouble the very next year. In August 1932, Palmeri, Sam DiCarlo and twelve other men were arrested and charged with the killing of John Bazzano, a Pittsburgh restaurant owner.[478] All fourteen men were cleared of the murder charges.

Whitney Avenue in Niagara Falls was the original "Mafia Row," with several members living on the street in close proximity. This is what Paul Palmeri's former home looks like today. *Photo by author.*

Palmeri was arrested again in 1934 after he and Salvatore Constantino attacked a patrolman who was investigating an accident in Niagara Falls.[479] Acting Police Justice Angelo F. Scalzo arraigned the pair and, two years later, posed for a photo with Palmeri and others at a testimonial dinner.[480]

Guarino Moretti, better known as Willie, grew up in East Harlem, New York, and was friends with Frank Costello, a well-known New York gangster. In the early 1920s, he moved to Niagara Falls, where he was known as Willie Moore, and ran a restaurant.[481] By 1927, Moretti had left Niagara Falls and headed back to New York, where his connections propelled him in the underworld. After the Castellammarese War ended, he relocated to New Jersey, where he became a major gambler and bookmaker. A young Frank Sinatra lived nearby, and the two became acquainted.

Moretti developed syphilis and began to speak out of turn, a no-no in mob circles. In December 1950, Moretti freely testified before a Senate committee investigating organized crime and acknowledged that he was a gambler but said he did not own any establishments.

Above: The first location of the Magaddino funeral home was on Pine Avenue in Niagara Falls. This is the building today. *Photo by author.*

Right: Willie Moretti lived in Niagara Falls for several years in the 1920s and was known as Willie Moore. Stefano Magaddino sent him to Florida to get his cousin Joe Bonanno out of some legal trouble. *Author's collection.*

Willie Moretti's days were numbered. On October 4, 1951, he arranged to have lunch with Dean Martin and Jerry Lewis, but he had to stop for a business meeting in Cliffside, New Jersey, first. He and four others met for a short while, and then, in what has been called a "mercy killing," they put two bullets in Moretti's head and walked out.[482]

On October 18, 1951, Paul Palmeri and Ralph Belvedere were taken into custody as material witnesses in the Moretti murder.[483] They were eventually freed, and no one was ever charged with Moretti's murder.

Palmeri's son Frank married Moretti's daughter. Frank and his brother Ernest were both involved in organized crime in the New Jersey area. Ernest was caught in some shady union dealings, and Frank was involved in an early 1970s detergent and labor fiasco.[484]

Paul Palmeri died on May 7, 1955, after a short illness and is buried in New Jersey.[485]

LUPO THE WOLF

It's nice that you came together because it shows harmony, that's all we need is harmony—peace—harmony—respect.[486]
—Stefano Magaddino

Frederico Garibaldi "Fred Lupo, The Wolf" Randaccio was born in Palermo, Sicily, on July 1, 1907. He said he earned his nickname because as a young man he had quite a reputation as a "wolf" with the girls.[487] He had a "low, mumbling voice" and often was inaudible on FBI wiretaps. He spoke both English and Sicilian.[488]

When Joe Valachi testified in 1963, he said Randaccio was Stefano's underboss. He controlled the Buffalo "Arm" for Magaddino and was classified as a "lieutenant and strong-arm man" by the FBI.[489]

His earliest arrest was in 1922 as a juvenile, but by 1924, he had been arrested for playing dice, for which he received a five-dollar fine, an amount that was common yet not much of a deterrent. In 1930, he was sentenced to ten years at Elmira Reformatory for robbery. He served a short sentence and was released but returned to complete the sentence after violating his parole.[490]

In the early 1940s, Randaccio was living above the Senate Grill on Rhode Island Street in Buffalo. When anti-saloon crusader Eddie Pospichal was murdered in January 1945, Randaccio was questioned by Buffalo Police. He said he had been at a party at the Senate and drove in a car owned by Willie Castellani, who killed himself just two months later, in March 1945.[491]

Fred Randaccio lived in several homes. This is his home on Richmond Avenue as it looks today. *Photo by author.*

With his close friend Fred S. Mogavero, he ran Delaware Vending Co., a cigarette vending machine business, and attempted to monopolize Buffalo's predominantly Italian West Side, sometimes legitimately and sometimes by their intimidating presence.[492] When Mogavero died, the funeral was held at Perna Funeral Home in Buffalo, but the Magaddinos ran the funeral, as the hearse bore the Magaddino emblem.

By 1955, Randaccio and his brother Victor were a powerful tandem. The mob had been running Laborers Local 210 for years, and Magaddino approved Victor taking over as secretary-treasurer. Fred could often be found meeting with Stefano at the Magaddino Memorial Chapel in Niagara Falls, where he frequently called him Uncle Steve.

According to mob rat Paddy Calabrese, Randaccio would hold court in the Senate Grill, where everyone who owed him or needed a favor paid a visit to plead their case. His closest associate was Pasquale "Patty" Natarelli,

Pat Natarelli was one of Fred Randaccio's closest aides in the 1960s. This is his former home on Manchester Place today. *Photo by author.*

known for using an ice pick in someone's ear to remind him that he owed him money. Natarelli was said to be behind the policy and numbers rackets in Buffalo and Niagara Falls in the 1960s and worked with Rochester, Syracuse and other areas to set up their rackets.[493] Natarelli and Randaccio were feared men and as dangerous a pair as there was in Buffalo. Randaccio was also involved in narcotics with Salvatore Rizzo, Roy Carlisi and Charles Cassaro, among others.

Randaccio was involved in a multitude of legitimate businesses over the years but was rarely seen actually working. One of those businesses, Vinsco

Amusement Co., operated lucrative bingo games until it was outlawed in 1958. Another operation he had with Natarelli and John Cammilleri was Frontier Lathers, Inc., a barricade sign rental company. When the Magaddinos took an interest in Pandoro Exterminators, Randaccio, Ernest Panebianco and Jerry Dorobiala also took an interest.[494]

Vito "Buck Jones" Domiano was a cousin of Fred Mogavero's and said to be head of the "numbers racket"[495] in Buffalo, but he still reported to Randaccio. Domiano operated a shoe store on Chippewa Street. According to one informant, he was a "reasonable and just man," whereas Randaccio used strong-arm techniques and was feared but did not earn the same respect. Domiano had been personally appointed by Magaddino, along with Samuel Freedman, who was a "principal financial backer behind all numbers operations in the Buffalo area prior to Domiano's death."[496] Freedman was also the president of Kaufmann's Bakery and co-owner of North Park Furniture in Buffalo.

Fred Randaccio's girlfriend Darlene lived in this home on Essex Street in the 1960s. The FBI had secretly installed a wiretap and listened in on his conversations nightly. This is the home today. *Photo by author.*

When Domiano died in April 1958, the funeral was handled by Joseph Spano and Sons Funeral Home, Inc., but the Magaddino Memorial Chapel actually ran it.[497] After Domiano's death, Randaccio took over all his business.

Randaccio's brother-in-law, Augustine J. "Willie" Territo, owned Augustines' restaurant on Washington Street in downtown Buffalo. He also owned the Char-Pit, a popular West Side barbecue restaurant.

One of Randaccio's amusing habits was faithfully visiting a friend every Thursday so they could watch *The Untouchables* television show. The FBI also caught him watching the televised hearings with Joe Valachi in the early 1960s at his girlfriend's house.

In 1959, a numbers operation that Randaccio was involved in operated out of two legitimate businesses in Buffalo, Keith's Theater and Bonnie Lou Candy Corp.[498] Randaccio was observed at both and other locations on a regular basis.

While Randaccio lived on Richmond Avenue, just east of Buffalo's West Side, he had a girlfriend who lived just a few blocks away. The FBI placed a wiretap in Darlene Grann's apartment in the early 1960s and listened in on their nightly conversations, which Randaccio assumed were private. He would often be heard telling Grann not to discuss anything over the phone in case it was bugged. With additional physical surveillance of the location, they knew almost all of Randaccio's moves during the time the tap was in place. Grann was employed by Buffalo attorney Salten Rodenberg and then attorney Nathan D. Seeberg. Randaccio did not like Seeberg, and on May 21, 1962, he told Grann that in five years Seeberg "would be nothing but a bum on the streets."[499] Both attorneys represented many of Buffalo's criminals.

Randaccio was listed in the 1963 Buffalo City Directory as a construction worker with Randaccio Builders. He readily admitted to FBI agents in 1963 that he was friends with many of Buffalo's bookmakers and gamblers but said that he felt that it was a "much better business…than…robbing people and burglarizing houses."[500] But he most likely made sure to take his cut from any of those who did choose those other professions. After all, he believed in the old school La Cosa Nostra values and was against "prostitution" and "dope."

Paddy Calabrese was one of Randaccio's associates who robbed the treasurer's office at Buffalo City Hall on December 29, 1964. Calabrese knew he had to kick a percentage, or "tax," for every job he did to Randaccio just to stay in his good grace.

Vito Agueci, whose brother Albert was killed in 1961, said Randaccio had initiated him into the Magaddino Family. According to an informant,

Randaccio lost respect from Stefano because of how he handled himself after the Panaro's raid. Magaddino was angry at him for the way he treated FBI agents.[501]

In July 1967, Randaccio made a move to smooth things over with the FBI and stopped an agent to talk with him. When he was asked about La Cosa Nostra, "he laughed and stated that all he knew about LCN he read in the newspaper."[502]

Randaccio was arrested and convicted in 1967 after Calabrese testified against him. Randaccio, sixty at the time of his sentencing, had lost his opportunity to become boss of the Magaddino Family. In November 1968, Magaddino and others were arrested. Randaccio was already serving time, and the vacuum left would eventually lead to family infighting for control.

On appeal, Randaccio was able to get his sentence reduced to sixteen years and was released in July 1979 after serving eleven years of his sentence. By the time he was released, Magaddino was dead, and Randaccio no longer commanded the same respect.

Fred Randaccio spent the last years of his life in a Buffalo nursing facility and died on October 4, 2004, at ninety-seven years of age.[503] Pat Natarelli was eighty-three when he died in 1993.[504]

HIDE IN PLAIN SIGHT

Freddy, take half. It's the least I can do under the circumstances.[505]
—*Paddy Calabrese talking to Fred Randaccio*

Perhaps two of the most important events related to organized crime activity in western New York occurred in the 1960s: the formation of the Witness Protection Program and the Strike Force.

It all started rather innocently, in theory at least. Pasquale "Paddy" Calabrese was a brash young hood from Buffalo's Italian West Side. He had an inside scoop that a bag containing close to $300,000 would be in the treasurer's office at Buffalo City Hall, waiting for him. So on December 29, 1964, he calmly walked in and hopped the fence. As he went to grab the bag, he was surprised to see two. He grabbed the wrong one, as there was only $16,000 in the bag, not the $300,000 he had hoped for.

Calabrese escaped unscathed and a few days later was called to meet Fred Randaccio at the Senate Grill. Randaccio and Pat Natarelli were meeting people in the closed bar to discuss business. Calabrese did not like being summoned there and was worried about how Randaccio would handle the heist.

When Paddy was called to the back room to meet the two mobsters, it was not to scold; instead, Randaccio wanted half the score, not his usual 10 percent. Paddy gladly gave him this. In return, he offered Paddy a chance at a big score in Los Angeles, California, where several former Buffalonians were now "working." The men were Stephen "The Whale" Cino; Charles

"Bobby Milano" Caci, a singer; and Lewis Sorgi, who worked at the hotel they were going to rob. They had all relocated to California in the 1950s. Caci's brother Sam was later Local 210 president, and his brother Vincent "Jimmy" would join him in the late 1970s and be named a leader in the Los Angeles mob.

Paddy, Natarelli and Randaccio also planned another robbery of the Marine Trust Co. branch on Fillmore Avenue in Buffalo and one at the Weirton, West Virginia Savings and Loan Co.

Natarelli and Randaccio gave Paddy plane fare, and off he went to meet his fellow Buffalonians in California. What happened after that changed everything related to the Buffalo Mafia. Paddy was finally identified for the city hall robbery, and Randaccio ordered him back to Buffalo to take the fall. After his arrest, he expected that Randaccio would provide bail money, a lawyer or something, but the Magaddino Family backed away, leaving Paddy's girlfriend and her kids hungry and scared and Paddy stuck in jail. "Magaddino was a cheap old man," one agent later recalled.[506]

Paddy was convicted of three counts of robbery, and the only one who seemed to care about him and his girlfriend was Buffalo Police detective sergeant Sam Giambrone. He felt he could get Paddy to turn on Randaccio, but Paddy held on to the belief that the mob would eventually help him.

In June 1967, Calabrese was named as co-conspirator in the Marine Trust robbery, along with Salvatore Pieri and Daniel J. Domino, and co-conspirator, along with Alfred Majrini, in the West Virginia plot. Randaccio, Natarelli and Nicholas Rizzo were named defendants. The last indictment named Calabrese as a co-conspirator and Cino, Vincent and Charles Caci, Sorgi, Randaccio and Natarelli as defendants.[507]

Other events were transpiring in western New York. The FBI had wiretaps in the Magaddino Memorial Chapel in Niagara Falls, Camellia Linen Supply in Buffalo, Fred Magavero's Texaco station in Buffalo and other locations, but President Lyndon Johnson ordered that these wiretaps be shut down. So Strike Force was created by lawyers and a combination of government agencies but not the FBI, as Director J. Edgar Hoover wanted no part. Buffalo was chosen as the first location because there had only been two mobsters prosecuted in the previous decade, so "anything we did was bound to be an improvement" and it was "a small enough target to be manageable,"[508] said Thomas Kennelly, the second-in-command attorney.

Giambrone finally convinced Calabrese to flip and brought him to the Strike Force. Paddy knew if he testified against Randaccio there would be a contract on his head, so he wanted protection for him, his girlfriend, Rochelle, and her kids. They agreed. This was before the Witness Protection Program was ever thought of.

Calabrese opened up about everything he knew, including the L.A. robbery, which was what they would hang Randaccio and Natarelli on. After they were arrested, there was a rumor that "Magaddino was offering $100,000 to anyone" who found Calabrese. His testimony would be the first major blow that Magaddino ever had, and he wanted to prevent it. According to Donald Campbell, one of the Strike Force attorneys, "several of us...began getting threatening phone calls. We were shocked,"[509] he would state, since the mob usually had an unwritten rule about going after police or federal agents.

In May 1967, Stefano Magaddino was supposedly upset with Randaccio for his treatment of FBI agents, which he felt brought heat on the family. This is Magaddino from that time period. *Courtesy Buffalo State College Archives*, Courier-Express *Collection*.

According to one source, Sam Giambrone and a Bureau of Narcotics agent drove to Lewiston to pay Magaddino a visit. When he came to the door, Giambrone shoved his revolver in Magaddino's mouth and told him the threats had better stop or "we are going to come back and blow your fucking head off."[510] The harassment stopped.

Calabrese and Rochelle had been hiding at a military base in another state. He finally got his day in court in late 1967. "It tore holes in Stefano Magaddino's chain of command,"[511] Detective Giambrone would later say.

Some of Buffalo's top defense attorneys worked the case. On November 21, 1967, after eight hours of deliberating, the jury foreman announced, "We find all five defendants guilty on both counts."[512] Natarelli and Randaccio were convicted and each received twenty-year sentences, later dropped to sixteen years. Cino also received twenty but had his dropped. Caci and Corgi each received ten years.

For his part, Calabrese, who had married his girlfriend Rochelle, and their kids were all given new identities and moved to a new state. The problem was that two of the children were from another marriage, and the father wanted to see his kids. This set off a whole other episode.

Thomas Leonhard had been married to Rochelle before Calabrese. After they went into hiding, Leonhard lost contact with his kids and spent eight years fighting the government to see them. He won custody and even sued the U.S. government. His lawyer, Sal Martoche, pushed a congressman to pass a bill to disclose Leonhard's kids' whereabouts or pay $1 million in restitution.[513]

Meanwhile, Calabrese and family were in Michigan and, later, Reno, Nevada, where he became a government witness in other cases. Rochelle divorced Paddy after years of abuse, and Leonhard finally got to see his kids. It was bittersweet, as he found out they had visited Buffalo three or four times over the years but had not been allowed to see him.

Vincent and Charles "Bobby Milano" Caci moved to Los Angeles in the 1970s. Bobby had a minor radio hit in the 1950s. This is their final resting place in Buffalo. Jimmy's name was not yet engraved on the stone. *Photo by author.*

Paddy moved to Seattle and operated an investigation firm. He died in 2005 at sixty-six years old.

As singer Bobby Milano, Charles Caci had one minor song hit in the 1950s and later married singer Keely Smith. His brother Jimmy was said to be a top mobster in Los Angeles after moving there in the 1970s. The brothers both served additional prison sentences on various charges over the years. Jimmy died on August 16, 2011, at eighty-six,[514] and Charles died in January 2006 at sixty-nine.[515] Their other brother, Sam, died in 2002 at seventy-two. Bobby and Jimmy are buried together in a Cheektowaga cemetery.

A GANGSTER, A HIT AND A REMBRANDT

Nobody did it.[516]
—*John Sacco, bleeding with two bullet wounds*

In 1971, three small ten-inch by eleven-inch Rembrandt paintings were stolen from Musée Bonnat in Bayonne, France. Robert LeBec, a young French art student, had been admiring a series of paintings on multiple visits and realized that about a dozen paintings were simply hanging by nails. On March 3, 1971, he came dressed "in a large, loose, long beige raincoat" and pocketed three paintings.[517]

LeBec was no master criminal, so he met a friend who ran drugs in Amsterdam, which led him to a German who ran in the same low-level circles. These were not the people needed to offload a Rembrandt. Due to a few missteps by the bungling thieves, two of the paintings were recovered without a fight, but LeBec kept the last painting. The painting went through some harrowing ordeals, including being buried, hidden in a false-bottom crate and eventually transported to Canada through LeBec's drug-dealer friend. This is where Johnny "Rio" Gandolfo came into the story.

Rio was a New York gangster hiding in Canada, and he wanted a piece of the drug dealer's trade. The dealer was loose-lipped, and Rio found out about the painting. Some months later, the dealer left Canada for a drug buy, and Rio was able to find the painting through some threats of violence.

In early 1976, Buffalo "cat burglar and safecracker"[518] Charles S. "Chuckie" Carlo was convicted of possessing burglary tools. When he was offered probation in exchange for becoming an FBI informant, he reluctantly accepted. The FBI was looking to do a sting operation in Buffalo and set up Operation Teepee, named after a Native American store Chuckie once ran. The Allentown section of Buffalo was filled with antique stores in 1976, which is exactly why the FBI opened its own store on Elmwood Avenue called the House of Tasha. The big difference was that this store was manned by Chuckie, an FBI informant. It had hidden microphones and video that was fed to a rented apartment three doors down.

With Chuckie's underworld contacts, it was his job to attract every burglar, fence and loan shark from Buffalo to Syracuse. Acting as a fence for the FBI, he quickly started bringing in stolen goods left and right.

One of his frequent customers was Gennarino "Jerry" Fasolino. In January 1977, Fasolino and Chuckie were "hanging at his house"[519] when Fasolino said he could get his hands on a stolen Rembrandt if Chuckie was interested. He was, and they agreed on a $200,000 price, half of which would go to Fasolino for his part as middleman. Chuckie immediately called his FBI handler, and they agreed to the purchase.

Apparently, Rio had met a Buffalo girl whose father had some mob connections in Buffalo. Fasolino was that connection. It took three months for Rio to make it to Buffalo, and on April 3, 1977, Chuckie, Rio, his girlfriend and Fasolino met at Fasolino's house. "Rio…grilled Chuckie about his criminal pedigree and underworld connections for a half hour."[520] Afterward, Rio agreed to sell the painting on April 11. The FBI sting operation had grown well beyond what they had anticipated, and they were in slightly over their heads at this point. Enter FBI undercover agent Thomas McShane of the New York office. McShane was an art expert and would pose as the buyer of the painting, making the charade all the more real.

Rio dropped off the painting for Chuckie's art "expert" to inspect as scheduled and was given $10,000 as collateral. That same day, McShane flew into Buffalo from New York, and everything seemed to be falling into place to pull off one of the biggest sting operations in Buffalo history.

When McShane was picked up at the airport, the Buffalo agents were surprised at who they met. McShane did not look like a typical FBI agent; he had long hair, sideburns and flashy clothes. When he asked the Buffalo agents questions about the operation, they seemed to talk around him, never giving the details he might need. This made the buy even more dangerous, since Rio was known to carry a gun.[521] It got to the point where the Buffalo agents started calling McShane "Inspector Clouseau," as they felt they were dealing with a bumbling idiot.

When the FBI set up a fake antique shop on Elmwood Avenue, they didn't expect to recover a Rembrandt, as well as find bribery going on in the district attorney's office. This is the building today. *Photo by author.*

He was driven to the apartment two streets away from Chuckie's shop, from where the operation was run. He was given an additional $13,000 to pay Rio, for a total of $23,000, not the $200,000 as was expected. After a short briefing, he was sent on his way, not even being told the name of Chuckie's shop or the address but simply that it was in the antiques district.

McShane walked two blocks, turned right onto Elmwood Avenue as they had told him and realized that there were many antique shops and he had no idea which one Chuckie was in. Luckily, Chuckie spotted him as he passed and called him into the shop. After a quick introduction, McShane got down to work inspecting the painting. He took photos, looked at it under a magnifying glass and under ultraviolet light, took measurements and closely studied the age of the paint and brushstrokes. He finally declared, "I'm ninety-five percent sure" it was a Rembrandt.[522] The buy was a "go," and the operation was set in motion. Chuckie made calls and went to meet Rio at Fasolino's house. When they returned, only Rio was with Chuckie.

After introductions, McShane dove right in and explained to Rio that he was not paying Rio's price for the painting. He went into details about the painting, explaining that this was only a "study" for a larger painting, which Rio could not have verified. After subtracting Chuckie's cut as the fence and the cost of restoration, after a while they were down to the amount McShane was authorized to spend. Rio was flabbergasted. He admitted he had "gently dabbed the surface with a damp cloth to spruce it up."

While the rest of the agents watched on the video feed three doors down, Rio said he couldn't take that low of a price for something he had babied for five years. "It's been a part of me. It's influenced a lot of things I've done."[523] McShane, unmoved by his tale of woe, offered his final price of $23,000.

Rio finally relented, saying, "I never want to see that face again." He took the $13,000 from McShane and started on his way out. He then turned around and said he could get his hands on a Picasso. "Would you be interested in that?" McShane paused, as he had been searching for that stolen painting prior to this operation, but declined. The two shook hands, and Rio left.

The agents were thrilled that McShane had pulled it off, and that night they went out to celebrate over some beers. When they asked McShane what he thought of Buffalo, he said that the gangsters he had met that day were the nicest people he had talked to all day.

The FBI shadowed Rio after he left the House of Tasha for two days until he slipped away and disappeared. It took two years to track him down, and he was finally arrested in Calgary, Alberta, Canada, on a drug violation. He was later extradited and charged with the Rembrandt sale. He made a deal and spent a short time in prison, only to disappear into the wind once again.

You may be wondering exactly what painting it was that made it to the little antique shop in Buffalo. It was created in 1665 and titled *Le Rabbin*, or *The Rabbi*. It is now worth well over the $1 million that Johnny Rio was hoping to cash in on in 1977.

Operation Teepee did not end with the Rembrandt recovery, though. On Monday June 25, 1977, the FBI finally shut down the operation, Chuckie went into hiding and the FBI began the arrests. It turned out to be a tremendous sting for the Bureau. Among those arrested were John Sacco, accused of possessing 1,672 records and cassettes stolen from Cavages, a former Buffalo record store chain; Thomas G. Gascoyne, for $100,000 in stolen jewelry (he would later become a government witness); Stanley Seneca and Ronald Carlisle, charged with third-degree burglary from a $3,000 dental office burglary; and Alfred T. "Big Al" Monaco, charged with a $19,000 antique store robbery on Allen Street. (Seneca and Monaco would both turn up dead from apparent mob hits.)[524]

Fasolino received a mere $3,000 for his part as middleman in setting up the Rembrandt sale.[525] John Sartori, whose daughter was dating Rio, was arrested for his part in the art heist. Both were charged with sale and transport of stolen property. Fasolino was later found guilty and sentenced to prison.

Joseph SanFratello was charged with multiple counts, including his part in a cigarette burglary and $45,000 robbery. He would be killed gangland style in 1985 in an apparent warning to others after it was determined that he was dealing drugs.

All these were impressive arrests, but the biggest were yet to come. A total of twenty-six people were arrested and $500,000 in stolen property was recovered. In addition, Erie County legislator James V. Arcardi, lawyer Thomas Amodeo and assistant district attorney Richard M. Mancuso,

In 1976, Buffalo criminal Faust Novino was lured to this building and five men, led by John Sacco, attempted to kill him. Instead, he shot first and escaped. This is the building today. *Photo by author.*

Arcardi's cousin, were charged with bribe receiving.[526] Arcardi was dumbfounded by the charges. "I'm as shocked and surprised as you are," he told reporters.

The FBI had wired everything they could think of, including Chuckie, who sometimes wore a wire when meeting people. There was a recorder in his car, and Sacco's phone was tapped.

On June 17, 1976, Frosty Novino, twenty-four, was lured to the former Connecticut Hall under the guise of picking up some burglary tools from Louis Pisa. It was evening when they entered the building, which was dark. Novino "noticed a shadow" and saw "a heavyset man" emerge from the shadows.[527] He said he thought the man was going to hit him, so he pulled his .45-caliber handgun out. "I felt like I was boxed in," he said, and started shooting at the heavyset man, who turned out to be John C. Sacco. He hit Sacco once.[528] He saw two more men crouched on the floor; one was Frank Billiteri, the brother of the man he had killed in 1974 in a botched drug deal. He fired again, hitting Sacco a second time. He saw three other men who had been identified as made men in high-ranking positions in the Buffalo Mafia. Chaos ensued, and Novino was able to run to the rear of the building and escape through a back door.

Sacco, bleeding from wounds to the upper chest and left hip, was dragged outside by the others and left. One of the men called the police from a pay phone and ran. Sacco yelled that he had been shot, but when a neighbor ran to his aid, he told her she "didn't see anything or hear anything."[529]

When asked by the police who shot him, Sacco said, "Nobody shot me." Officers asked if the assailants were still in the building, and Sacco said, "There's nothing to go in the building for." Police searched it anyway and found multiple shotguns, hunting knives, ammunition, six ski masks, clothesline and pairs of gloves.[530] Homicide Chief Leo J. Donovan said the weapons were "generally used in holdups or contract killings."

It turned out that Sacco and the others had lured Novino there to kill him in retaliation for the Billiteri murder. They were going to torture him with the clothesline and knives before finishing him off. Sacco refused to say who had shot him or what happened. He did eventually recover but was convicted of having illegal guns in the building.[531]

On March 22, 1977, in the midst of Operation Teepee, Sacco was heard discussing how to kill Novino with his brother Richard, a Buffalo Police officer. On the wiretap, John admitted asking for the contract to hit Novino. "Let me handle it. I'll let my son drive and I'll shoot him." Richard said, "You look around, you go to a bar, he walks out, you walk out, boom that

John Sacco was a loan shark and burglar. When he was shot by Faust Novino in 1976 and lay bleeding on the sidewalk, the only thing he would tell the police was, "Nobody shot me." *Courtesy* Buffalo Evening News.

is it, all over, one solid day, no big thing. If you are going to do a job, do it right. Blow his head right off, from here to Delaware."[532]

It wasn't until the sting operation ended in June that FBI officials revealed the taped conversations. Richard Sacco immediately resigned from the police force, ending a long career. He later confirmed the conversations during grand jury testimony.

In 1978 John Sacco was tried for the Novino shooting, but Novino could not be located and it ended in a mistrial. In August 1978, John Sacco was given immunity to testify before a federal grand jury but refused and was sentenced to fourteen months in prison. In late January 1979, he began plea negotiations on multiple charges. He pleaded guilty to first-degree assault on the Novino shooting and to multiple stolen property charges from Operation Teepee. He served time for all those charges.

In July 1989, Sacco was again arrested, and FBI agents convinced him to become an informant. In exchange for several thousand dollars per month, he would wear a wire and try to get local mob members to discuss unsolved killings.[533] Because the feds did not completely trust Sacco, he was also secretly recorded. An associate of Sacco's, Buffalo drug dealer Michael Ress, was apparently "becoming a headache," according to Buffalo loan shark Leonard Falzone.[534] During one conversation, Sacco was heard telling Ress to "Get my money…get it or I'm going to hurt you bad." Ress disappeared on August 9, 1989, and his burned-out automobile was found on Chandler Street.[535]

In February 1990, Sacco was exposed as an informant and went into hiding. The events that unfolded became a disaster. Dennis Vacco, the U.S. attorney in Buffalo, said that Sacco would not get out of prison, even though the FBI had made him a deal. Parole officials claimed he had violated his parole by consorting with known criminals.[536]

Sacco was testy, and the FBI never knew if he was providing them with false information. Then, in June 1990, Sacco was arrested on a drug charge from prior to his stint as an FBI informant, and his life as an informant was over.

While in custody in a Lockport jail, John Sacco suffered a heart attack and died. While in jail, he had been married, and a battle over his estate between his two adult children and wife ensued. His estate was said to include $300,000 in cash and jewelry, three houses and thirty-one wedding rings.[537]

Frosty Novino, having survived Sacco's murder attempt in 1976, was allegedly shot at outside a Forest Avenue bar a few years later but again escaped unharmed. The Buffalo Mafia apparently gave up trying to kill him, and he moved to Arizona, returning in the 1980s.[538]

In 1991, Novino was charged with drug trafficking. During this time, multiple informants started ratting each other out, and Novino was caught in the middle, finally pleading guilty to the 1974 Billiteri murder. He testified against another gangster for his own 1976 ambush. Novino was sent to prison for eight and one-third to twenty-five years and may have died in 2001.

VALACHI AND HIS SWEETHEART

They know everything under the sun. They know who's back of it, they know Amici, they know Capodecina, they know there is a Commission. We got to watch right now, this thing, where it goes and stay as quiet as possible.[539]
—Stefano Magaddino

In the early 1950s, Fred Randaccio met John "Johnny Pops" Papalia of nearby Hamilton, Ontario, and became "more mentor than friend."[540] In 1955, Papalia was told by Stefano that he was taking over Ontario, and Stefano asked Papalia if he wanted to be his lieutenant, which he accepted. From then on, he "kept a flow of tribute money" going to Buffalo.[541]

Papalia became involved in a "number of illicit enterprises" with Albert Agueci, a native of Sicily who arrived in Canada in 1950.[542] Agueci also wanted to get into narcotics, specifically heroin, where the profits were tremendous. Papalia wanted a piece of the action.

A meeting in Palermo, Sicily, at the Grand Hotel des Palmes supposedly took place from October 12 to 16, 1957, to discuss the growing drug trade and how the Mafia planned to handle it. Joe Bonanno mentions a trip to Sicily during that time (but not the meeting) in his book, and one journalist, Claire Sterling, claims it took place, but there is little corroborating evidence to validate such a meeting. The very next month, the Apalachin summit took place in Apalachin, New York, and it has long been thought that the drug trade was discussed at the pre-summit meeting.

A meeting was said to take place in Sicily at the Grand Hotel des Palmes in October 1957, the month before Apalachin, to discuss the drug business. This is the building today. *Photo by author.*

By October 1958, Agueci was using his Sicilian contacts and a crooked travel agent to have heroin shipped in the luggage of unsuspecting immigrants traveling to Toronto and New York City.[543] It would then be split, with most going to New York. The ring had thirty-two people in three countries, and Papalia was "the money man."[544]

All the parties needed to get permission from their godfathers, including Vito Genovese and Joe Bonanno in New York and Magaddino, to participate. Agueci and Papalia visited Magaddino and paid him $4,000 as tribute, and Magaddino in turn assured them of his support and expected 50 percent of the profit.[545] Both Magaddino and Bonanno outwardly opposed the drug trade, but both were involved and accepted its windfall.

Police on both sides of the border had been slowly putting together the pieces of the ring. It was during this time that Genovese soldier Joe Valachi became part of the puzzle. He had been sentenced to five years for a heroin charge in 1956 but was released on appeal. An associate of his involved in the dope ring, Ralph Wagner, was arrested in 1959 and ratted out Valachi to reduce his sentence. While out on bail, Valachi decided to leave the country and met Albert Agueci. Valachi made his way to Buffalo, where he stayed at the Statler-Hilton for four days and met Randaccio. With Albert's help, he was then able to make it into Canada.

Eventually, too many mistakes were made in the drug ring, and two men were arrested in New York. The men made a deal to give up everyone involved in return for reduced sentences. In late May 1961, the arrests began. The U.S. district attorney announced that a $150 million heroin smuggling ring, dubbed the French Connection, had been broken up. Valachi, Papalia, the Aguecis and many others were arrested.

Albert Agueci thought that Stefano would provide bail or a lawyer, but Magaddino never kept his end of the deal. This would prove to be a turning point for the Buffalo family and the Mafia nationally.[546] When Albert Agueci demanded that Magaddino spring for his $20,000 bail, it fell on deaf ears. Agueci told Valachi that "he was going to declare himself [inform] if Steven Magaddino don't get his brother out."[547]

Agueci's wife sold their home and gathered enough money to bail him out of the New York City jail, and Agueci jumped bail. On October 31, 1961, a confidential FBI informant said that Fred Mogavero had contacted Pat Natarelli to tell him "Al" was at his service station in Buffalo after taking a taxi from New York City.[548]

On Thanksgiving Day, November 23, 1961, a body was found in the Rochester suburb of Penfield by two hunters. The body was badly burned. The arms were tied behind the back, clothesline was around the neck, "the jaw [was] broken and eight teeth knock[ed] out [and] roughly 40 pounds of flesh…had been sliced" off the body while he was still alive.[549] The body was so badly burned that officials had to remove the fingers to get fingerprints. Two days later, the FBI identified the body as that of Albert Agueci.

On November 27, an informant told the FBI that Randaccio and Sansanese had been discussing someone but never mentioned Agueci by name. Randaccio said they were supposed to "burn the fingers even if they had to get a blowtorch." They had dug a hole, but some hunters came by and jokingly asked if they were going to bury someone. They then poured five gallons of gasoline over his head and burned him.[550]

Vito Agueci blamed Magaddino and Randaccio, but police believed it was actually done by the Rochester mob family as a favor to Magaddino.[551]

While in jail, Valachi claimed that Genovese, with some prodding from Vito Agueci, thought he was an informant. Valachi, in his paranoia, killed an innocent man in prison and now had a murder charge added to the others. He thought there was a price on his head and felt he had only one option: become an informant. Valachi was put in seclusion and testified before the Senate Rackets Committee, where he named people, places and events dating back to his earliest days in crime. His memory was amazing, but even he could not have known all those people. It is believed that the FBI helped him fill in some blanks. His testimony, along with that of Buffalo Police commissioner William H. Schneider, Lieutenant Michael A. Amico and Detective Sergeant Samuel Giambrone, helped to put Buffalo and the Magaddino Family on the map. Those named were Magaddino, John Montana, Randaccio, Carlisi, Lagattuta, Nino, Pascal Politano and others.

Nothing substantial ever came from his Buffalo testimony, other than more awareness by the public and law enforcement. After it was all over, Valachi was sent to LaTuna Military Prison in Texas, where he was held prisoner, more for his own safety than anything. While there, he cultivated a love affair with a Niagara Falls woman, Marie K. Jackson. She was divorced and he was still married, but apparently their love was real. She said they had met at a mutual friend's house in Niagara Falls in the 1950s. Their affair was unknown to the outside world, but according to Jackson,

Joe Valachi's last days were spent sending love letters to his Niagara Falls girlfriend, Marie Jackson. When he died in 1971, she claimed his body and had it buried in Lewiston. When she died, she was buried next to him. *Photo by author.*

"Joe was always good to me." She said, "He gave me gifts and money, and we took a lot of trips" before he went to prison. Afterward, "I wrote to him everyday."[552]

During his time in prison, Valachi wrote his memoirs, which he thought could be sold. Instead, he and Jackson claim, they were stolen by a U.S. senator and never returned.[553]

Joe Valachi died on April 3, 1971, at sixty-six years of age. His body went unclaimed for three days; neither his wife nor his son wanted him. That was when Marie Jackson went public. She claimed his body and had it shipped to Niagara Falls. After a private ceremony at Our Lady of Mount Carmel Church, he was secretly buried right in Stefano's backyard at Gate of Heaven cemetery in Lewiston.[554]

Jackson was named Valachi's executor and beneficiary, and his will stipulated that his burial site be secret, as he did not want his former comrades desecrating his remains. She tried to get his manuscript back from the government but was constantly stonewalled. She earned royalties from *The Valachi Papers*, a book about his life, and possibly the movie, which starred Charles Bronson.

Valachi was the perfect scapegoat for the government to use to open up the public's eyes to organized crime. He paid with his freedom, but the love of his life would never be forgotten. He wrote to her, "I am thinking of you day and night...I love you darling...Joe."[555]

Two years after Valachi died, Jackson had a small stone placed on his grave site and the one next to it, where she would be buried in 1999.

DEADLY NIGHTS

THE UNION, THE MURDER AND THE INFORMANT

I abhorred the mob.[556]
—Ron Fino

Laborers Local 210 was chartered in 1913 from the International Hod Carriers' and Building Laborers' Union to provide the construction industry with laborers.[557] Over time, Local 210 became synonymous with the Buffalo Mafia, and although it was difficult to see where one ended and the other began, it was generally considered to be run by the mob, even though evidence of such was scarce.

According to testimony given during Senate hearings in 1963, Lieutenant Michael Amico of the Buffalo Police said that in the early 1950s, in order to work in the union, "it was necessary...to partake of some of their gambling activities," and if you did so while on the job, you "would remain on the job for longer periods of time."[558]

Joe Fino rose through the mob ranks from a soldier to capo under Stefano. He was a bookmaker and had his brothers Nick and Anthony "operating horse books" for him.[559] After Stefano's arrest in 1968, Fino aligned himself with John Cammilleri and Sansanese Sr. as part of a faction attempting to wrest control of the crime family from Magaddino.

Fino's son Ron graduated from high school in 1964 and began working as a laborer for Local 210 while attending classes at University at Buffalo.[560] During this time, he also did undercover work for the government. According to Ron, "Starting in 1964, I provided the Department of Justice and the FBI

For years, law enforcement suspected that Laborers Local 210 was controlled by the local Mafia, but no evidence was ever found. It no longer occupies this fortress at 481 Franklin Street in Buffalo. This is the building today. *Photo by author.*

with information relating to the control"[561] of the union and its organized crime ties.

In 1971, *Time* magazine exposed the corrupt union in an article about the much-delayed federal building construction. The article blamed Local 210 for the problems, saying, "Fully 90 percent of Buffalo Mafia members belong to Local 210."[562]

Samuel Lagattuta served as union official and timecard keeper. Workers generally showed up well after starting time, but timecards showed that they were on time. When the contractors complained, there were walk-offs and sick calls, and even a fire broke out.

As a last resort, the Dallas contractor, J.W. Bateson Co., hired Cammilleri as a "job coordinator." He was born on October 17, 1912, and was a typical Mafioso. He wore expensive clothes and shoes and a pinky ring, gambled and had girlfriends. His legitimate employment was vice-president of Vin James Builders, Inc., but he also had a stake in Nairy's Social Club on West Ferry Street, which was coveted by Sansanese Sr.[563]

His affiliation with Local 210 dates back to about 1939, but "no one can remember him ever lifting a shovel." He implemented new job standards, telling workers they could not take toilet breaks out of order, could not have surgery since "we hired you as you are" and could not die without two weeks' notice and first training a replacement. The workers kicked into high gear and the building was completed, albeit a year late.

In 1970, at age twenty-three, Ron Fino became a business agent for Local 210 as Victor Randaccio's way to get closer to Joe Fino, who was heading a defecting faction of the Magaddino Family.[564] It was during this time that Ron realized how corrupt the union was, and in 1973, he decided to run for business manager on a reform ticket.

Without thinking, he was going against the mob itself, and this put his life in danger. Joe was worried, but a deal was brokered to let Fino run, since they figured he couldn't win. Even law enforcement officials said that Fino would not have been able to attempt this if Magaddino had not been arrested in November 1968 and Fred Randaccio imprisoned. "Do you really think there'd be this election if there was an organization?" a local policeman commented.[565]

Fino recruited Salvatore "Sammy" Caci, brother of Charles and Vincent, to run as president and said the union was "fighting for its life" to represent all the members, "not just a handful."[566] Caci brought along Cammilleri, whom Joe wanted involved, and also recruited Sansanese Sr., so Ron had to promise Sansanese's son, Dan Jr., and Ralph Velochi jobs if he won the election.[567]

Ron Fino believes that the union's American Indian and Irish members of South Buffalo brought in the votes. Over 2,700 of the 3,000 members showed up, and Ron won the election by a two-to-one vote.

Secretly, Ron had been meeting with government agents while traveling and working for the union. Not long after the election, Cammilleri went to Ron and asked him for a job inside the union. Ron declined, and Cammilleri was not happy.

One day, Ron received a call to have a sit-down at the Turf Club, owned by Roy Carlisi. Carlisi congratulated Fino and then told him he had no power, that he would be told who to give no-show jobs to and whose pensions to pad; in essence, he was to be the union's figurehead leader because the Mafia still controlled it. Ron gave Carlisi some lip and was berated.

In 1972, Joe Fino was acting as if he were boss and was summoned to appear before the Mafia Commission to explain why, since Magaddino was still the boss. Sansanese, Frangiamore and Carlisi accompanied him, and they all agreed to stick together with their decision. When told that Magaddino was still boss, Fino told the Mafia Commission their decision, but the others said they would abide by the commission's ruling, leaving Fino with little choice but to eat crow and backpedal on his decision. He now realized that they had never planned on backing him for the long term, and he had to reconsider who he could trust. Sam Frangiamore was chosen as boss by the commission.

In April 1974, Joe decided to make a move to try to take over the family. His crew, Cammilleri and some of the Rochester faction agreed that they would not recognize Frangiamore as boss and would attempt to wrest control from him. Before Fino and Cammilleri could make their move, Frangiamore found out, and Charles Cassaro, Albert Billiteri Sr., Angelo Massaro and Sam Cardinale turned on Cammilleri.

Meanwhile, Cammilleri had been demanding a meeting with the mob's union leaders, and they agreed to meet him on May 8, 1974, his sixty-third birthday. It's not believed that the meeting went well, as Cammilleri said they refused him a job. That night, he met some friends for dinner and drinks at Roseland Restaurant, a popular West Side Italian eatery, to celebrate his birthday.

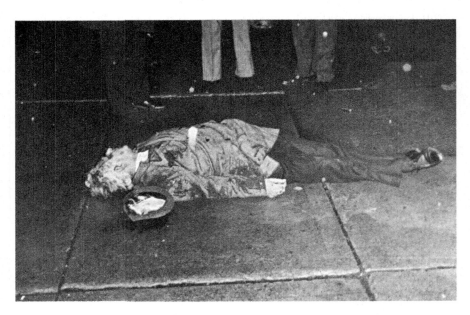

John Cammilleri's time as a made member of the Buffalo Mafia ran out on his sixty-third birthday in 1974. As he was returning to his party at Roseland Restaurant on Rhode Island Street, a car pulled up, and he was shot and killed. *Courtesy Mike Kaska.*

Roseland Restaurant was already well known for its Italian food when John Cammilleri was gunned down outside in 1974. This is the building today. *Photo by author.*

After dinner, he excused himself, saying he had to attend the wake of Sam Pieri's brother-in-law, but he told his friends to wait, as he would return. Cammilleri attended the wake, along with numerous underworld figures. As is common among Italians, the men greeted one another with kisses on the cheek. Cammilleri would soon find out that one of the kisses he received was *il bacio della morte*, the kiss of death.

He left the wake and drove back to Roseland about 9:30 p.m. He parked his car in the lot across the street and headed back to his birthday celebration. As he crossed the street, a car sped up, and a man or men jumped from the car and shot Cammilleri, hitting him in the head. He fell onto the sidewalk in front of the restaurant and died. The killers sped away down Chenango Street and were not identified. Years later, Cammillieri's nephew and former county legislator Michael J. Alessi was arrested and pinned the murder on Vincent S. "Jimmy" Sicurella.

That same night, Joe Fino was scheduled to die, but another mob member convinced Frangiamore that only Cammilleri needed to go. Joe, who had little power by then, was spared. Joe died in 1984 at sixty-nine years old.[568]

175

Sansanese Sr. promptly took over Cammilleri's stake in Nairy's Social Club, as well as part of his crew, including Billy Sciolino, who had been under Joe, Rinaldo and Sam Cardinale. Cassaro took over the rest of Cammilleri's crew, including Angelo Massaro and Albert Billiteri.

Ron left the union in 1988 to start an environmental waste firm, which he said the mob muscled in on. Others say Fino lived an extravagant life and drove the business into the ground.

In 1988, Dennis Vacco became U.S. attorney in Buffalo with support from the local mob leadership. Not long after, Fino had a close friend, Dan Domino, see if the mob knew anything about his undercover work. That same night, he found out they knew he was an informant and decided to leave town. Once his cover was blown, it all came out. Most people could not believe that he was an informant. Others, like attorney Paul Cambria, who had represented Fino in the past, said, "He wanted to be a much bigger player in the union, and they didn't want it."[569] Fino disagrees. "I just did not like what they were doing to it and limiting who was taken care of just to their family members and cronies."[570]

Ron testified in other cities and put several suspected mob members in jail, but in his hometown of Buffalo, it was proving much more difficult. He said he "had many fights with" Vacco, who did not want to prosecute anyone in Local 210 and told Fino he would never have him testify in Buffalo.[571]

By June 1996, things had finally come to a head at Laborers' International Union of North America (LIUNA). They said twenty-eight members of Local 210 were either mobsters or mob associates and had to be removed from the union. Those named included Leonard F. Falzone, Joseph Todaro Jr. and Frank "Butchie Bifocals" Bifulco, among others.[572]

Ron had been working closely with LIUNA, and as he got closer to the top, he realized they weren't really interested in cleaning up Local 210 or any locals. Someone gave his unlisted telephone number to national reporter Michael Isikoff, as well as leaked information (some of which Ron says was false) to try to discredit him.[573]

In April 1996, LIUNA put a trustee in charge of Local 210 as part of an effort to clean out organized crime.[574] LIUNA only agreed to this after the Justice Department threatened action. LIUNA conducted a disciplinary hearing in Buffalo on the mob allegations, and Fred Saia, a former union member and FBI informant, testified that he was given a construction job without any experience simply because he visited a Mafia leader at a restaurant. He also worked on Stefano's home while he was a paid contractor for a State Thruway project.[575] His testimony helped force six of the accused to resign.

In March 1998, LIUNA cleared six men and found "credible charges" against seventeen, including the six who resigned. The remaining five had their charges dismissed.[576]

LIUNA, however, felt that "organized crime figures or their associates" wanted back in control, so LIUNA proposed tighter controls. Members of the old guard protested in front of the longtime union hall on Franklin Street, garnering publicity, claiming that it was a witch hunt against Italians.

In January 2000, John J. "Jack" McDonnell, a former FBI special agent, took over as the union's court-appointed liaison officer.[577] The first time he walked into the union hall on Franklin, he took a look around and said, "Hey, I've never seen this place in the daytime!" joking about times the FBI had planted bugs in the office. It broke the ice, and he was able to work with the new leadership. On January 26, 2006, McDonnell ended his job, saying the union was finally clean. He said that only "a handful of corrupt people had been running 210."[578]

When Ron Fino first ran for business manager of the union in 1973, there were 2,300 members paying $500,000 a year in union dues. When the government control ended in 2006, there were just 750 members, and according to McDonnell, "I think they are savvy enough to keep mob influences out."[579]

MYSTERIOUS MURDERS

If any police officer still doubts the existence and power of the Mafia, the Cosa Nostra, or whatever you want to call it, just let him read this case.[580]
—*Sergeant Peter N. Bagoye, Los Angeles Police Department*

Crime in Buffalo during the 1920s was as frequent and reckless as in any bustling city in America. Prohibition was in full swing, and criminals were busy doing everything they could to quell the thirst of the average citizens. Many deaths would be attributed to bootleg wars and the vast sums of money they made. What are believed to be wars between rival gangs for the lucrative bootleg profits also waged across the Canadian border for most of Prohibition.

John Sciabore of Hamilton, Ontario, was found dead with five bullets in his body on a Buffalo street in 1923.[581] His wife said he left home looking for work six days earlier, but as was often the case, no one claimed to have seen anything.

In April 1925, the residents of Meadow Place in suburban Cheektowaga lived in fear as an unknown assailant shot and killed Giuseppi Scioscia of Buffalo on their street.[582] It may have been a case of mistaken identity, as days before, shotgun blasts had been targeted at Frank Morreale's home on the street.

Just a few months later, John Gambino felt the wrath of a suspected "feud among gangsters"[583] and was shot eight times by two men just outside Buffalo's Little Italy. Gambino had been held for questioning in two previous murders in Buffalo, and his number was up.

Police believed that a "bootleggers' war"[584] was in full swing in 1926, when four gang-related murders took place starting on July 2. Joseph Cicatello was shot five times while sitting in front of his store. On July 15, Peter Rizzo, forty-nine, was shot ten times, and on July 20, Anthony Vasallo was shot five times. Frank Polizzi was the fourth victim of the suspected war and was part owner of a "drinkery"[585] in Buffalo. He was shot dead while walking on Carolina Street at 1:30 a.m. on August 14.

Filippo "Philip" Mazzara was a "popular and wealthy chieftain"[586] and had been bondsman for Joe DiCarlo. His brother-in-law Giuseppe "Joseph" DiBenedetto was his "heir apparent."[587] They

Joe DiCarlo Jr. was labeled Buffalo's Public Enemy No. 1. Police pressure eventually forced him and his crew to leave Buffalo for Youngstown, Ohio. *Courtesy Joe DiCarlo's granddaughter.*

were thought to be Stefano's chief lieutenants in Buffalo, all from the same Sicilian town. With Angelo Palmeri, they led the Buffalo "Arm" of the Magaddino Family.

Mazzara was well known in the Italian community. He was believed to be involved in bootlegging, was a "cafe proprietor"[588] and had an office at the Elk Market in Buffalo. On December 22, 1927, Joseph Ruffino lent his automobile to Mazzara. Police later said that he was riding in a car owned by Joseph DiBenedetto, "his trusted lieutenant and confidante."[589]

While driving on Maryland Street near Cottage Street in Buffalo, two cars with "six or eight men" forced Mazzara's car to the curb and ambushed him. With shotgun blasts to the head and revolver shots from the rear, the men made sure Mazzara was dead and then fled.

DiBenedetto took over until February 27, 1929, when he was gunned down in a store in Buffalo's Little Italy.[590] More than one thousand curious onlookers gathered outside the store, and police were forced to stand guard to keep them at bay.[591]

Mazzara's younger brother Antonio and DiBenedetto's brother Antonio had both been killed on November 11, 1917, in Brooklyn as part of an ongoing Sicilian feud,[592] tied to the Good Killers after Stefano was arrested in 1921.[593]

Giuseppe "Joseph" DiBenedetto (left) was one of Magaddino's (right) top aides in the 1920s. *Courtesy Sharon Manning.*

In May 1928, Luigi Lozzi was "shot down by murderers"[594] near his home in Buffalo. The following day, his cousin Santo Falsone was walking from his cousin's wake when he was struck by a volley of bullets from two men and killed.[595] Police were able to trace one of the autos used in the shooting to Pasquale "Patsy" Corda of Erie, Pennsylvania, who was living in Buffalo at the time of the murder.

On January 27, 1928, Phillip Mannor, another restaurateur of Erie, Pennsylvania, was shot to death by a lone gunman.[596] Police believed it was a "black hand," extortion-related murder. Mannor had been a partner of Mazzara's in a café.

Patsy Corda was arrested by police in Buffalo, charged with Mannor's murder and also believed to be linked to Mazzara's killing.[597] All these deaths were believed to be tied to the liquor racket, or bootleg war, going on in Buffalo and the surrounding area.[598] The bootleg war took many lives, and these men paid with theirs.

In April 1919, Anthony "Baby Face" Palmisano, Corda, Salvatore Marino and two others robbed the State Bank of Randolph, New York, of $3,000.[599] During the robbery, a shootout took place, but the gang escaped, only to be caught later that same day. Palmisano eluded police until December 1919, when he was arrested in Brooklyn and sentenced to seven years in Auburn Prison.

In 1929, he was arrested on a narcotics charge involving morphine and sentenced to two years in Atlanta Prison. Although he had no lawyer, someone with influence convinced a congressman and a prominent Buffalo attorney to make pleas to the court, but it was for naught.

Palmisano was listed at number 6 on Buffalo's Public Enemy list and was said to be close to Angelo Palmeri and "engaged in various activities" with him. When Palmeri died in 1932, Joe DiCarlo Jr. and Palmisano may have been at odds with each other over control of some underworld activities.

Sometime on the cold night of February 20, 1934, Palmisano was "taken for a ride" on River Road, two miles north of the city line, near the new abutments of the Grand Island Bridge in Tonawanda. A patrol car found Palmisano literally ten to fifteen minutes after he was gunned down inside his own auto. He was sitting in the passenger seat, and twelve bullets had been pumped into his head, probably from behind and the driver's seat. Robbery was not a motive, and police believed that "two men hailing from Niagara Falls" were behind his murder.[600] The following day, two former drivers for Palmisano were questioned, but the police stated, "If the Mafia, as we suspect, was behind Palmisano's death, we'll probably never get to the bottom of it."[601]

Early October 1930 found Niagara County sheriffs searching for a killer when Salvatore "Sam" Frangipani's bullet-ridden and beaten body was found in a wheat field near Lewiston, New York. Frangipani was from Rome, New York, where he had a long arrest record. He had come to Niagara Falls six weeks prior and was planning to open a soft drinkery on Pine Avenue.[602] Police believed it was a vendetta killing, as both of his ears had been slit, indicating "that he had been told something that he did not heed."[603]

While authorities could find no clues to Frangipani's murder, another body turned up, this time in Walmore, near Sanborn, New York. Francis Falcony, thirty-nine, was the proprietor of a "cabaret and soft drink store" who was "taken for a ride." Not long before, men had demanded money from him. Police believe he met his slayers in a large sedan bearing Ohio license plates at about 11:00 p.m. on Sunday, October 23, 1930. He was not seen again until his body was found in the ditch early Monday morning[604] along Old Church Road in Walmore, with two bullets in the back of his head.[605]

Police were never able to solve the murder, but less than a year later, Falcony's brother Anthony, also a "cabaret" owner, was paid a visit by four men from Buffalo who said Angelo Palmeri had sent them and attempted to "shake him down."[606] Falcony turned them down, and when they returned, they were arrested.

Another Niagara Falls resident, thirty-five-year-old Marcello "Monk the Gambler" Ventrigo, a professional gambler, was found with two bullets in his head on September 4, 1931.[607] Residents heard the shots, but no one saw anything. Ventrigo had run a gambling joint on Ontario Avenue a few

Salvatore and Vincenzo Callea were running a saloon on Connecticut Street in 1933. The brothers were lured to the saloon in June and both gunned down by unknown assailants. This is the building today. *Photo by author.*

years prior, was heard to brag that he was owed more than $10,000 and had several gambling arrests.[608] Robbery was a possible motive, as was the theory that local gangsters offed him. It was never solved.

Two brothers who may have come from Ohio made their way to Buffalo around 1921. Salvatore "Sam" and Vincenzo "Big Jim" Callea opened a fish store in Buffalo's Little Italy on Dante Place when they first arrived. Six years later, they opened a "drinkery," also on Dante Place, that operated until 1932, when they supposedly "retired."[609] While living in Little Italy, they were known as the Valentones.[610]

In January 1933, a gun duel took place in front of the former Dante Place restaurant the Calleas owned. In that duel, Angelo Porello, son of one of the dead Porello brothers of Cleveland, was killed by a Buffalo politician who claimed self-defense after a "quarrel over a game of pool."[611]

Around June 1933, the Callea brothers moved to Buffalo's West Side and opened a new drinkery on Connecticut Street. It is believed that the Callea brothers were involved in bootlegging, and their storefronts may have been a cover, or else they retired with their bootlegging profits. Newspapers reported that one of their distilleries had been "knocked off" by federal agents.[612] In turn, they made a deal with a Cleveland gang, but when the Cleveland distillery was raided, the Calleas refused to provide any additional funds.

On Friday, August 25, 1933, Sam, thirty-seven, and Big Jim, thirty-two, both received "telephone messages asking them" to meet at their saloon.[613] Several theories as to what prompted the meeting were never fully explored, but what followed was as coldblooded as it got in Buffalo during those days.

Although witness accounts vary, it is believed that the brothers parked their cars on Connecticut Street and headed toward their saloon, where they met a man outside. One witness, Norman Mitchell, said he "saw a fat man [Big Jim] running east on the north side of Connecticut Street, holding his stomach and yelling."[614] Big Jim ran across the street and fell in front of a shoe repair store. The man walked up and put another bullet in him while he lay dying on the sidewalk. Meanwhile, Sam had jumped into a parked coupe in front of the saloon. Sam covered his face as the men approached and began shooting him, pinned inside the car. At least two bullets lodged in his head.

It was a sloppy job, as two bystanders were hit by stray bullets, though neither was fatal. "After that I saw all the five men get back into the car again."[615] The car drove about five feet before it stalled. Unable to start it, the men left the car and "ran down Fourteenth Street."[616]

Big Jim was dead at the scene, but Sam was rushed to Columbus Hospital, where he died a short time later. It was a bloody double murder, and police had few clues. Robbery was not the motive, as Sam had a bankbook on him showing $5,000 and Big Jim wore a $1,500 ring.

Several men were arrested within hours but yielded no additional clues. Several days later, two men were arrested in Jamestown, New York, for questioning, including John Porello, a relative of the Porello Gang. No connection to the Calleas could be made, though it was believed that the Cleveland gang may have been muscling its way into western New York and the Calleas were caught in the middle of the battle.[617]

Three men—Cerio DeSalvo, thirty-three, Joseph Mangus, thirty-six, and Anthony Perna, twenty-nine—were arrested on September 11, 1933, and held for two days but were released after police could not link them to the murders. Perna was listed as Public Enemy No. 9 in Buffalo.[618]

The dead bodies would continue to pile up, even before Buffalo Police had a chance to finish their investigation. Just days later, the body of James M. DiStefano, fifty-one, was found in a shed in suburban Cheektowaga. He had been hit over the head with an iron bar and his throat slit from ear to ear.[619] DiStefano lived near the Calleas, and police thought there might be a connection, but again, there were few leads.

The trail grew cold until Wednesday, September 27, 1933, when an explosion ripped through a garage owned by Vincent Marinello, smashing windows nearby and destroying several cars in the garage.[620] Marinello, who owned the Jamestown Grill on Allen Street, was moments from stepping into the garage when it exploded.

Police began searching for four men for whom DiStefano had posted bonds, three of whom police had wanted to question regarding the Callea killings. As is usually the case, no killer was ever caught for DiStefano, and no specific tie to the Calleas was ever found.

On Sunday, April 29, 1934, Marcantonio "Mike the Undertaker" Palamara, forty-four, was at Caruso's restaurant on Chippewa Street, long known as a gangsters' paradise. Mike was playing cards with a few "friends" in the second-story restaurant when several of the men got up and left. A few minutes later, two strangers entered and shook hands with the men at the table, but they only spoke to Palamara. One man calmly walked behind him and put a bullet in his head. The other man opened fire, shooting six times, hitting Palamara with three shots and killing him.

Palamara had been Anthony Palmisano's chauffeur, and police attributed both their deaths to the same "group."[621] Palamara's brother Anthony rose in underworld stature due to his brother's death but feared for his life from the day his brother was gunned down. On August 17, 1935, Anthony, thirty-two, left his home about seven o'clock, told his wife goodbye and never returned. He was shot seven times at close range while sitting in his automobile in Tonawanda. Six of the bullets passed through his head.[622] Two revolvers were found in the car. The keys were still in the ignition, and other keys were lying on the running board of the car.[623] His fear of death was not unwarranted.

Other murders occurred over the years, and rarely were they solved. In early 1938, John J. Barbera, thirty-eight, was Buffalo's Public Enemy No. 3 and at one time Joe DiCarlo's first lieutenant. Known as "John the Barber" and "John the Greek," Barbera was involved in bookmaking and had a falling out with DiCarlo around 1937. The theory that he was trying "to take over control of Buffalo's racketland"[624] while DiCarlo was in prison may have played into his murder.

As Barbera sat at the front table of a tavern at Carolina and Niagara Streets, two "dark-clad men" entered the tavern. They walked directly to Barbera, who had his back to them, pulled out revolvers and unloaded them into Barbera. Six bullets entered his head and back. The front window of the tavern was shattered by a bullet. The men then jumped over the body and left in a waiting car in front. None of the witnesses could identify the shooters. Questioned in the murder were Anthony Perna, Joseph Santasiero, Joseph Ruffino, Joseph Aleo, Joseph Albanese and Joseph Dipasquale. None was charged.[625]

This list is by far not complete, as many more have died as the result of liquor wars, gang wars, extortion, cheating and a litany of other reasons that the underworld may have had for ending the life of a man. These are just some of the long list that made the headlines.

A LESSON FROM THE MOB

Anything, any scheme [to] make money. You got to come to us.[626]
—*Stefano Magaddino*

S tefano ruled western New York with a quiet iron fist. According to one report, his power was so great that "his underlings and even some law enforcement officials believed his grip could not be weakened."[627] He was a powerful force, and few ever crossed him.

Frank C. Buttitta, twenty-five, a "racketeer in gasoline and alcohol black markets,"[628] was suspected of operating a still on Buffalo's West Side. On Wednesday, June 7, 1944, he was trailed by members of the U.S. Alcohol Tax Unit, but the agents lost him. About 12:30 a.m., he was shot while sitting in his auto in Buffalo. He had been arrested in a counterfeit gasoline coupon racket and said he would name the higher-ups if given a break, but he suddenly changed his mind.

Pasquale Quagliano, known as Patsy Collino, was said to be Niagara Falls mayor William Lupton's right-hand man. Quagliano was also a known bookmaker and apparently challenged Magaddino's monopoly on gambling in Niagara Falls.[629] He disappeared in April 1949 and was never seen again. An anonymous tipster said he was clubbed and killed on Easter Sunday and his body was dumped in a sewer, but after a thorough search, they found no body.[630]

Angelo "The Baron" Ciambrone was reported as missing on August 2, 1953. An anonymous tip to Niagara Falls Police superintendent Charles J. Gorman's unlisted number said that Ciambrone was dead.[631]

Brothers Fred "The Fox" and Frank Aquino were small-time burglars who hung around Allen Street and were known to frequent the Allentown Grill, run by made man Pascal "Lucky Pat, Pantaloons" Politano in Buffalo. The brothers were involved in a burglary ring that included James Delmont, Charles Miller and Richard Battaglia. It is believed that Fred Aquino tipped off Eugene Francis Newman to the Brink's garage on College Street in Buffalo, just around the corner from the Allentown Grill. On August 4, 1955, Newman, Anthony Pettinato of Baltimore and

This is another surveillance photo of Magaddino, location unknown. *Courtesy Buffalo State College Archives, Courier-Express Collection.*

Sylvester Mazzella of the Bronx staged a daring robbery at the garage.

At about 7:00 p.m., an armored truck carrying almost $500,000 in U.S. and Canadian currency (just over $4 million in 2010 dollars) had just arrived from Fort Erie Race Track in Ontario, Canada. As the truck was backing into the garage, the three men, all with silk stockings over their heads, "showed up out of nowhere."[632] The bandits ordered the four guards out, and Newman opened fire with a German machine gun for no apparent reason, striking one guard in the arm and chest. A mêlée broke out, during which the thieves tossed two boxes of money out a window while the injured guard activated the alarm. With time ticking away, the thieves attempted to make their escape, only to find their car blocked in by other guards. The bandits grabbed their loot, raced into the street and stole a car, with the Buffalo Police in hot pursuit.

A gun battle ensued until the bandits jumped from the car and ran into private homes on Buffalo's West Side. Police tear-gassed the homes, and two of the three bandits were captured, but Newman (who was thought to be James Salemerio at the time) managed to elude the police and went into hiding. The FBI took over the case and was able to identify Newman as the third bandit within hours. By 1956, Newman's name was added the FBI's Ten Most Wanted list. On June 11, 1965, he was removed from the list and the charges were dropped, most likely because they believed he was dead.

Early in the morning on March 14, 1957, witnesses say they heard an argument on the street and then shots. The body of Dominic Mafrici, thirty-eight, of Cleveland, was found on Whitney Avenue in Buffalo. "There was money all over the place," one witness recalled.[633] Mafrici was suspected in a $15,000 robbery in Amherst with the Aquinos. Not long after the killing, Fred Aquino purchased a new Cadillac, which led police to believe he was at least involved in, if not responsible for, the murder.[634] Fred Randaccio said "everyone on the West Side of Buffalo knew" that Aquino did it.[635]

The Aquino brothers were also known to run a lucrative bookmaking racket in local factories, and Frank was "often seen in Lackawanna,"[636] home to several large factories at the time. In October 1952, Frank and another man were "pistol-whipped"[637] by two men, possibly as a warning to the reckless brothers.

They were not made men in the Magaddino Family, but word of their profitable operation found its way to Magaddino, who, it is believed, sent Randaccio to pay them a visit.[638] Randaccio told the brothers they had to either give up the business or start kicking a percentage to Magaddino. They ignored the warning.

On Thursday, September 11, 1958, Fred went out drinking with some "companions," who drove him home. He disappeared on either Friday the twelfth or Saturday the thirteenth. On Saturday, his brother Frank was last seen at 3:00 a.m. after receiving a late-night telephone call.[639] About 11:00 a.m. on Saturday, September 13, 1958, two boys found Frank's body stuffed in the front seat of his mother's Lincoln Continental in a parking lot in Lackawanna. He had been beaten, choked and then shot through the heart.[640] He had been dead for several hours. He was just twenty-eight years old.[641] Authorities began looking in vain for Fred, who they feared may have also been in danger, but there was no sign of him.

On Wednesday, September 17, 1958, Frank's funeral was held. At 6:30 p.m., two boys found Fred's body dumped in a field off Two Mile Creek Road in Tonawanda.[642] The younger Fred, twenty-five, had wire or heavy cord looped around his neck and through his mouth. He had been tortured to death, and then acid was poured over his head to disfigure the man once called "The Fox." He was partially nude and decomposing and had been left where he would be found. It was a terrific killing that police believe was a warning to other gangsters.[643]

Police later surmised that Fred was killed first and Frank was an "insurance killing"[644] to keep him from talking. At the time, Magaddino was still not a household name, and the "syndicate"[645] or Black Hand were mentioned as possible connections.

The brothers' mother, Belle Conley, offered a $10,000 reward for information to find her sons' killers. She believed they were killed "over a woman"[646] but also said a man from Boston had checked into her hotel on Main Street the night before and then disappeared. Fred had received several calls from Boston the week before he was killed.

Police were never able to tie any of these clues together, and they didn't have much more time before another body turned up. Arthur DeLuca, twenty-three, an unemployed bricklayer, disappeared on October 8 and was found stuffed in the trunk of his 1957 Cadillac on October 14, 1958. He was killed in the same fashion as Fred Aquino, with a wire or cord wrapped around his neck and through his mouth.[647] He was most likely killed the night he went missing, since it was determined that his car had been in the same lot for six days before it was noticed. He had been killed from behind, as his shoes were not even scuffed, and his coat was pulled down over his shoulders as a way to hold his arms still.

Despite countless hours of detective work in Buffalo, Niagara Falls and Tonawanda, all three murders grew cold. Multiple people were questioned, including Guido D'Antuono, Leo J. Bartolomei[648] and a friend of the Aquinos, Pascal Politano.[649] D'Antuono, twenty-nine, and Bartolomei, twenty-three, themselves both disappeared on March 3, 1959, without a trace. D'Antuono had been stabbed during a fight outside a bar that catered to hoodlums on Allen Street in Buffalo the previous year and two Niagara Falls men were held, but no charges were ever filed.[650]

On November 29, 1958, Angelo J. "Rico" Cicatello, thirty-two, also believed to be acquainted with DeLuca and the Aquinos, disappeared.[651] Police, as well as his ex-wife, were sure he was dead. One of his cars was found a short distance from his home in Buffalo.

On May 23, 1959, the body of Richard R. Battaglia, twenty-nine, the last of the Aquino burglary gang, was found shot through the head in a car on a Buffalo street.[652]

On July 23, 1961, Nicholas C. Tirone was killed at close range while walking on Buffalo's West Side. He had spent the previous night with Vincent

Santangelo, twenty-two, who, along with Anthony Palestine, twenty-one, was found murdered on August 12, 1961.[653] The men had been held down and beaten. "Their hands were tied behind their backs and their legs trussed behind them with the knees bent back. A length of rope was then tied to their ankles and looped around their necks. As their legs tired and straightened, the noose tightened around their necks strangling them," in what is known as a "West Side necktie."[654] They were then dragged and dumped in a field in suburban Lancaster.[655]

One of those questioned by the police was former Public Enemy Number 1 in Buffalo, Joe DiCarlo, who had returned to Buffalo from his Miami home. He denied any knowledge of the killings.[656]

Pat Politano was also questioned after the killings. Politano himself would end up on the wrong side of a gun on July 23, 1962. While walking home from his bar at four o'clock in the morning, the forty-two-year-old was ambushed by Pasquale Santangelo, who believed Politano responsible for his brother Vincent's murder in 1961.[657] Politano was shot six times in front of his home from a moving vehicle. He knew Santangelo was his assailant and, thinking he was dying, named him.[658] When he miraculously recovered from his wounds, he refused to again name Santangelo, who had surrendered after the shooting and was charged with the crime. Santangelo was convicted in 1963. Politano was charged with perjury as a result of the shooting and tried three times, the first two ending in a hung jury, but he was convicted of one count of perjury at the third trial.[659]

Politano was known as an arsonist, safe cracker and possibly murderer. He was arrested numerous times on various charges but always acquitted. He was also named during the Valachi hearings as one of Buffalo's top mobsters. He would eventually be arrested as the result of a narcotics bust, and he died in 2001.

On September 21, 1965, Town of Tonawanda realtor Charles S. Gerass, thirty-six, left his home to show someone a house and never returned home. His body was found in the trunk of his Cadillac the following day in the parking lot of Sheridan Plaza in Tonawanda. His uncle, Cosmo Battaglia, found the body, tied with clothesline and shot through the head and chest.[660] His suit was dirty, his face had been "bashed" and "lacerations on his chest indicated he had been dragged a considerable distance."[661] Gerass and Richard Battaglia were cousins. In a bizarre conclusion, Cosmo Battaglia, fifty-three, was found stabbed to death in his ransacked home on November 12, 1973. His murder is also unsolved.[662]

On June 11, 1970, the bullet-riddled body of Gino Albini, thirty-five, was found in a parked car in Buffalo. He had been shot eighteen times. In 1977, Frank J. Tripi was charged with his murder.[663]

Richard J. Falise, twenty-three, was found tied and strangled at the rear of a vacant gas station on Buffalo's West Side on November 11, 1970.[664] Two years later, his girlfriend was dropped off at Lafayette General Hospital with a gunshot wound to the head, from which she died.[665]

In February 1972, Frank J. D'Angelo and another man robbed Sid Birzon jewelers on Pearl Street in Buffalo. They escaped with more than $300,000 worth of jewelry, a haul that attracted the likes of the Buffalo mob. D'Angelo was supposedly contacted and told to hand over a cut to the mob for operating in their territory, but it is believed he disliked the mob and refused.

Two years after the jewelry heist, D'Angelo's luck finally ran out. On October 5, 1974, the thirty-one-year-old was partying at Mulligans Night Club and left around 2:30 a.m. with his girlfriend. Three ski-masked gunmen emerged from the bushes, and seeing them, he ran down the sidewalk. Shots were fired from .38-caliber pistols and a twelve-gauge shotgun. They hit

Mulligan's was probably Buffalo's biggest disco bar in the 1970s. Everyone from O.J. Simpson to Frank D'Angelo frequented the place. D'Angelo was gunned down leaving the Hertel Avenue disco in 1974. This is the building today. *Photo by author.*

parked cars, buildings, store windows—and D'Angelo, four times. He died from his gunshot wounds. Buffalo Police had several suspects, and twelve hours after the killing, guns and ski masks were recovered in the Erie Canal in Tonawanda.[666] It wasn't until the 1990 trial of Philip LaRosa, under witness protection, that he admitted to helping arrange the murder, but no one was ever convicted and it is still an unsolved crime.

On February 17, 1976, convicted burglar William "Butch" Esposito, thirty, was found dumped in a muddy field behind an apartment complex in suburban West Seneca.[667] Esposito was an associate of Frank D'Angelo and Stanley Seneca, both also murdered. It was believed to be "revenge for a dispute Esposito had with a mob associate."[668] In October 1994, Ronald Carlisle was charged with his murder. He said that he lured Esposito to his death but others committed the murder.[669]

Robert H. Reingold was convicted of conspiracy charges for his part in the killing of a man set to testify against him in 1972.[670] He was involved in narcotics and also dated a girl who was dating "an organized crime figure."[671] After he took a few shots at the man's house, a contract was put out on Reingold. On May 29, 1976, forty-two-year-old Reingold's bullet-riddled body was found stuffed in the trunk of his Pinto in the Black Rock section of Buffalo.

Reingold and Esposito were killed in a "West Side necktie."[672] Reingold had also been shot twice in the head.[673]

On April 19, 1979, one of Buffalo's budding entrepreneurs was killed in a building on Elmwood Avenue. Peter Piccolo, thirty-two, had been a well-known Buffalo hair stylist since the late 1960s. He was no stranger to the law, having been arrested at least once in 1964 after breaking into a home in Niagara Falls.[674] With his business partner, Louis Fumerelle (a cousin of Ron Fino), Piccolo opened the Sculpture Room in Buffalo. In 1975, they opened the Peter Piccolo School of Hair Design in the Wilson Building on Main Street, and in 1979, he opened a new salon in Allentown.[675]

While his employees were busy with customers on the morning of April 19, 1979, in the second-floor Allentown salon, his body lay in a hallway on the first floor. He had been shot at least four times in what police termed "an execution."[676] There were several theories, including the possibility that Piccolo was overextended and owed people money, but Fumerelle said that was not the cause. Police believed Piccolo was killed over a botched cocaine deal.[677] Fumerelle continued operating the school at least until 1990, when he was convicted of tax evasion after selling a miracle hair growth product in the early 1980s.[678]

On March 7, 1980, two men had their lives taken. William Sciolino was killed in a construction trailer on Main Street. The same day, Carl J. Rizzo, sixty-four, a dental consultant who was selling dental contracts to Local 210 as part of a bigger scheme, did not return home. His body was not found until April 1980, when a car was being towed from an apartment parking lot in Buffalo. His decomposing body was found stuffed into the trunk. He had been killed in similar fashion as Esposito and Reingold. Police believe he was actually killed before Sciolino. The dental clinic he worked for was tied to a dentist who later became a government witness against New Jersey mob members.

A "longtime professional burglar," Alfred Monaco, forty-one, was found on a secluded road in Evans in 1981. He left his mother's home on March 30, and his bullet-riddled body was found April 2. He was a member of Local 210 and a heavy gambler, known to carry $5,000 to $10,000 on him.[679] At six foot three inches and 290 pounds, he was not an easy prey.

In June 1977, dozens were arrested as part of the FBI sting Operation Teepee. Joseph San Fratello was a local criminal arrested numerous times over the years, including for trying to sell $2 million in stolen bonds, for the theft of four thousand cartons of cigarettes and for bank robbery. He was also arrested as part of the FBI sting. He served time for several of the crimes.

He was at a club on Allen Street on February 2, 1985, and at 3:30 a.m., forty-five-year-old San Fratello and a barmaid left the club and headed to his car, parked a few houses down on North Pearl Street. As he approached his car, a lone gunman appeared and put two bullets in his head and two in his back, killing him on the spot.[680] The barmaid only gave a "vague description."[681] Initially, police were unsure of the motive, but two days later, they recovered $100,000 in cocaine in an apartment San Fratello had rented in suburban West Seneca under an assumed name.[682] Police speculated that he had been dealing cocaine from that apartment since July 1984 and may have been cheating the mob out of their cut, so the murder was a message to others.

Alan "the Tuxedo Kid" Levine was a high-rolling drug dealer in Buffalo during the 1980s. He had been arrested numerous times for drug sales, stolen property and other charges but was always able to pay high-priced lawyers to keep him out of jail.[683] On September 18, 1986, thirty-three-year-old Levine was lured to a garage on Lafayette Avenue to complete a $75,000 drug deal. While there, he was shot twice in the head. His body was then wrapped in a heavy moving blanket and dumped in a field on the East Side. The murder remained unsolved until 1991, when several local dealers flipped against one another. Levine was supposedly killed because he kept pushing another dealer to repay an $87,000 debt owed him. The testimony of these dealers solved several unsolved murders, and one man pled guilty to Levine's killing.

From 1984 through 1986, there were five mob-related murders in Buffalo, and most would be linked to one local mobster who spent time in prison for several of them.

In 2004, the Buffalo FBI decided to look into six unsolved mob-related murders in the Buffalo area. They figured that with new technologies like DNA, they might be able to solve some of the crimes. They contacted local police agencies to see what evidence was available.

The FBI wrote to Buffalo Police and found that several key pieces of evidence were missing and the FBI had never received them. A few days later, Buffalo Police commissioner H. McCarthy Gipson ordered the evidence unit to search for it, and it was found in the basement of police headquarters. The guns from the Sciolino killing were sent for DNA analysis, but there is still no answer to this crime. Frank D'Angelo's evidence was also thought missing, but the murder weapon was found, although it has not yielded the killer.

Unless specifically mentioned, none of these murders has been solved.

WHERE TO FIND EVERYTHING

Like an iceberg…the part of Magaddino's income which shows on the surface is but a fraction of the whole. [684]
—Criminal Intelligence Digest

This chapter is really what this book is all about. If you are in western New York, you can jump in your car and drive around town, looking at where these guys (and a few girls) lived, worked, hung out and, for the unfortunate ones, died. You can also just type the addresses into Google Maps and take a look around. A good number of the addresses still have homes or businesses at the site. Imagine the streets bustling with activity and men coming and going, new cars at the curb, gambling joints, arrests being made, payrolls robbed, escapes, scheming, police listening in on wiretaps and more.

Almost every address has been verified, but some of the locations are the best guess based on searches through multiple sources. Some of the older addresses no longer exist, and urban renewal did its fair share of demolishing many properties.

As a reminder, these properties are privately owned, so please don't traipse across the property or do any damage. Also, use common sense when driving through neighborhoods, as they all have their own distinctive look and feel.

Lastly, if you are interested in learning more, you can take walking tours in Buffalo that highlight some of the stories in the book. Visit NakedBuffalo. com for more information.

THE GANGSTER ERA

The Blonde Bandit

HERMAN CHEIFFETZ, 68 Brunswick Boulevard, Buffalo
LOAN SHOP OF HERMAN CHEIFFETZ, 154 Seneca Street, Buffalo
DAVID L. GLICKSTEIN JEWELRY STORE, 1159 Broadway, Buffalo
PETER DOMBKIEWICZ, 954 Sycamore Street, Buffalo
EDDIE IZZYDORCZAK, 197 Titus Street, Buffalo
MORRIS A. KATZMAN, 388 William Street, Buffalo
ANTHONY KULAND, 882 Fillmore Avenue, Buffalo
RELIABLE JEWELRY & LOAN COMPANY, 158 Seneca Street, Buffalo
SALLY JOYCE RICHARDS, 954 Sycamore Street, Buffalo
EDWARD SAMUELS, 333 Benzinger Street, Buffalo
FRANK SMIGIERA, 1925 Clinton Street, Buffalo

The Korney Gang

ART WORK SHOP, 828 East Ferry Street, Buffalo
JOSEPH BARTKOWIAK, 130 Coit Street (1922), Buffalo
FRANCIS BIEBER, 710 Walden Avenue (1928), Buffalo
BINGHAM & TAYLOR CORPORATION, 575 Howard Street, Buffalo
BOLLY TAVERN, 1204 Sycamore Street (1928), Buffalo
BROWNING & BROTHERS, 1203 Broadway Street, Buffalo
BUFFALO POLICE, FIFTH PRECINCT, 291 W Delavan Avenue, Buffalo
BUFFALO POLICE HEADQUARTERS, 74 Franklin Street, Buffalo
BUFFALO POLICE, SEVENTEENTH PRECINCT, 98 Colvin Avenue, Buffalo
VICTOR CHOJNICKI, 114 Beck Street, 28 Woltz Avenue, Buffalo
VINCENT J. CONNORS, 165 Como Avenue, Buffalo
ALVIN J. DAIGLER, 330 Woodlawn Avenue (1922), Buffalo
DUFFY SILK MILL, 207 Guilford Street, Buffalo
FEDDERS MANUFACTURING COMPANY, 57 Tonawanda Street, Buffalo
GARAGE FOR STOLEN AUTO, 350 Potomac Avenue, Buffalo
WILLIAM GROBLEWSKI, 49 Harmonia Street (1928), Buffalo
ANTHONY KALKIEWICZ, 40 and 50 Loepere Street, 428 Sweet Avenue,
    Houghton Street, Buffalo; 37 Wendell Avenue, Depew
JOE KORNACKI, 183 Miller Street (1928), Buffalo
KORNEY BOTTLING PLANT, 487 Penora Street, Depew

KORNEY FAKE ADDRESS, 71 Ellicott Road (Walden Avenue), Lancaster
KORNEY SALOON, 49 Main Street, Depew
KORNEY STILL, 29 Neoga Street, Depew
LEON KOSEK, 1134 Sycamore Street, Buffalo
JOHN KWIATKOWSKI, 968 Sycamore Street, 42 Littlefield Street, Buffalo
LANG'S BREWERY, 400 Best Street at Jefferson Avenue, Buffalo
EDWARD LARKMAN, 689 Eagle Street, Buffalo
LOOSE-WILES BISCUIT COMPANY, 1380 Niagara Street, Buffalo
WARD MCCARTNEY, killed at Chicago and Elk Streets, Buffalo
PEACOCK INN, 554 Washington Street, Buffalo
JOHN PERRATON, Canada
WARD PIERCE, 751 7th Street, Buffalo
ZYGMUND "ZIGGY" PLOCHARSKI, 185 Sweet Avenue, Buffalo
ROYAL LINEN SUPPLY COMPANY, 200 Terrace Street, Buffalo
STORE ROBBERY, 1255 Jefferson Avenue, Buffalo
STEPHEN WOJCIECHOWSKI, 145 Baitz Avenue (1928), Buffalo
STEPHEN ZIOLKOWSKI, 68 A Street, 1315 Broadway Street, 95 St. Joseph
     Avenue, Buffalo

The Blue Ribbon Gang

DUNLOP PLANT, 3115 River Road, Tonawanda
FERDINAND FECHTER, 984 East Delavan Street, Buffalo
GANG HEADQUARTERS, 92 Franklin Street, Sloan
MICHAEL GEORGE, 214 Maryland Street, Buffalo
STANLEY GONCIAZCZ, 104 Gibson Street, Buffalo
EDWARD GRZECHOWIAK, 64 Sobieski Street (1922), 58 Sobieski Street (1928),
     Buffalo
STEPHEN GRZECHOWIAK, 119 Hirschbeck Street (1922), 116 Fay Street (1928),
     Buffalo
PEACOCK INN, 554 Washington Street, Buffalo
STEPHEN PILARSKI, 87 Lathrop Street (1920), Buffalo
MAX RYBARCZYK, 250 Wilson Street (1928), Buffalo
ST. STANISLAUS CHURCH, 123 Townsend Street, Buffalo

Buffalo's Molls

BEULAH BAIRD, Amiantus Apartments, Buffalo
GEORGE BITTLE, 180 Pratt Street, 236 Adams Street, Buffalo
ELSIE PIERI DICARLO, 274 Prospect Avenue (1933), Buffalo
BERNICE FRANK, 143 Wohlers Avenue (1928), Buffalo
HELEN GROBLEWSKI, 49 Harmonia Street, Buffalo
BLANCHE GRZECHOWIAK, 16 Fay Street (1929), 174 May Street (1934), Buffalo
HOYLER'S JEWELERS, 313 Genesee Street, Buffalo
CLARA MACKOWIAK, 16 Loepere Street (1910), Buffalo; Albion State Training
    School (1930), Albion
CARMELA MAGADDINO, 5118 Dana Drive, Lewiston
BESSIE PERRI, Canada
MARGARET WHITTEMORE, Baltimore

Apartment 821

AMIANTUS APARTMENTS, 18th and Rhode Island Streets, Buffalo
CHARLES ARTHUR FLOYD, ADAM RICHETTI, JUANITA BAIRD, ROSE BAIRD, not
    in Buffalo

The $93,000 Question

BANK OF BUFFALO, Main and North Division Streets, Buffalo
MARION CARSON/GOULD, 230 Prospect Avenue, Buffalo
CITY HALL, 92 Franklin Street, Buffalo
LEVY JEWELERS, 483 Main Street, Buffalo
MANUFACTURERS AND TRADERS TRUST COMPANY, Main and Swan Streets,
    Buffalo
WIRE WHEEL CORPORATION, 1700 Elmwood Avenue, Buffalo

The Millionaire Kid

BERNICE FRANK, 979 Main Street, Buffalo
GANG HIDEOUT, 31 Best Street, Buffalo
MARKEEN HOTEL, 979 Main and Utica Streets, Buffalo

ETHEL MASON, 629 Fillmore Avenue, Buffalo

EDDIE PRZYBYL, 46 Hirschbeck Street (1920), 629 Fillmore Avenue, Delwood Apartments (Prospect and Georgia Streets), Buffalo

STANLEY PRZYBYL, 46 Hirschbeck Street (1920), Buffalo

AGNES RENAUD, Delwood Apartments (Prospect and Georgia Streets), Buffalo

TED ROGACKI, 856 Broadway Street, Buffalo

WILLIAM SEINER, 170 Kosciuszko Street, Buffalo

Bobbed-Haired Beauty

GEORGE BITTLE, 236 Adams Street, Buffalo

RUFUS ELLER, 566 Elm Street, Buffalo

HOYLER JEWELERS, 313 Genesee Street, Buffalo

AUGUST HOYLER, 61 Pershing Avenue, Buffalo

STELLA MACKOWSKA, Cleveland, 180 South Division Street, Buffalo; home in Painesville, Ohio

FRANK MINNICK, 47 East Mohawk Street, 217 East Eagle Street, Buffalo; home in Virginia

NORWOOD CARS, 121 Norwood Avenue, Buffalo

CATHERINE PATTERSON, 180 South Division Street, Buffalo

ORCHARD INN, Orchard Park and Fisher Road, West Seneca

THE MAFIA, PART I

The Barrel Murder

GIUSEPPE DIPRIEMO, New York City

GARIBALDI GARDEN, Sicily

BENEDETTO MADONIA, 47 Trenton Avenue, Buffalo; body found at 11th Street and Avenue D, New York

GIUSEPPE "CLUTCH" MORELLO, 362 East 116th Street, New York

SERGEANT JOSEPH PETROSINO, New York; Sicily

Early Mafia Families

JOHN J. BARBERA, 270 Prospect Avenue (1930), Buffalo

GAETANO CAPODICASO, 234 Myrtle Avenue, Buffalo

JULIUS CAPUTO, 341 Niagara Street, Buffalo (not home)

WILLIAM E. CASTELLANI, 240 North Division Street (1933), Buffalo

SAM COPPOLA, 77 Dante Place, Buffalo

FRANK DEFUSTO, 419 Prospect Avenue (1922), Buffalo

GIUSEPPE DICARLO SR., 274 Prospect Avenue (1919), Buffalo

JOE DICARLO JR., 166 Front Avenue (1920), 274 Prospect Avenue (1919–22), Buffalo; 7310 Grey Avenue (1959), Miami[685]

SAM DICARLO, 274 Prospect Avenue (1934), Buffalo; 5363 LaGorce Drive (1959), Miami [686]

DICARLO'S BUFFALO ITALIAN IMPORTING CO., 161 Court Street, Buffalo[687]

PETER GIALLELLI, 68 Dante Place, Buffalo

HAMLIN TERRACE NURSING HOME, 1014 Delaware Avenue, Buffalo (1980)

LITTLE HARLEM RESTAURANT, 496 Michigan Avenue, Buffalo

ANTHONY LOMBARDO, 270 Swan Street (1930), Buffalo

ANGELO PALMERI, 556/8 Portage Road, Niagara Falls (1920); 295 Jersey Street (1921–32), 284 Seventh Street (1922), Buffalo

PALMERI SALOON, 211 Court Street, Buffalo

JOE PATTITUCCI, 132 Main Street (1920), Buffalo

ANTHONY PERNA, 246 Massachusetts Avenue (1930), Buffalo

JOSEPH PIERI, 359 Busti Avenue (1929), Buffalo

SALVATORE PIERI, 359 Busti Avenue (1929), Buffalo

EDWARD J. POSPICHAL, 98 Halstead Street (1938), Cheektowaga

RITZ RESTAURANT, 387 Washington Street (1924), Buffalo

JOSEPH RUFFINO, 341 Niagara Street, 944 Niagara Street, Buffalo

STELLA RESTAURANT, The Terrace (1924), Buffalo

JOHN TRONOLONE, 838 Prospect Avenue (1922), 79 Seventh Street (1930), Buffalo; 8090 Hawthorne Avenue (1959), Miami[688]

The Magaddino Family

CAMELLIA LINEN SUPPLY, 460 East Delavan Street, Buffalo

CAMELLIA LINEN SUPPLY LAUNDRY, 1782 Fillmore Avenue, Buffalo

CAPITOL COFFEE SHOP, 1302 Niagara Street, Niagara Falls

FALLS BOTTLING WORKS, 831 Linwood Avenue, Niagara Falls

MICHAEL FARELLA, 829 19th Street, 1190 Haberle Avenue, Niagara Falls

FBI (CURRENT), 1 FBI Plaza, Buffalo
FBI (OLD), 68 Court Street, Buffalo
GUARINO & MAGADDINO BAKERY, 1811 Ferry Street (1939), Niagara Falls
NICHOLAS LONGO, 1653 Whitney Avenue, Niagara Falls
LORELEI CLUB, Fort Erie, Ontario
PETER MACK, 1744 100th Street, Niagara Falls
ANTONIO MAGADDINO, 2404 South Avenue, lower (1945–60), 1528 Whitney Avenue, Niagara Falls (1960–71)
GASPARE MAGADDINO, 1653 Whitney Avenue (1936), 1649 Whitney Avenue, (1938–42), 740 17th Street (1942–50), Niagara Falls
PETER A. MAGADDINO, 1653 Whitney Avenue (1920–46), 1123 22nd Street, Niagara Falls
PETER J. MAGADDINO (COUSIN), 2404 South Avenue (1939), 3038 Orleans Avenue (1946), 2494 Independence Avenue (1956), Niagara Falls; 1029 Carter Road, Grand Island
STEFANO MAGADDINO, 1101 East Falls Street (1923),[689] 1653 Whitney Avenue, Niagara Falls; (1923–58), Buffalo; 5118 Dana Drive, Lewiston (1958–74)
STEFANO MAGADDINO, handed arrest warrant at 2806 Ferry Avenue, Niagara Falls
MAGADDINO FUNERAL HOME, 1710 Pine Avenue, Niagara Falls (1940–55)
MAGADDINO MEMORIAL CHAPEL, 1338 Niagara Street, Niagara Falls (1955–92)
MAGADDINO SUMMER HOME, 3588 Lower Mountain Road, Cambria
MAGADDINO & URSO FUNERAL CHAPEL, 1010 South Avenue (1992–96), Niagara Falls
DOMINIC MANTELL, 415 16th Street (1941), 532 17th Street (1946), Niagara Falls; 3538 Sherwood Avenue (1958), 902 Dana Drive, Lewiston
MANTELL'S CARROUSEL OF FLOWERS, 1310 Niagara Street, Niagara Falls
GINO MONACO, 6831 Pine Avenue, Niagara Falls
MOUNT SAINT MARY'S HOSPITAL, 5300 Military Road, Lewiston
NIAGARA FALLS MEDICAL CENTER, 621 10th Street, Niagara Falls
NIAGARA SUNDRY SHOP, 1216 Niagara Street, Niagara Falls
BENJAMIN NICOLETTI JR., 2654 North Avenue, Niagara Falls
BENJAMIN NICOLETTI SR., 2719 Independence Avenue (1946), 5903 Buffalo Avenue (1958), Niagara Falls; 35 Fort Gray Drive (1963), 455 Cayuga Street (1968), 1002 Hewitt Avenue, Lewiston
OUR LADY OF MOUNT CARMEL CHURCH, 27th and Independence Avenue, Niagara Falls
AL PACINI, 109 Dorchester Road, Buffalo
PACINI, NERI AND RUNFOLA, 1006 Morgan Building (1957), Buffalo

PASQUALE PASSERO, 2895 Lewiston Road, Niagara Falls

DR. VICTOR PELLICANO, 760 Main Street, Niagara Falls

PINE BOWL BOWLING ALLEYS, 9594 Niagara Falls Boulevard (was Pine Avenue), Niagara Falls

POWER CITY DISTRIBUTING COMPANY, 200 9th Street (1954–58), 1113 LaSalle Avenue (1933–54), Niagara Falls

SAM PUGLESE, 177 61st Street, Niagara Falls

SAM RANGATORE, 614 Hyde Park Boulevard, 610 31st Street (1966), Niagara Falls

AUGUSTINE RIZZO, 257 Witmer Road, North Tonawanda

ROUND-THE-CLOCK RESTAURANT, 829 Main Street, Niagara Falls

JOSEPH RUNFOLA, 1131 Niagara Street (1942), Buffalo; 463 Woodland Drive (1957), Tonawanda

ANGELO F. SCALZO, 608–14 Niagara Building, 43 Falls Street (1946), Niagara Falls

ST. JOSEPH'S CEMETERY, 3806 Pine Avenue, Niagara Falls

ST. JOSEPH'S CHURCH, 14th and Pine Avenue, Niagara Falls

LOUIS TAVANO, 5308 Elm Drive, Lewiston; 1625 South Avenue (1966), Niagara Falls

U.S. DISTRICT COURT (CURRENT), 2 Niagara Square, Buffalo

U.S. DISTRICT COURT (OLD), 68 Court Street, Buffalo

The Magaddino Relatives

CHARLES DISTRIBUTION CORP., 1115 11th Street, Niagara Falls

ANGELINE AND JAMES V. LADUCA, 1653 Whitney Avenue (1940s), Niagara Falls; 5114 Dana Drive, Lewiston

ARCANGELA AND NICHOLAS LONGO, 1651 Whitney Avenue, Niagara Falls

PETER AND FRANCES MAGADDINO, 1103 22nd Street, 2204 Woodlawn Avenue, Niagara Falls

PETER J. MAGADDINO, 2494 Independence Avenue, Niagara Falls

MAGADDINO FUNERAL HOME, 1710 Pine Avenue, Niagara Falls

CHARLES A. MONTANA, 25 Kemp Road, Cheektowaga

FRANCES MONTANA (MAGADDINO), 278 Baynes Street (1942), Buffalo

JOSEPHINE AND CHARLES A. MONTANA, 5124 Dana Drive, Lewiston

PANDORO EXTERMINATORS, 351 Fox Street, 1216 Genesee Street, Buffalo

RICHFORD HOTEL, 210 Delaware Avenue, Buffalo

ARCANGELA AND VINCENT SCRO, 5130 Dana Drive, Lewiston

The Crime Family

AMERICAN DRY CLEANERS, 341 First Street, Niagara Falls

SALVATORE BONITO, 49 Antoinette Drive, Depew

C&C MARKET, 515 Busti Avenue (1964), Buffalo

STEVE CANNAROZZO, 29 Danforth Place, 87 Mariner (late 1950s), Buffalo

ROY CARLISI, 20 Anderson Place, lower (1957), 107 Pennsylvania Avenue (1934), 230 Prospect Avenue (1935), 138 Depew Avenue (1951), Buffalo; 64 Smallwood Drive (1967), 1693 Orchard Park Road, 510 Center Road, West Seneca; 865 North French Road, Tonawanda

CARLISI CLAM BUSINESS, 290 Trenton Avenue (1960s), Buffalo

CARLISI RESTAURANT, 97 Mortimer Street (1935), Buffalo

CHARLES CASSARO, 200 Busti Avenue (1960s), 793 Busti Avenue (1977), Buffalo

ANGELO CIAMBRONE, 1950 Cudabach Street (1934), Niagara Falls

DOMINICK D'AGOSTINO, 2226 Ontario Avenue, Niagara Falls

JAMES DELMONT, 257 Hudson Street (1957), Buffalo

JOSEPH FINO, 873 Worthland Avenue, Buffalo; 3404 McKinley Parkway, Blasdell; 266 Pellman Place, West Seneca

NICK FINO, 280 Carlton Street (1950s), Buffalo

SALVATORE FRANGIAMORE, 471 Seventh Street (1957), 334 Seventh Street (1960), Buffalo

THOMAS GASCOYNE, 216 Ross Street, Buffalo

SAM GRANA, 1211 East Falls Street (1934), Niagara Falls

HERMAN'S GARAGE, 409 Niagara Street, Buffalo

LAUREL HOTEL, 436 First Street, Niagara Falls

MADISON TAXI, 516 Rhode Island Street, Buffalo

GEORGE MERANTO, 1730 Elmwood Avenue (1934), 635 Twenty-first Street (1943), Niagara Falls

ROSARIO MOSCATO, 202 Dewey Avenue (1942), Buffalo

PANARO, 15 Ladner Street (1967), Buffalo

PANARO'S RESTAURANT, 319 Hampshire, Buffalo

PEACE BRIDGE MOTEL AND BOWLING ALLEYS, Fourth Street and Porter Avenue, Buffalo

ANTHONY PERNA, 246 Massachusetts Avenue, 720 7th Street, Buffalo

PERNA FUNERAL HOME, 1306 Hertel Avenue, Buffalo

JOSEPH PIERI SR., 41 Massachusetts Avenue (1957), Buffalo

SALVATORE PIERI, 22 17th Street (1977), 596 West Avenue (1963), 3 Massachusetts Avenue (1970), 370 West Ferry Avenue (1971)

NICHOLAS RIZZO, 69 Livingston Street, Buffalo

SALVATORE RIZZO, 412 Vermont Street, 12 Brayton Street (late 1950s), Buffalo
JOSEPH SAN FILIPPO, 101 Fifteenth Street, Buffalo
DANIEL SANSANESE SR., 208 Lexington Avenue, 414 Porter Avenue, 489 Norwood Avenue, Buffalo
EDWARD SCILLIA, 362 Rhode Island Street, Buffalo
STANLEY SENECA, 145 16th Street, 234 Georgia Street (1971), Buffalo
JOHN SIMONE, 530 20th Street (1934), Niagara Falls
JOE TODARO SR., 95 Joseph Drive (1967), Tonawanda
HERMAN WEINSTEIN, 352 Lincoln Parkway, Buffalo

APALACHIN

November 14, 1957

DOMINICK D'AGOSTINO, 2226 Ontario Avenue, Niagara Falls
SAM LAGATTUTA, 555 Lafayette Avenue, 94 Parkdale Avenue, 170 Lovering Street (1971), Buffalo

Kidnapping Cousins

BILL BONANNO, New York
JOSEPH BONANNO, Brooklyn
SAM DECAVALCANTE, New Jersey
GASPAR DIGREGORIO, New York
GASPARE MAGADDINO, killed in Brooklyn
PETER J. MAGADDINO MALT SHOP, 482 19th Street, Niagara Falls
STEFANO MAGADDINO, 1653 Whitney Avenue, Niagara Falls
MAGADDINO FARMHOUSE, 3588 Lower Mountain Road, Cambria
JOE MASSERIA, New York
COLA SCHIRO, New York

The Montana Affair

ANGELO ACQUISTO, 216 Front Street (1922), Buffalo
BUFFALO AIRPORT, Genesee Street, Cheektowaga

BUFFALO BEVERAGE CORP., 1040 Sycamore Street, Buffalo
BUFFALO TAXI SERVICE & SIGHTSEEING CO., INC., 218 Niagara Street, Buffalo
EMPIRE STATE BREWING CORP., 301 West Henley Street (1937), Olean
FRONTIER LIQUOR CORP., 381 Niagara Street, Buffalo
JOHN C. MONTANA, Arlington Hotel, 138 Exchange Street (1922), 175 North Street (1930), 228 Busti Avenue (1936), 495 Paderewski Drive (1942), 340 Starin Avenue (1957), Buffalo
MONTANA MOTORS, 369 Niagara Street, Buffalo
MONTANA WORLD TRAVEL SERVICE, INC., 367 Niagara Street, Buffalo
NEW YORK CENTRAL TERMINAL, 495 Paderewski Drive, Buffalo
POWER CITY DISTRIBUTING, Niagara Falls
ANDY SCIANDRA, 211 Court Street, Buffalo[690]
STATLER HOTEL, Niagara Square, Buffalo
FREDERICK VAN DYKE, The Stuyvesant, Buffalo
VAN DYKE TAXI, 125 Erie Street (1930), Central Terminal Building, Buffalo

BOOKIES AND GAMBLERS

The Major Players

MATT BILLITERI, 712 Richmond Avenue (1960s), Buffalo
BLUE BANNER SOCIAL CLUB, 858 Prospect Avenue, Buffalo
MIKE BONA, 285 Pennsylvania Avenue (1977), Buffalo
ANGELO BONITO, 716 Lafayette Avenue, Buffalo
SALVATORE BONITO, 49 Antoinette Drive, Depew
BRIDGE COFFEE SHOP, Zacaria's Barber Shop, Ontario Avenue, Niagara Falls
BRUNDO'S MUSIC STORE, 1907 Pine Avenue (1969), Niagara Falls
COFFEE JOE'S, 1816 Niagara Street (1969), Niagara Falls
CONNECTICUT HALL, 372 Connecticut Street, Buffalo
DELMAR GRILL, 919 North Avenue (1969), Niagara Falls
DON DiCARLO, 52 Days Park, Buffalo
JACK H. EHRENREICH, 432 Michigan Avenue (1930), Buffalo
FINO BOOKIE ROOM, 19 Allen Street, Buffalo
FIVE STAR ATHLETIC CLUB, 644 19th Street, Niagara Falls
GAMING ROOM, 1932 Main Street, third floor, Niagara Falls
GAMING ROOM, 1803½ Main Street (1943), Niagara Falls
GAMING ROOM, 245 Elmwood Avenue, sixth floor, Buffalo
GAMING ROOM, 469 Broadway, Buffalo

Gaming room, 196 East Ferry Street, Buffalo

Gaming room, 294 William Street, Buffalo

Gaming room, 364 William Street, Buffalo

Gaming room, 365 Military Road, second floor, Buffalo

Gaming room, 1268 West Avenue, first floor, Buffalo

Gaming room, 1546 South Park Avenue, Buffalo

Gaming room, 60 Days Park, Buffalo

Gaming room, 196 Prospect Avenue, rear apartment, Buffalo

Gaming room, 47 Lovering Avenue, Buffalo

Gaming room, 249 South Elmwood Avenue, Buffalo

Gaming room, 444 Hudson Street, Buffalo

Gaming room, Friar's Lounge, 110 Genesee Street, Buffalo

Holy Cross Church, Maryland and Seventh Streets, Buffalo

Samuel Izzo, 216 Ellicott Street, Batavia

Samuel Izzo, killed at 242 Seventh Street, Buffalo

Norman Joseph, 919 Ontario Avenue, Niagara Falls; 50 Garlow Road, Lewiston (1954–59)

Laconia Social Club, 1427 Pine Avenue, Niagara Falls

Lenny's Cleaners, Colvin/Eggert Plaza, Tonawanda

Little White House, 5877 Main Street, upper, Williamsville

Frank LoTempio, killed at Maryland and Seventh Streets, Buffalo

Nicholas Mauro, 61 Kenwood Road, Kenmore, 161 Washington Highway, Amherst

Gaetano Miceli, 410 Massachusetts Avenue (1977), Buffalo

Nairy's Social Club, 314 West Ferry Avenue, first floor, rear, Buffalo

Oh Boy's Social and Athletic Club, 714 West Market Street, Niagara Falls

Oliver Street Social Club, 383 Oliver Street, North Tonawanda

Alfred Panepinto, 1523 Pine Street, 630 17th Street (1936), Niagara Falls; 1 Thorpe Street (1928), Batavia

Pasttime Poolroom, 1116 East Falls Street, Niagara Falls

Salvatore J. Pieri, 596 West Avenue, Buffalo

Nick Rinaldo, 380 Rhode Island Avenue, Buffalo

Rizzo's Cataract Barber Shop, 2024 Pine Avenue, Niagara Falls

Savoy Club, 2024 Pine Avenue, Niagara Falls

Benny Spano, 858 Prospect Avenue, Buffalo

Toyshop, 11 North Division Street, Buffalo

Turner Social and Athletic Association, 416 Chicago Street, Buffalo

Louis Viale, 111 Pearl Street, Buffalo

James Vona, 55 Walter Avenue, Tonawanda

LEONARD WELCH, 1213 Maple Avenue (1952), Niagara Falls
WHIRLPOOL CLUB, 237 24ᵗʰ Street, Niagara Falls

The Whirlpool Club

WHIRLPOOL CLUB, 237 24ᵗʰ Street, Niagara Falls

THE MAFIA, PART II

The Business of Funerals

JOHN BAZZANO, Pittsburgh
JOHN BAZZANO, killed in Brooklyn
SALVATORE CONSTANTINO, 1012 East Falls Street, Niagara Falls
SAM DiCARLO, 133 Seventh Street (1920), Buffalo
THE IMPERIAL HOTEL, northwest corner of Falls and Second streets, Niagara Falls
MAGADDINO FUNERAL HOME, INC., 1710 Pine Avenue (1942), Niagara Falls
PAUL PALMERI, 1538 Whitney Avenue (1926–34), 1727 Walnut Avenue (1941), Niagara Falls; 455 Passaic Avenue (1945), Passaic, New Jersey
PALMERI & AUGELLO, 1710 Pine Avenue (1940), Niagara Falls
PANEPINTO AND PALMERI FUNERAL HOME, 496 19ᵗʰ Street (1936), Niagara Falls

Lupo the Wolf

DELAWARE TEXACO SERVICE STATION, 453 Delaware Avenue, Buffalo
DARLENE GRANN, 51 Essex Street, Buffalo
JOSEPH SPANO & SONS FUNERAL HOME, 470 Niagara Street, Buffalo
FRED MOGAVERO, 40 Cortland Avenue, Tonawanda
PAT NATARELLI, 85 Plymouth Street (1930), 20 Manchester Place, 60 Manchester Place, Buffalo
PEACE BRIDGE TEXACO SERVICE STATION, 7ᵗʰ and Porter Streets, Buffalo
FRED RANDACCIO, 934 Niagara Street (1930–40s), 157 Auburn Avenue, 181 Rhode Island Street, upper, 562 Richmond Avenue, Buffalo
RANDACCIO OFFICE, 200 West Tupper Street, Buffalo
SALVATORE P. RIZZO, 412 Vermont Street, 12 Brayton Street (1960s), Buffalo

Hide in Plain Sight

BUFFALO CITY HALL, Niagara Square, Buffalo
CHARLES CACI, 82 Tenth Street (1967), Buffalo
SALVATORE CACI, 166 Seventh Street (1942), Buffalo
VINCENT CACI, 71 Tioga Street, Buffalo
PASQUALE CALABRESE, 28 North Jesella Drive, North Tonawanda
STEVEN CINO, 45 Chatham Avenue (1967), Buffalo
DANIEL DOMINO, 355 University Avenue, Town of Tonawanda
THOMAS LEONHARD, 57 Lardner Court (1964), 366 Woodstock Avenue, Tonawanda
FRED MAGAVERO, 96 Cottage Street (1957), Buffalo
SAL MARTOCHE, 74 Niagara Street, Buffalo
VICTOR RANDACCIO, 157 Auburn Street (1942), 282 Sterling Avenue, Buffalo
SENATE GRILL, 181 Rhode Island Street, Buffalo

A Gangster, a Hit and a Rembrandt

THOMAS AMODEO, 60 Virgil Street, Buffalo
JAMES V. ARCADI, 26 Ripley Place, Buffalo
ALBERT M. BILLITERI JR., 23 Commonwealth Avenue, Buffalo
ALBERT M. BILLITERI JR., body found on Aero Drive, Cheektowaga
BLUE BANNER SOCIAL CLUB, 374 Connecticut Street, Buffalo
CHARLES CARLO, 278 Hampshire Street (1972), Buffalo
GENNARINO FASOLINO, 399 Jersey Street, Buffalo
HOUSE OF TASHA ANTIQUE SHOP, 168 Elmwood Avenue, Buffalo
RICHARD M. MANCUSO, 31 Longleat Drive, Amherst
FAUSTINO NOVINO, 48 Granger Place (1972), Buffalo
JOHN C. SACCO JR., 519 Inwood Place (1977), 245 Bedford Avenue (1971), Buffalo
JOHN A. SARTORI, 349 Longmeadow Drive, Amherst
STING OPERATION, 168 Elmwood Avenue, Buffalo

Valachi and His Sweetheart

GATE OF HEAVEN CEMETERY, 500 Riverdale Avenue, Lewiston
MARIE K. JACKSON, 3026 Panama Street (1956), Niagara Falls
OUR LADY OF MOUNT CARMEL CHURCH, 2703 Independence Avenue, Niagara Falls

DEADLY NIGHTS

The Union, the Murder and the Informant

JOHN CAMMILLERI, 542 Richmond Avenue, Buffalo; 584 Cornwall Avenue (1966), Tonawanda

JOE FINO, 462 Seneca Street, 873 Northland Avenue (1960), Buffalo; 236 Pellman Place, West Seneca

NICK FINO, 1921 Abbott Road (1974), Lackawanna; 224 Pellman Place, West Seneca

RON FINO, 32 Rolling Hills Drive (1974), Orchard Park

LABORERS LOCAL 210, 481 Franklin Street, Buffalo

NICK RINALDO, 380 Rhode Island Street, Buffalo

ROSELAND RESTAURANT, 490 Rhode Island Street, Buffalo

WILLIAM SCIOLINO, 381 Cornwall Avenue, 403 Somerville Avenue, Tonawanda

WILLIAM SCIOLINO, killed in lot at Main Street at Ferry Avenue, Buffalo

VIN JAMES BUILDERS, 472 Connecticut Street, 428 Connecticut Street, Buffalo

Mysterious Murders

JOHN J. BARBERA, 27 Penfield Street, Buffalo

JOHN J. BARBERA, killed at 272 Niagara and corner of Carolina Street, Buffalo

SALVATORE CALLEA, 95 Seventh Street (1925), 27 Dante Place (1927), 95 Seventh Street (1929), 179 Auburn Avenue, Buffalo

VINCENZO CALLEA, 38 Evans Street (1921), 258 Terrace Street (1925), 27 Dante Place (1927), 309 Potomac Avenue (1929), Buffalo

VINCENZO AND SALVATORE CALLEA, killed at 372 Connecticut Street, Buffalo

CALLEA SALOON, 78 Dante Place and 38 Evans Street, Buffalo

CALLEA SALOON, 367 Connecticut Street (1933), Buffalo

CARUSO'S RESTAURANT, 93 West Chippewa Street, Buffalo

CHIPPEWA INN (Phillip Mannor), 85 West Chippewa Street (1927), Buffalo

JOSEPH CICATELLO, 83 Dante Place (1926), Buffalo

JOSEPH CICATELLO, killed at Virginia and Niagara Streets (1931), Buffalo

PATSY COLLINO, 309 15th Street (1939), Niagara Falls

COLUMBUS HOSPITAL, 300 Niagara Street, Buffalo

PASQUALE CORDA, 1501 Walnut Street (1917), Erie, Pennsylvania; 174 South Elmwood Avenue, Buffalo

GUISEPPE DIBENEDETTO, 418 Front Avenue (1922), Buffalo

GUISEPPE DIBENEDETTO, killed at 116 Dante Place, Buffalo

JAMES M. DISTEFANO, 170 Seventh Street (1934), Buffalo

JAMES M. DISTEFANO, found on Pinehurst, Cheektowaga

ANTHONY FALCONY, 245 Main Street (1917), 345 Main Street (1930), Niagara Falls

FRANCIS FALCONY, 205 Main Street (1917), Niagara Falls

FRANCIS FALCONY, killed at Old Church Road, Walmore

SANTO FALSONE, 1242 Niagara Street, Buffalo

SANTO FALSONE, killed at 168 Georgia Street, Buffalo

SALVATORE FRANGIPANI, 18th and Pine Avenue, Niagara Falls

FRONTIER HOTEL, 981 Niagara Street, Buffalo

JOHN GAMBINO, 53 Seventh Street (1925), Buffalo

JOHN GAMBINO, killed at Lower Terrace and Church Street, Buffalo

JOHN LOMBARDO, killed at Busti and Virginia Streets (1936), Buffalo

LUIGI LOZZI, 68 Efner Street (1928), Buffalo

MAYOR WILLIAM LUPTON, 245 73rd Street, Niagara Falls

JOSEPH MANGUS, 190 Efner Street (1922), Buffalo

PHILLIP MANNOR, Erie, Pennsylvania

VINCENT MARINELLO, Jamestown Grill, 248 Allen Street, Buffalo

VINCENT MARINELLO, 383 Hudson Street, 809 Amherst Street (1950), Buffalo

PHILIP MAZZARA, 203 Porter Avenue (1929), Buffalo

PHILIP MAZZARA, killed at Maryland near Cottage Street, Buffalo

FRANK MORREALE, 62 Clover Street (1930), Cheektowaga

JAMES PALADINO, 29 Evans Street (1930), Buffalo

ANTHONY PALAMARA, 860 Niagara Street (1934), Buffalo

ANTHONY PALAMARA, killed at Fargo, southeast corner of Porter Avenue, Buffalo

MARCANTONIO PALAMARA, 860 Niagara Street, Buffalo

ANTHONY PALMISANO, 501 Front Avenue, 232 Connecticut Street (1934), Buffalo

ANTHONY PALMISANO, killed on River Road near Grand Island Bridge, Tonawanda

FRANK POLIZZI, 174 Seventh Street (1930), Buffalo

FRANK POLIZZI, killed at Carolina and Seventh Streets, Buffalo

ANGELO PUMA, 981 Niagara Street, Buffalo

PETER RIZZO, 83 Dante Place, 70 Efner Street, Buffalo

PETER RIZZO, killed at 53 Front Street near Georgia Street (1926), Buffalo

JOSEPH RUFFINO, 944 Niagara Street (1930), Buffalo

JOHN SCIABORE, killed at 145 Carolina Street, Buffalo

GIUSEPPI SCIOSCIA, Efner Street, Buffalo

GIUSEPPI SCIOSCIA, killed on Meadow Place, Cheektowaga

ANTHONY VASSALLO, 202 Seventh Street (1926), Buffalo

ANTHONY VASSALLO, killed at 544 Seventh Street, Buffalo

MARCELLO VENTRIGO, 1131 Center Avenue and 2723 South Avenue, Niagara Falls
MARCELLO VENTRIGO, gambling joint, 922 Ontario Avenue, Niagara Falls
MARCELLO VENTRIGO, killed at 56th Street and Girard Avenue, Niagara Falls

A Lesson from the Mob

JOSEPH ALBANESE, 193 Trenton Avenue (1930), Buffalo
GINO ALBINI, 181 15th Street, Buffalo
GINO ALBINI, found in car at Bradley and Dewitt Streets, Buffalo
JOSEPH ALEO, 144 Seventh Street (1922), Buffalo
ALLENTOWN GRILL, 256 Allen Street, Buffalo
FRANK AQUINO, 996 Main Street (1958), Buffalo
FRANK AQUINO, found on Steelawanna Avenue (1958), Lackawanna
FRED AQUINO, found on Two-Mile Creek Road, Tonawanda
JOHN BARBERA, 27 Penfield Street, Buffalo
JOHN BARBERA, killed at saloon, 272 Niagara Street, Buffalo
LEO J. BARTOLOMEI, 2737 Independence Avenue (1959), Niagara Falls
RICHARD R. BATTAGLIA, 635 Loretta Street, Town of Tonawada
RICHARD R. BATTAGLIA, killed on Reynolds Alley, Buffalo
BRINK'S ARMORED CAR GARAGE, 80 College Street, Buffalo
FRANK C. BUTTITTA, 330 Vermont Street, Buffalo
FRANK C. BUTTITTA, found in car on Malta Place, between West Avenue and Maryland Street, Buffalo
ANGELO CIAMBRONE, 213 Second Street, Niagara Falls
ANGELO J. CICATELLO, 769 Seventh Street, Buffalo
BELLE CONLEY, Virginia Hotel, 996 Main Street, Buffalo
FRANK D'ANGELO, 161 Belmont Avenue, Tonawanda
FRANK D'ANGELO, killed at 1669 Hertel Avenue, Buffalo
GUIDO D'ANTUONO, 2217 Cudaback Avenue, 548 Seventh Street (1959), Niagara Falls
ARTHUR DELUCA, 636 21st Street, upper apartment (1958), Niagara Falls
ARTHUR DELUCA, found in car in Begole Chevrolet parking lot, 27 Main Street (1958), North Tonawanda
EMERGENCY HOSPITAL, 108 Pine Street, Buffalo
WILLIAM ESPOSITIO, 577 Ward Road, North Tonawanda
WILLIAM ESPOSITIO, found 77 South Fisher Road, West Seneca
RICHARD J. FALISE, found in lot at 15th and Vermont Streets, Buffalo
CHARLES GERASS, 85 Glenside Avenue, Tonawanda

CHARLES GERASS, found in car at Sheridan Plaza, Tonawanda
INNER CIRCLE, 26 Allen Street, Buffalo
JAMESTOWN GRILL, 248 Allen Street, Buffalo
LAFAYETTE HOSPITAL, 113 Lafayette Avenue, Buffalo
ALAN LEVINE, found at Welker and East Ferry Streets, Buffalo
ALAN LEVINE, killed at 1034 Lafayette Avenue, Buffalo
DOMINIC MAFRICI, Cleveland
DOMINIC MAFRICI, killed at 52 Whitney Place, Buffalo
ALFRED MONACO, found on Carpenter Road, Evans
ANTHONY PALESTINE, 222 Efner Street, Buffalo
PALESTINE AND SANTANGELO, found on William Street near Bowen Road
in Lancaster
ANTHONY PERNA, 246 Massachusetts Avenue (1934), Buffalo
PETER PICCOLO SCHOOL OF HAIR DESIGN, Wilson Building, 695–711 Main
Street, Buffalo
PETER PICCOLO, 156 14th Street, Buffalo (1964); 138 Lorelee Drive,
Tonawanda
PETER PICCOLO, killed at 124 Elmwood Avenue, Buffalo
PASCAL POLITANO, 51 Days Park, 234 Prospect Avenue, Buffalo
ALBERT PREVITE GAMBLING HOUSE, 502 Nineteenth Street, Niagara Falls
ROBERT REINGOLD, 217 Irving Terrace, Tonawanda; 1457 Hertel Avenue,
Buffalo
ROBERT REINGOLD, found in car at Joslyn Place near Austin Street, Buffalo
CARL RIZZO, 629 Busti Avenue (1980), Buffalo
CARL RIZZO, found in parking lot at 578 Taunton Place, Buffalo
JOSEPH SAN FRATELLO, 501 Crescent Avenue, Buffalo
JOSEPH SAN FRATELLO, killed at 72 North Pearl Street, Buffalo
PASQUALE SANTANGELO, Bosco's Hotel, 249 Trenton Avenue (1956), 159
South Division Street (1963), Buffalo
VINCENT SANTANGELO, 736 Niagara Street, Buffalo
JOSEPH SANTASIERO, 48 Seventh Street (1922), 25 Maiden Lane (1925), Buffalo
SCULPTURE ROOM, Delaware and Chippewa Streets, 332 Elmwood
Avenue, Buffalo
STANLEY SENECA, 145 16th Street, Buffalo
SID BIRZON JEWELERS, 320 Pearl Street, Buffalo
NICHOLAS C. TIRONE, 222 Efner Street, upper, Buffalo

NOTES

PROLOGUE

1. FBI files, "Fred Randaccio," 11-8-1962.
2. Wikipedia, "Gangster," en.wikipedia.org/wiki/Gangster.
3. Mottram, *Public Enemies*, 120.
4. "The Assassination of President John F. Kennedy and Organized Crime, Report of Ralph Salerno, Consultant to the Select Committee on Assassinations," 95th Congress, 2nd Session, January 2, 1979.
5. *New York Times*, "4 Indicted in Scheme to Bilk New York on AIDS Research," 12-11-1984.
6. Rizzo, *Through the Mayors' Eyes*.

THE BLONDE BANDIT

7. *Courier-Express*, "Pleads for Lip-Stick," 2-10-1930, 4.
8. *Buffalo Evening News*, "Auto of Wounded Girl Bandit Found," 11-7-1929, 1.
9. Ibid.
10. *Courier-Express*, "Lad Uses His Shotgun," 12-29-1929, 1.
11. *Courier-Express*, "Store Owner Robbed of Trousers $75 and Goods," 1-21-1930, 22.
12. *Buffalo* [NY] *Times*, "Girls Vary Holdup Roles About Town," 1-25-1930, 10.
13. *Buffalo* [NY] *Times*, "Robber Queen Stages Daring East Side Job," 1-27-1930, 1.

14. *Buffalo Evening News*, "Blonde Bandit with Two Pals En Route Here," 2-10-1930, 1.
15. *Buffalo Evening News*, "Girl Bandit, 2 Pals Now in Local Cells," 2-13-1930, 1, second section.
16. *Courier-Express*, "…Girl's Pal Admits Part in 64 Burglaries," 2-18-1930, 11.
17. *Buffalo Evening News*, "'Sally' Recites Crimes," 2-26-1930, 1.
18. *Buffalo Times*, "Dombkiewicz Wields Razor on Glickstein," 2-26-1930, 1.
19. *Buffalo Evening News*, "'Blonde Bandit' Gets 20 Years," 2-28-1930, 3.
20. [Auburn, NY] *Citizen-Advertiser*, "Noted Female Felons Soon to Leave Auburn," 6-22-1933, 7.
21. *New York Times*, "Mother Aids Girl Bandit," 5-18-1930, N1.
22. *Courier-Express*, "Terms of Bittle, 'Blonde Bandit' Are Commuted," 12-21-1938, 1.
23. *Niagara Falls Gazette*, "Denies Guilt in Stabbing," 7-7-1964, 14.

THE KORNEY GANG

24. Rizzo, *They Call Me Korney*, 161.
25. Ibid.

THE BLUE RIBBON GANG

26. *Courier-Express*, "Two of Three Enter Chair Denying Guilt," 7-18-1930, 1.
27. *Courier-Express*, "Gunmen Slay Man, Wound Four Others in Downtown Cabaret," 1-2-1928, 1.
28. *Buffalo Evening News*, "Fechter Murder Auto Recovered," 8-7-1929, 1.
29. *Buffalo Evening News*, "Detectives Hunting Driver of Car in Fechter Murder," 11-6-1929, 1.
30. *Courier-Express*, "…Smoke Out Blue Ribbon Gunmen," 9-9-1929, 1.
31. *Buffalo* [NY] *Times*, "Double Cross Given Terror by Korney Pal," 9-11-1929, 1.
32. *Buffalo Evening News*, "Three Convicted Gangsters Sentenced to Die in Chair," 11-6-1929, 3.

BUFFALO'S MOLLS

33. *Buffalo Evening News*, "Moore to Press Murder Charges," 5-12-1924, 1.
34. Poulsen, *Don't Call Us Molls*, x.

35. Wikipedia, "Gun moll," en.wikipedia.org/wiki/Gun_moll.

36. Lay, *Hooded Knights on the Niagara*; [NY] *Daily Journal*, "Klansmen Visit 'Jew Minnies' and Compels Orchestra to Play," 3-17-1924.

37. *New York Times*, "Whittemore Hangs; Slayer Dies Calmly as Last Plea Fails," 8-13-1926.

38. *New York Times*, "Accuses Mrs. Whittemore. Ex-Cashier in Baltimore Hold-Up Says She Robbed Store," 3-23-1926, 3.

39. *New York Times*, "Whittemore Offers to Bare All Crimes If His Wife Is Freed," 3-26-1926, 1.

40. *Courier-Express*, "Gem Theft Evidence Submitted, Jury to Receive Case Today," 1-14-1930, 1.

41. *Courier-Express*, "Four Convicted in Carson Theft," 1-15-1930, 1.

42. *Buffalo* [NY] *Times*, "Stan Przybyl to Face Quick Trial for Carson Job," 1-22-1930, 1.

43. *New York Times*, "Gets Life Sentence for $300,000 Robbery," 3-1-1930, 14.

APARTMENT 821

44. The Outlaw Journals, "8 miles and a sandwich," www.babyfacenelsonjournal.com/floyds-death-2.html.

45. Wikipedia, "Kansas City Massacre," en.wikipedia.org/wiki/Kansas_City_massacre.

46. FBI files, "Charles Arthur Floyd."

47. Ibid.

THE $93,000 QUESTION

48. *Buffalo* [NY] *Times*, "Buffalo Police Confident Their Prisoner Will Confess Bank of Buffalo Murder-Holdup," 4-2-1926, 1.

49. *Buffalo Evening News*, "3 Robbers Steal $6000 Payroll," 9-10-1925, 1.

50. *Buffalo Evening News*, "Crimson Trail Points to Girl as Gang Victim," 11-7-1929, 1.

51. *Buffalo Evening News*, "Arrest of Two 'Super-Criminals' Clears Up Buffalo Payroll Robberies," 10-7-1925, 1.

52. *Buffalo Evening News*, "Bandits Wife, Out on Bail, Also Missing," 10-21-1925, 1.

53. *Buffalo Morning Express*, "Wife of Harry Harris Jumps Bail," 10-30-1925, 13.

54. *Buffalo Evening News*, "Harris and Gang Back; Slay One, Wound Two in $93,000 Bank Holdup," 10-29-1925, 1.

55. Ibid.

56. *New York Times*, "Bandits Get $93,000 from Armored Car," 10-30-1925, 1.

57. *Buffalo* [NY] *Times*, "Kozak Boasts of Buffalo Robbery," 1-19-1926, 1.

58. *Buffalo Morning Express*, "Buffalo Cops Return Here from Detroit," 1-22-1926, 4.

59. *New York Times*, "Slayer and His Gang Admit 6 Gem Thefts with $386,000 Loot," 3-21-1926, 1.

60. *Buffalo Evening News*, "Witnesses Link Pair with Bank Murders," 3-25-1926, 1.

61. *Buffalo* [NY] *Times*, "Robbers to Face Trial at Once," 4-1-1926, 1.

62. *Buffalo* [NY] *Times*, "Whittemore's Alibi Witnesses Close Defense," 4-23-1926, 1.

63. *Medina* [NY] *Daily Journal*, "Harris, Suspected of Bank of Buffalo Holdup, Killed in Florida," 10-12-1926, 1.

THE MILLIONAIRE KID

64. *Buffalo* [NY] *Times*, "Million Dollar Kid Takes Cake as Buffalo's Famous In-Out Crook," 12-5-1929, 1.

65. Ibid.

66. *Buffalo* [NY] *Times*, "Police from Buffalo Trap Stan Przybyl," 1-21-1930, 1

67. *Buffalo* [NY] *Times*, "Gem Bandit Manhunt Sweeps County," 11-15-1929, 1.

68. Ibid.

69. *Courier-Express*, "Allied Forces Move on Mob; Woman in Net," 11-30-1929, 1.

70. *Courier-Express*, "Jewelry Sold in New York," 12-1-1929, 1.

71. *Courier-Express*, "Deputies with Machine Guns Form Escort," 1-21-1930, 11.

72. *Buffalo* [NY] *Times*, "Police from Buffalo Trap Stan Przybyl," 1-21-1930, 1.

73. Ibid.

74. *Auburn* [NY] *Citizen*, "'Blonde Bandit' Given 20 Years Here; Her Pal and the 'Millionaire Kid' Get Life," 2-28-1930, 11.

BOBBED-HAIRED BEAUTY

75. *Buffalo* [NY] *Times*, "Minnick Says Bad Women to Blame," 5-12-1924, 1.

76. Ibid.

77. *Buffalo* [NY] *Times*, "Didn't Know What I Was Doing," 5-12-1924, 1.

78. Ibid.

79. *Buffalo Evening News*, "Virginian's Trial for Murder Gets Under Way in County Court," 5-20-1924, 1.

80. *Buffalo* [NY] *Times*, "Jury Out But 23 Minutes," 5-21-1924, 1.

81. *Sandusky* [OH] *Star-Journal*, "Blames Girl for Enticing Husband," 5-24-1924.

82. *Buffalo Morning Express*, "Governor Suggests New Trial for Bittle After Hearing Plea for Life," 6-4-1926, 5.

83. *Buffalo Evening News*, "Moore to Press Murder Charges," 5-12-1924, 1.

84. *Buffalo Evening News*, "Bittle Sentenced to Death in Chair," 5-28-1925, 1.

85. *New York Times*, "Escapes Execution; Family Before Cell," 6-13-1926, 20.

86. *Tonawanda* [NY] *News*, "George Bittle, 8 Others Freed by Governor Lehman," 12-21-1938, 6.

THE BARREL MURDER

87. *New York Herald*, "Petrosino Stood Always in the Shadow of Death," 3-21-1909, 7.

88. Dash, *First Family*, 4.

89. Ibid., 29.

90. Ibid., 3.

91. Ibid., 10.

92. Gangrule.com, "The Barrel Murder," www.gangrule.com/events/the-barrel-murder-1903.

93. *New York Times*, "'Barrel' Murder Plot and Victim Known," 4-21-1903.

94. Gangrule.com.

95. Gangrule.com.

96. Dash, *First Family*, 178.

97. The American Mafia, "Chronology—Section III, 1920–1931," www.onewal.com.

98. Dash, *First Family*, 287.

EARLY MAFIA FAMILIES

99. Yans-McLaughlin, *Family and Community*, 127.

100. Ibid.

101. *Courier-Express*, "Blast, Razing Hotel, Traced to Vendetta," 4-27-1929, 15.

102. Thomas Hunt and Michael A. Tona, "Men of Montedoro," *Informer: The History of American Crime and Law Enforcement* (April 2011): 8.

103. Thomas Hunt and Michael A. Tona, "The Good Killers: 1921's Glimpse of the Mafia," www.onewal.com.

104. Hunt and Tona, "Men of Montedoro," 32.

105. *Courier-Express*, "Hunt for Joe DiCarlo," 11-5-1939, 1.

106. Ibid.

107. *Buffalo Evening News*, "Record Funeral Is Expected as Hundreds Mourn Palmeri," 12-22-1932.

108. Wikipedia, "Buffalo Crime Family," en.wikipedia.org/wiki/Buffalo_crime_family.

109. B.F. Ruby, "DiCarlo—'Public Enemy.'" *Town Tidings*, September 1933, 28.

110. *Courier-Express*, "Hunt for Joe DiCarlo," 11-5-1939, 1.

111. Ruby, "DiCarlo," 28.

112. *Buffalo* [NY] *Express*, "Three Guilty in Dope Case; Are Sentenced," 2-12-1924, 1.

113. *Buffalo Times*, "DiCarlo to Give Himself Up," 4-9-1925, 1.

114. *Buffalo* [NY] *Express*, "Two Sicilians Are Arrested by U.S. Agents," 4-13-1924, 1.

115. Ruby, "DiCarlo," 29.

116. Michael Tona, author correspondence.

117. *Buffalo Evening News*, "Record Funeral Is Expected as Hundreds Mourn Palmeri," 12-22-1932.

118. [Tonawanda, NY] *Evening News*, "Men Absolved," 2-24-1933, 3.

119. *Niagara Falls Gazette*, "'Public Enemy' Is Convicted, Jailed on Bad Bill Count," 4-20-1933, 18.

120. *Niagara Falls Gazette*, "Two Buffalo Men Are Acquitted on Charge of Assault," 3-4-1937.

121. *Niagara Falls Gazette*, "Joe DiCarlo Gets Year, $500 Fine," 4-1-1938, 30.

122. *Niagara Falls Gazette*, "Buffalo Police Official Fined and Transferred," 5-9-1938, 24.

123. *Geneva* [NY] *Daily Times*, "Police Seek Distributor of Machines," 9-11-1939, 4.

124. *Courier-Express*, "U.S. Agents Seek to Learn Where DiCarlo Was Hiding," 6-1-1940, 15.

125. Ibid.

126. [Amsterdam, NY] *Evening Recorder*, "Erie Democratic Leader Held on Perjury Charge," 10-31-1939, 5.

127. *Utica* [NY] *Daily Press*, "Buffalo Case Nearing Close," 10-10-1939, 10.

128. *Buffalo Evening News*, "Court Gives Caputo Limit, Lashes Politics-Crime Tie," 11-9-1939.

129. [Tonawanda, NY] *Evening News*, "Shootings, Kocemba Hushed in Buffalo," 1-22-1945, 1.

130. Ibid.

131. [Tonawanda, NY] *Evening News*, "Gambling Data Is Sent to Governor Lehman," 2-13-1945, 1.

132. Ibid.

133. [Tonawanda, NY] *Evening News*, "Buffalo Murder," 1-31-1945, 5.

134. *Kingston* [NY] *Daily Freeman*, "Crusader's Slayer Hunted by Police," 1-29-1945, 9.

135. *Buffalo Evening News*, "Police Question Wife, Sister and Others in House; Victim in Emergency Hospital in Critical Condition," 3-16-1945, 1.

136. Ibid.

137. *Tonawanda* [NY] *News*, "Pistol Found Is Not One Used in Killing," 4-6-1956, 7.

138. *Binghamton* [NY] *Press*, "Policeman Guilty in Gambling Case," 4-24-1945, 20.

139. [Auburn, NY] *Citizen-Advertiser*, "Police Captain Found Guilty: Wins New Trial," 1-10-1946, 2.

140. [Gloversville, NY] *Morning Herald*, "Review Exonerates Buffalo Policeman," 2-9-1946, 9.

141. Michael Tona, author correspondence.

142. *Courier-Express*, "DiCarlo Finding Returns from Crime Diminishing," 6-19-1960, 2B.

143. Ibid.

144. *Courier-Express*, "DiCarlo Tied to Two Major Crime Gangs," 3-1-1951, 30.

145. *United States v. DiCarlo*, 102F.Supp. 597(1952), *United States v. DiCarlo*, Cr. 20299.

146. *Courier-Express*, "DiCarlo Finding," 6-19-1960, 2B.

147. [Auburn, NY] *Citizen-Advertiser*, "Buffalo Police Continue Quiz on Deaths," 8-17-1961, 7.

148. *Courier-Express*, "Rites Today for DiCarlo; Tied to Mob," 10-14-1980, 2.

149. Porello, *To Kill the Irishman*, 205.

150. "Organized Crime: 25 Years after Valachi, Hearings Before the Permanent Subcommittee on Investigations of the Committee on Governmental Affairs, United States Senate," 100th Congress, U.S. Government Printing Office, Washington, D.C.: 1988, Statement of Angelo Lonardo, 535.

151. Porello, *To Kill the Irishman*, 206.

152. Wikipedia, "John Tronolone," en.wikipedia.org/wiki/John_Tronolone.

153. Porello, *To Kill the Irishman*, 207–8.

THE MAGADDINO FAMILY

154. *Courier-Express*, "Arraignment Is Conducted in Bedroom of Defendant," 11-30-1968.

155. *Buffalo Evening News*, "Family Man Magaddino Shunned Violence," 2-25-1974.

156. *Buffalo Evening News*, "68 Arrest, Lost Union Control Spelled End for Magaddino," 2-27-1974.

157. Mary Ferrell, "Steve Magaddino," 1-29-1963. www.maryferrell.org/ mffweb/archive/docset/getList.do?docSetId=1447.

158. *Buffalo Evening News*, "68 Arrest."

159. *Buffalo Evening News*, "Magaddino Empire Only Legend Now," 2-24-1974.

160. *Buffalo Evening News*, "68 Arrest."

161. Hunt and Tona, "Good Killers."

162. Ibid.

163. FBI files, "Stefano Magaddino," 92-61.

164. Ferrell, "Fred Randaccio," NARA 124-10335-10076, 53. www. maryferrell.org/mffweb/archive/docset/getList.do?docSetId=1502.

165. FBI files, "Stefano Magaddino," 92-61.

166. *Niagara Falls Gazette*, "Magaddino—A $10,000 a Day Salesman?" 12-15-1968, 2C.

167. *Niagara Falls Gazette*, "Area Guests at Apalachin Have Local Business Ties," 3-9-1958, C1.

168. Onewal.com, "Chronology—Section III, 1920–1931," www.onewal.com.

169. Critchley, *Origin of Organized Crime*, 165.

170. Ibid., 191.

171. FBI files, "Peter J. Magaddino," BU 92-210.

172. Ibid.

173. FBI files, "Stefano Magaddino," 92-61.

174. Ibid.

175. Ibid.

176. FBI files, "Antonio Magaddino," BU 92-57.

177. *Niagara Gazette*, "Peter Magaddino's Funeral Thursday," 8-17-1976.

178. FBI files, "Antonio Magaddino," BU 92-57.

179. Ibid.

180. Ibid.

181. FBI files, "Stefano Magaddino," 92-61.

182. *Niagara Falls Gazette*, "Magaddino, Reputed Crime Lord, Lives Quietly in Niagara Area," 10-13-1963, 6-C.

183. *Utica Observer-Dispatch*, "Magaddino Worlds: One a Niagara Suburb of Family, Friends; Another in Shadows with Falcone in Wings," 12-18-1968.

184. Michael Tona, author correspondence.

185. *Niagara Falls Gazette*, "Hundreds Attend Magaddino Rites at St. Joseph's," 8-21-1950, 19.

186. FBI files, "Antonio Magaddino," BU 92-57.

187. Ibid.

188. Griffin, *Mob Nemesis*, 66.

189. Ibid.

190. *Niagara Falls Gazette*, "Probe of Apalachin Is Linked to Case of Willie Moretti," 7-13-1958, 3C.

191. FBI files, "Stefano Magaddino," 92-61.

192. *Niagara Falls Gazette*, "Grenade Tossed at Magaddino Home," 11-10-1958.

193. *New York Times*, "Apalachin Witness Balks Ninety Times," 1-15-1959, 67.

194. *Niagara Falls Gazette*, "10 May Be Queried on Falls Fugitives," 8-2-1959, 2-C.

195. FBI files, "Stefano Magaddino," 92-61.

196. Reid, *Grim Reapers*, 53–54.

197. FBI files, "Antonio Magaddino," BU 92-57.

198. *Buffalo Evening News*, "Magaddino Empire Only Legend Now," 2-24-1974.

199. FBI files, "Stefano Magaddino," 92-61.

200. *Niagara Falls Gazette*, "Magaddino Too Ill to See Press, Wife Says," 10-3-1963.

201. Ferrell, "Vincent Scro," www.maryferrell.org/mffweb/archive/docset/getList.do?docSetId=1475.

202. FBI files, "Stefano Magaddino," 92-61.

203. Ibid.

204. Ibid.

205. *Niagara Falls Gazette*, "Hospital Releases Magaddino," 5-26-1965.

206. Griffin, *Mob Nemesis*, 66.

207. *Niagara Falls Gazette*, "Lewiston Gambler Is Linked to Ring," 6-15-1962, 1.

208. FBI files, "Peter A. Magaddino," BU 92-288.

209. Ibid.

210. Ibid.

211. Ibid.

212. Ibid.

213. FBI files, "Antonio Magaddino," BU 92-57.

214. *United States of America, Plaintiff, v. Stefano Magaddino Et Al., Defendants.* Cr-1968-196.

215. Ibid.

216. FBI files, "Peter J. Magaddino," BU 92-210.

217. *Buffalo Evening News*, "68 Arrest, Lost Union Control Spelled End for Magaddino," 2-27-1974.

218. *Courier-Express*, "'Don' Retired in '69, But Mob Only Now Has Chiefs in Line," 2-11-1973.

219. FBI files, "Peter J. Magaddino," BU 92-210.

220. *Courier-Express*, "Magaddino Decline Outlined to Senators," 5-3-1980.

221. *Courier-Express*, "Arraignment Is Conducted in Bedroom of Defendant," 11-30-1968.

222. *United States of America, Plaintiff, v. Stefano Magaddino Et Al., Defendants.*

223. FBI files, "Antonio Magaddino," BU 92-57.

224. *United States of America, Plaintiff, v. Stefano Magaddino Et Al., Defendants*; letter from Dr. Eugene J. Lippschutz dated March 31, 1970.

225. FBI files, "Peter A. Magaddino," BU 92-288.

226. FBI files, "Antonio Magaddino," BU 92-57.

227. *Niagara Falls Gazette*, "Antonino Magaddino's Final Rites Are Held," 4-15-1971, 17.

228. FBI files, "Stefano Magaddino," 92-61.

229. *United States of America, Plaintiff, v. Stefano Magaddino Et Al., Defendants*, order dated 7-17-70.

230. Ibid.

231. Ibid.

232. Ibid.

233. Ibid.

234. Ibid.

235. Ibid.

236. *United States of America, Plaintiff, v. Stefano Magaddino Et Al., Defendants.* Cr-1968-196.

237. FBI files, "Peter A. Magaddino," BU 92-288.

238. Ferrell, "Steve Magaddino," www.maryferrell.org/mffweb/archive/docset/getList.do?docSetId=1447.

239. *United States of America, Plaintiff, v. Stefano Magaddino Et Al., Defendants.*

240. *United States of America, Plaintiff-Appellant, v. Stefano Magaddino Et Al., Defendants-Appellees*, 496 F.2s 455 (2nd Cir. 1974).

241. *United States of America, Plaintiff, v. Stefano Magaddino Et Al., Defendants.*

242. *Niagara Falls Gazette*, "Crowd Views Magaddino Cortege," 7-22-1974.

243. *United States of America, Plaintiff, v. Passero and Rizzo, Defendants*, Order, 11-19-1975.

244. FBI files, "Peter A. Magaddino," BU 92-288.

245. Ibid.

THE MAGADDINO RELATIVES

246. Ferrell, "Vincent Scro," www.maryferrell.org/mffweb/archive/docset/ getList.do?docSetId=1475, 2-19-63.

247. FBI files, "Stefano Magaddino," 92-61.

248. *Niagara Falls Gazette*, "Trail of Panepinto's Killers Is Leading to Buffalo, Police Feel," 8-17-1936.

249. *Geneva Daily Times*, "Batavian Shot by Gunmen in Buffalo, Dies," 8-26-1936, 1.

250. *Niagara Falls Gazette*, "Pay Last Respects to Mrs. Longo," 5-25-1936, 1.

251. *Niagara Falls Gazette*, "Niagara Topics," 5-17-1959, 1C.

252. *Niagara Falls Gazette*, "Area Guests at Apalachin Have Local Business Ties," 3-9-1958, C1.

253. FBI files, "Peter J. Magaddino," BU 92-210.

254. Ferrell, "Steve Magaddino," www.maryferrell.org/mffweb/archive/ docset/getList.do?docSetId=1447.

255. FBI files, "Antonio Magaddino," BU 92-57.

256. Amigone Funeral Home, "Rose Mary Longo," obit.amigonefuneralhome. com/obit-954773.

257. *Buffalo News*, "James V. LaDuca, Retired Bakery Employee," 9-27-1993, A6.

258. *Washington Post*, "Vincent Scro," obituary, 7-25-2009.

THE CRIME FAMILY

259. FBI files, "Stefano Magaddino," 6-1963.

260. Kurek, *Troopers Are Coming*, 175.

261. *Courier-Express*, "Big Boss Had Title of 'Don,'" 10-17-1963, 9.

262. Ferrell, "Steve Magaddino," www.maryferrell.org/mffweb/archive/ docset/getList.do?docSetId=1447.

263. FBI files, "Herman Weinstein," BU 92-421.

264. *Niagara Falls Gazette*, "Admits He Killed Wife by Striking Her on the Head," 10-20-1930, 1.

265. [Tonawanda, NY] *Evening News*, "Judge Hackett Imposes Severe Penalties on 4," 9-19-1934, 3.

266. *Buffalo Evening News*, "68 Arrest, Lost Union Control Spelled End for Magaddino," 2-27-1974.

267. *Niagara Falls Gazette*, "Body of Murdered Falls Man Taken from Barge Canal in Erie County," 12-20-1943, 1.

268. [Tonawanda] *Evening News*, "Slain Thug from Falls Involved Here, Is Claim," 12-21-1943, 1.

269. *Niagara Falls Gazette*, "Area Guests at Apalachin Have Local Business Ties," 3-9-1958, C1.

270. *Niagara Falls Gazette*, "Italian Accuses Two Compatriots," 4-29-1931, 14.

271. *Schenectady* [NY] *Gazette*, "Release Six Men Held in Buffalo for Extortion," 5-8-1931, 19.

272. Bill Davidson, "How Mafia Killers Got Their Man," *Saturday Evening Post*, 10-31-1964, 38–40.

273. Ibid.

274. Ibid.

275. Ibid.

276. Ibid.

277. Ibid.

278. Ferrell, "Steve Magaddino," www.maryferrell.org/mffweb/archive/docset/getList.do?docSetId=1447.

279. Ibid.

280. Ibid.

281. FBI files, "Fred Randaccio," 6-12-1967.

282. Griffin, *Mob Nemesis*, 84.

283. Ibid., 84–85.

284. Ibid., 85.

285. *Courier-Express*, "Some Hide in Storeroom," 5-9-1967, 1.

286. *Niagara Falls Gazette*, "36 LaCosa Nostra Figures Arrested in Buffalo Raid Are Freed by Court," 5-9-1967, 1.

287. FBI files, "Fred Randaccio," 6-12-1967.

288. *Courier-Express*, "21 More Officers Named in Suit," 8-4-1967.

289. *Tonawanda* [NY] *News*, "Todaro Claims Ethnic Motive Causes Raid," 10-3-1967, 1.

290. Ron Fino, personal correspondence with author.

291. Ibid.

292. *Buffalo News*, "Sacco Gave Information on Unsolved Crimes, Official Says," 10-26-1990, B8.

293. Ron Fino, personal correspondence with author.

294. Ibid.

295. *Buffalo Evening News*, "Magaddino Court Victory Has a Hollow Ring to It as His Empire Crumbles," 5-19-1973.

296. *Niagara Falls Gazette*, "Buffalo Dinner Was Incomplete; Magaddinos Did Not Attend," 8-2-1970, C1.

297. Griffin, *Mob Nemesis*, 95.

298. Ibid., 96.

299. Ibid., 97.

300. FBI files, "Samuel Lagattuta," BU 66-1988.

301. Ibid.

302. Ibid.
303. Ibid.
304. Ibid.
305. Ibid.
306. Ibid.
307. Ibid.
308. Ancient Faces, "Albert M Billiteri (1926–1998)," www.ancientfaces.com/ research/ person/9736727/ albert-m-billiteri-profile-and-genealogy.
309. Ron Fino, personal correspondence with athor.
310. FBI files, "Samuel Lagattuta," BU 66-1988.
311. Ferrell, "Steve Magadino," www.maryferrell.org/mffweb/archive/ docset/getList.do?docSetId=1447.
312. Kurek, *Troopers Are Coming*, 179.
313. Family Tree Maker, "Benjamin Nicoletti (b. 28 Jan 1911, d. 22 May 1982)" familytreemaker.genealogy.com/users/c/a/f/Lindy-Jaye-Cafaro/ WEBSITE-0001/UHP-0059.html.

NOVEMBER 14, 1957

314. Kurek, *Troopers Are Coming*, 176.
315. "Hearings before the Select Committee on Improper Activities in the Labor or Management Field," 85th Congress, 1st session, 1957; 85th Congress, 2nd session, 1958; and 86th Congress, 1st Session, 1959, 12213.
316. Ibid.
317. Ibid.
318. *Niagara Falls Gazette*, "Falls Apalachin Guests Clam Up, Mum to 109 Questions," 12-15-1957, 1.
319. "The Assassination of President John F. Kennedy and Organized Crime, Report of Ralph Salerno, Consultant to the Select Committee on Assassinations," 95th Congress, 2nd Session, January 2, 1979.
320. Griffin, *Mob Nemesis*, 62.
321. *Buffalo Evening News*, "Key Session Shaping Up in Apalachin Quiz," 3-26-1958.
322. *Niagara Falls Gazette*, "Falls Apalachin."
323. *Tonawanda News*, "Falls Mortician Gives Testimony to Grand Jury," 4-10-1958, 11.
324. *Binghamton* [NY] *Press*, "Offer of Immunity to D'Agostino Indicated by Tioga Jury Action," 2-25-1958, 4.
325. Kurek, *Troopers Are Coming*, 177.
326. *Niagara Falls Gazette*, "10 May Be Queried on Falls Fugitives," 8-2-1959.

327. Sifakis, *Mafia Encyclopedia*, 20.

328. *Niagara Falls Gazette*, "Appalachin [*sic*] Figure Dies in Memorial," 8-18-1970, 12.

329. *Binghamton* [NY] *Press*. "Lagatutta [*sic*] of Apalachin Fame, Dies," 9-12-1964, 9.

KIDNAPPING COUSINS

330. Bonanno, *A Man of Honor*, 141.

331. Ibid., 26.

332. Ibid., 55.

333. Ibid., 57.

334. Ibid., 56.

335. Ibid., 142.

336. Bonanno, *Last Testament of Bill Bonanno*, 168.

337. Bonanno, *Bound by Honor*, 20.

338. Talese, *Honor Thy Father*, 22.

339. Bonanno, *Man of Honor*, 249.

340. Ferrell, "Fred Randaccio," Nara 124-10335-10076, 54. www.maryferrell.org/ mffweb/archive/docset/getList.do?docSetId=1502.

341. FBI files, "Peter J. Magaddino," BU 92-210.

342. Bonanno, *Last Testament of Bill Bonanno*, 203.

343. Ibid., 205.

344. Ibid., 206.

345. Ibid., 207.

346. Ibid., 209.

347. Ferrell, "Steve Magaddino," 92-61, 10-14-1964, NARA, 6. www.maryferrell.org/ mffweb/archive/docset/getList.do?docSetId=1447.

348. Raab, *Five Families*, 164.

349. Bonanno, *Last Testament of Bill Bonanno*, 210.

350. FBI files, "Stefano Magaddino."

351. *Life*, "How Joe Bonanno Schemed to Kill—and Lost," September 1, 1967, 18.

352. Bonanno, *Bound by Honor*, 214.

353. Ibid.

354. Ibid., 215.

355. *Life*, "How Joe Bonanno."

356. Bonanno, *Last Testament*, 213.

357. Bonanno, *Bound by Honor*, 215.

358. Ibid.

359. Ibid., 216.

360. *New York Times*, "Alleged Mafia Triggerman Shot to Death on a Street in Brooklyn," 4-22-1970, 32.

361. Social Security Death Index.

THE MONTANA AFFAIR

362. "Hearings before the Select Committee on Improper Activities in the Labor or Management Field," 85th Congress, 1st session, 1957; 85th Congress, 2nd session, 1958; and 86th Congress, 1st Session, 1959, 12311.

363. Hunt and Tona, "Men of Montedoro," 8–9.

364. Forgotten Buffalo, "John Montana—The BOSS of Buffalo Central Terminal: The Reason Why the Trolley Lobby Was Never Used," www.forgottenbuffalo.com/forgottenbflofeatures/trolleylobbythemafia.html.

365. Bonanno, *A Man of Honor*, 126.

366. Ibid., 127.

367. Ibid., 128.

368. Ibid.

369. "Hearings before the Select Committee on Improper Activities in the Labor or Management Field," 85th Congress, 1st session, 1957; 85th Congress, 2nd session, 1958; and 86th Congress, 1st Session, 1959, 12294.

370. Ibid.

371. Ibid., 12296.

372. *Buffalo Evening News*, "Magaddino: Velvet Glove Hid Iron Fist," 2-26-1974.

373. Ibid.

374. "Hearings before the Select Committee on Improper Activities in the Labor or Management Field," 85th Congress, 1st session, 1957; 85th Congress, 2nd session, 1958; and 86th Congress, 1st Session, 1959, 12301.

375. Ibid.

376. Ibid., 12306.

377. *New York Times*, "Wire Fence Aided Raid in Apalachin," 11-14-1959, 144.

378. *Binghamton* [NY] *Press*, "Montana Leads off Probable Tioga Jury 'Parade of Silence,'" 2-4-1958, 7.

379. "Hearings before the Select Committee on Improper Activities in the Labor or Management Field," 85th Congress, 1st session, 1957; 85th Congress, 2nd session, 1958; and 86th Congress, 1st Session, 1959, 12311.

380. *Tonawanda* [NY] *News*, "Taxi Baron Dies of Heart Attack," 3-19-1964, 8.

381. *Niagara Falls Gazette*, "Apalachin Agenda Believed Included Dope," 2-22-1958, 5.

382. *Evening* [Binghamton, NY] *Press*, "Valachi to Describe Upstate Crime, Cosa Nostra Links," 10-3-1963, 19.

383. *Utica* [NY] *Observer-Dispatch*, "Left Estate of $839,581," 8-30-1968, 12.

THE MAJOR PLAYERS

384. *Batavia* [NY] *Times*, "Police Center Probe of Two Killings in Batavia," 9-3-1936, 1.

385. American Mafia, "Pistone testimony," americanmafia.com/pistone_ testimony.html.

386. Wikipedia, "Italian Lottery," en.wikipedia.org/wiki/Italian_ lottery#Italian_lottery.

387. *Niagara Falls Gazette*, "Niagara Topics," 5-17-1959, 1C.

388. *Niagara Falls Gazette*, "Second Important Anti-Gambling Raid in Week Nets 17 Men," 2-22-1932, 22.

389. *Niagara Falls Gazette*, "Anti-Gambling Drive Is Opened by Police Here," 4-21-1943, 1.

390. *Niagara Falls Gazette*, "New Falls Squad Cracks Down on Gambling, Vice," 7-25-1944, 1.

391. *Niagara Falls Gazette*, "Is Falls Crimes Organized? Gazette Digs for Answers," 3-8-1958, 1.

392. *Niagara Falls Gazette*, "Man Caught in Raid Faces His 10th Gambling Charge," 4-1-1954, 22.

393. *Niagara Falls Gazette*, "Forty-Eight Men Arrested and $8,000 Seized in Lumber City Gambling Raid," 3-22-1948.

394. *Niagara Falls Gazette*, "40 Arrested in Gambling Raids Here," 6-1-1946, 1.

395. *Niagara Falls Gazette*, "Man Caught."

396. Humphreys, *The Enforcer*, 60–62.

397. *Niagara Falls Gazette*, "Gambling Raid Spurs City Move for Crackdown," 5-15-1959, 1.

398. *Niagara Falls Gazette*, "Gambler No 'Mr. Big'—Gorman," 5-23-1959, 1.

399. *Niagara Falls Gazette*, "City Has Vice, but Views on Its Extent Vary Widely," 3-11-1958, 1.

400. [Tonawanda] *Evening News*, "N.T. Police Will Confer with D.A. on Gambling Data," 3-25-1949, 1.

401. [Tonawanda] *Evening News*, "Marinelli and Sillman Get 6-Month Sentences in Pen," 1-4-1951, 1; 12-12-1950.

402. [Tonawanda] *Evening News*, "Marinelli."

403. [Tonawanda] *Evening News*, "8 4-Corner 'Wheels' Also Plead Guilty," 12-12-1950, 1.

404. *Niagara Falls Gazette*, "Falls Police Think 'Blackie' Previte May Still Be Alive," 8-21-1953, 1.

405. Ibid.

406. *Tonawanda* [NY] *News*, "Tip on 'One-Arm Blackie' Reveals No New Evidence," 2-29-1956, 1.

407. Ehrenreich Obituary.

408. *Niagara Falls Gazette*, "Falls-Buffalo Gambling Links Traced at State Crime Hearing," 9-29-1960, 1.

409. *Niagara Falls Gazette*, "Falls' Few Bookmakers Claim Business Is Bad," 3-10-1958, 1.

410. FBI files, "Stefano Magaddino."

411. *Niagara Falls Gazette*, "Nab 46 in Gaming Raid on East Side Poolroom," 2-8-1959, 1.

412. *Niagara Falls Gazette*, "Owner of Gambling House Fined $250," 2-9-1959, 12.

413. *Niagara Falls Gazette*, "$10,000 Seized by Police in Pine Ave. Gaming Raid," 4-5-1959, 1.

414. Ibid.

415. *Niagara Falls Gazette*, "Falls Man Fined $1,250 on Gaming, Smut Charges," 5-7-1959, 1.

416. *Niagara Falls Gazette*, "34 Defendants Deny Gambling Charges," 6-22-1959, 13.

417. *Tonawanda* [NY] *News*, "State and NT Police Smash Their Way into Suspected Gambling Establishment," 10-16-1964, 1.

418. *Niagara Falls Gazette*, "Benjamin Nicoletti Sr. Admits Gaming Charges," 4-12-1971, 10.

419. *Niagara Falls Gazette*, "'Operation Bookie' Well-Kept Secret," 8-23-1959, 1.

420. *Niagara Falls Gazette*, "16 Are Arrested in Crackdown," 8-23-1959, 1.

421. *Niagara Falls Gazette*, "State Unit Plans Hearing in Buffalo," 10-25-1959, 1.

422. *Niagara Falls Gazette*, "Big-Stake Gaming Dens in Buffalo Described," 6-30-1960, 19.

423. Griffin, *Mob Nemesis*, 66.

424. Ibid., 75.

425. Ibid.

426. *Courier-Express*, "Suspects Allegedly Held for Lensmen," 12-10-1969, 45.

427. *Courier-Express*, "3 Men Arrested in Gambling Raid," 12-9-1969, 1.

428. *Niagara Falls Gazette*, "Falls-Buffalo Gambling Links Traced at State Crime Hearing," 9-29-1960, 1.

429. Ibid.

430. *Niagara Falls Gazette*, "Jury Quizzes Falls Man on Gambling," 5-11-1966, 40.

431. *Buffalo Evening News*, "T-Men Seize 6 in Betting Room Raid," 5-12-1961, 1.

432. Ibid.

433. *Buffalo Evening News*, "Bonito, Two Others Arrested in $450,000 Bookie Setup," 10-22-1963, 1.

434. FBI files, "Stefano Magaddino," 92-61.

435. FBI files, "Fred Randaccio," 10-8-1966.

436. Ibid.

437. Ibid.

438. Ibid.

439. Ibid.

440. *Courier-Express*, "46 Arrested in Club on Gambling Charges," 12-9-1967, 1.

441. *Niagara Falls Gazette*, "City Gambling Raids Bring 24 Arrests," 8-17-1969, 1.

442. *Niagara Falls Gazette*, "U.S. Roster of Mafia Is New Blow to Magaddino," 8-22-1969, 15.

443. *Tonawanda [NY] News*, "2 Gambling Suspects Arrested," 12-14-1970, 18.

444. *Tonawanda [NY] Evening News*, "Gambling Probe Leads to Cache of $96,700," 12-19-1970, 6.

445. Griffin, *Mob Nemesis*, 80.

446. *Courier-Express*, "Betting Parlor Operations, Principals Told in Affidavits," 3-15-1975.

447. Ibid.

448. *Tonawanda [NY] News*, "FBI Agent Uncovers Crime Ties in Buffalo," 3-14-1975, 1.

449. *Courier-Express*, "Betting Parlor Operations, Principals Told in Affidavits," 3-15-1975.

450. Ibid.

451. Ibid.

452. Ibid.

453. Ibid.

454. Ibid.

455. *Tonawanda [NY] News*, "FBI Agent Uncovers Crime Ties."

456. *Courier-Express*, "New Charges Filed Against Social Club," 4-12-1975.

457. *Buffalo Evening News*, "Pieri, Reputed Mafia Boss, End Federal Jail Term," 6-11-1976, 15.

458. *Buffalo Evening News*, "Police Kept an Eye on Clubs in Probe," 3-17-1975.

459. *Tonawanda [NY] News*, "Town Man Among 4 Arrested by FBI on Gambling Charges," 3-24, 1977, 8.

460. *Courier-Express*, "Reputed Local Mob Czar, Cronies Netted in Raid," 3-25-1977, 1.

461. *Courier-Express*, "Gambling Trial Ends in Blast at Evidence," 2-15-1978.

462. *Tonawanda* [NY] *News*, "2 Are Guilty of Gambling," 2-16-1978, 10.

463. *Courier-Express*, "37 Face Gambling Charges After Raid in Williamsville," 4-23-1977, 3.

464. *Courier-Express*, "12 More Grabbed on Gaming Counts," 4-24-1977, 1.

465. *Courier-Express*, "Gambling Flourishes Despite Magaddino Deaths," 4-26-1977, 1.

The Whirlpool Club

466. "Hearings before the Permanent Subcommittee on Investigations of the Committee on Government Operations. United States Senate," 88th Congress, 1st session, 1963; 2nd session, 1964, 604.

467. *Niagara Falls Gazette*, "Gambling Place Closed," 7-29-1962, 18.

468. *Niagara Falls Gazette*, "Whirlpool Club Charter Revoked in Court Action," 9-10-1955, 11.

469. *Niagara Falls Gazette*, "'Club' Roundup in 24th St. Led by Gorman, DA," 4-16-1955, 1.

470. *Niagara Falls Gazette*, "2 Men Tried to Bribe Him, Officer Says," 4-16-1955, 1.

471. *Niagara Falls Gazette*, "Heavy Bail Set as 10 Men Deny Guilt in Gambling Raid," 5-18-1955.

472. *Niagara Falls Gazette*, "Gaming Revival in Falls Denied by City Officials," 1-27-1956, 15.

473. *Niagara Falls Gazette*, "Gambling Place Closed."

474. *Niagara Falls Gazette*, "29 Seized in 24th St. Gambling Raid," 7-28-1962, 1.

The Business of Funerals

475. Chiocca, *Mobsters and Thugs*, 82.

476. *Niagara Falls Gazette*, "Sensational Rumors Set Afloat by Falls Undertaker's Arrest," 11-11-1931, 1.

477. Ibid.

478. *Niagara Falls Gazette*, "Falls Man Is Held with 13 Others on Charge of Homicide," 8-18-1932, 1.

479. *Niagara Falls Gazette*, "Bail Bonds for Pair Increased," 5-21-1934, 19.

480. *Niagara Falls Gazette*, "Mrs. Scrufari Honored at Dinner," 8-13-1936, 18.

481. *Niagara Falls Gazette*, "Area Guests at Apalachin Have Local Business Ties," 3-9-1958, C1.

482. Gangsters Inc., "Whack Out On Willie Moretti," gangstersinc.ning. com/profiles/blogs/whack-out-on-willie-moretti.

483. *Niagara Falls Gazette*, "Former Falls Man Material Witness in Murder Case," 10-19-1951, 1.

484. *Herald Statesman* [Yonkers], "Crime, Soap: Group Probes A&P Problem," 10-9-1971.

485. *Niagara Falls Gazette*, "Former Falls Funeral Home Operator Dies," 5-12-1955.

LUPO THE WOLF

486. FBI files, "Stefano Magaddino," 3-31-1964.

487. FBI files, "Fred Randaccio," BU 92-174

488. FBI files, "Steve Magaddino," 1-29-1963.

489. FBI files, "Fred Randaccio," BU 92-174.

490. *Courier-Express*, "Randaccio's Record Dates Back to 1922," 10-11-1963, 27.

491. FBI files, "Fred Randaccio," BU 92-174.

492. Reid, *Grim Reapers*, 54.

493. Ferrell, "Steve Magaddino," 92-61, www.maryferrell.org/mffweb/ archive/docset/getList.do?docSetId=1447.

494. Ibid.

495. FBI files, "Fred Randaccio," BU 92-174.

496. Ibid.

497. FBI files, "Stefano Magaddino," 92-61.

498. FBI files, "Fred Randaccio," BU 92-174.

499. Ferrell, "Fred Randaccio, www.maryferrell.org/mffweb/archive/ viewer/showDoc.do?docId=94023&relPageId=2, 5-25-1962.

500. FBI files, "Fred Randaccio," BU 92-174.

501. FBI files, "Fred Randaccio," 9-18-1967.

502. Ibid.

503. Genealogybank, "Fred Randaccio," www.genealogybank.com/gbnk/ ssdi/doc/ssdi/v1:113097CAD9DA8E45.

504. Genealogybank, "Pasquale Natarelli," www.genealogybank.com/ gbnk/ssdi/doc/ssdi/v1:112F1E016CAA3B6D.

HIDE IN PLAIN SIGHT

505. Waller, *Hide in Plain Sight*, 46.

506. Earley and Shur, *Witsec*, 48.

507. *Tonawanda* [NY] *News*, "Calabrese Named in Robbery Plot," 6-30-1967, 12.

508. Earley and Shur, *Witsec*, 47.

509. Ibid., 50.

510. Ibid., 51.

511. Waller, *Hide in Plain Sight*, 162.

512. Ibid., 184.

513. Ibid., 246.

514. *Buffalo News*, "'Jimmy' Caci, 86, dies; had ties to local mob," 9-4-2011.

515. Jazzhouse, "Bobby Milano," www.jazzhouse.org.

A GANGSTER, A HIT AND A REMBRANDT

516. *Courier-Express*, "'Nobody Did It,' Shot Underworld Figure Tells Police," 6-18-1976.

517. McShane, with Matera, *Stolen Masterpiece*, 3.

518. Ibid., 14.

519. Ibid.

520. Ibid.,16.

521. Ibid., 18.

522. Ibid., 25.

523. Ibid., 28.

524. *Courier-Express*, "11 Are Indicted on Charges in 'Fence' Probe," 7-1-1977, 1.

525. *Courier-Express*, "FBI Bares Alleged Talks About Billiteri 'Hit,' Others," 6-28-1977, 12.

526. *Courier-Express*, "Officials, Others Accused in Attempted Briberies," 6-28-1977, 12.

527. *Buffalo News*, "Novino Describes Escape from Ambush in 1976 and Identifies 4 of 5 Suspects," 4-13-1993.

528. Ibid.

529. *Buffalo Evening News*, "Sacco Faces Term on Guilty Plea in Mob Shooting," 2-28-1979, 12.

530. *Buffalo Evening News*, "'Nobody Did It,' Shot Underworld Figure Tells Police," 6-18-1976.

531. *Buffalo News*, "Novino Set to Testify as Federal Witness Sicurella Perjury Trial Seen as Part of Effort Against Organized Crime," 11-23-1992.

532. *Buffalo News*, "The Words of John Sacco," 3-4-1990, A10.

533. *Buffalo News*, "Reputed Gangland Killer Sacco Is FBI Informant," 2-21-1990, 1.

534. *Buffalo News*, "Sacco's Death May Undermine U.S. Probe; FBI, U.S. Attorney's Office Are Left with a Mountain of Unanswered Questions," 12-11-1990.
535. Ibid.
536. *Buffalo News*, "Sacco Triggers Tug of War for FBI, Parole Officials," 3-10-1990.
537. *Buffalo News*, "Wife of Late Mob Informant Battles for His Estate Two Children of Secretly Married Sacco Want Legacy Estimated at $700,000," 3-10-1991.
538. *Buffalo News*, "Novino Set to Testify."

VALACHI AND HIS SWEETHEART

539. JFK EXHIBIT F-629 F.B.I. surveillance of Stefano Magaddino, May 23, 1963.
540. Humphreys, *The Enforcer*, 70.
541. Ibid., 79.
542. Ibid., 103.
543. Ibid., 108.
544. Ibid.
545. Ibid.
546. Edwards and Nicaso. *Deadly Silence*, 50.
547. Ibid.
548. FBI files, "Albert Agueci," Buffalo Office, 1-31-1962.
549. Edwards and Nicaso, *Deadly Silence*, 55.
550. FBI files, "Albert Agueci," Buffalo Office, 11-29-1961.
551. *Niagara Falls Gazette*, "Feud Has Grisly Climax," 12-17-1968, 13.
552. *Buffalo News*, "Falls Woman Tells of Love Affair with Hit Man Had Decades-Long Relationship with Mobster Turned FBI Informer," 6-25-1995, C1.
553. Niagara County Historical Society, "Marie Jackson notes."
554. *Buffalo News*, "Falls Woman."
555. Niagara County Historical Society, "Marie Jackson notes."

THE UNION, THE MURDER AND THE INFORMANT

556. Ibid.
557. Laborers International Union of North America Local 210, "About Laborers Local 210," www.laborers210.org/index.cfm?fuseaction=page.display&page_id=22.

558. "Hearings before the Permanent Subcommittee on Investigations of the Committee on Government Operations. United States Senate, 88th Congress, 1st session, 1963; 2nd session, 1964, 605.

559. Ferrell, "Steve Magaddino," 92-61. www.maryferrell.org/mffweb/archive/docset/getList.do?docSetId=1447.

560. *Buffalo News*, "Fino's Double Life Recalls Father's Warning on Mob; Ron Fino: Turning His Back on a Lifetime with the Mob," 4-17-1989, 1.

561. Laborers.org, "Letter to Patrick J. Fitzgerald," www.laborers.org/Fino_Fitz_2-17-04.htm.

562. *Time*, "Building with the Buffalo Boys," 8-30-1971, 22.

563. Ron Fino, personal correspondence with author.

564. Ibid.

565. *Buffalo Evening News*, "'8 Arrest, Lost Union Control Spelled End for Magaddino," 2-27-1974.

566. *Front Page* [Hamburg, NY], "Local 210" ad, 3-29-1973, 13.

567. Ron Fino, personal correspondence with author.

568. Ibid.; Social Security Death Index.

569. *Buffalo News*, "Ex-Local 210 Official Who Aided Probe See Vindication in Deal to Reform Union," 2-19-1995, B1.

570. Ron Fino, personal correspondence with author.

571. Ibid.

572. *Buffalo News*, "Union Links 28 Members of Local 210 to Mob," 6-19-1996, B1.

573. Ron Fino, personal correspondence with author.

574. *Buffalo News*, "Union Links 28 Members."

575. *Buffalo News*, "Informant Causes Stir with Tales of Mob Activity," 8-7-1996.

576. *Buffalo News*, "Power Struggle at Local 210—Hearing Held on Trustee for Union," 3-24-1998, 1.

577. *Buffalo News*, "Local 210 Gets Clean Bill of Health—10-year, Government-enforced Cleanup of Union Ends Today with the Retirement of Its Overseer," 1-26-2006, 1.

578. Ibid.

579. Ibid.

Mysterious Murders

580. *Saturday Evening Post*, "How Mafia Killers Got Their Man," 10-31-1964.

581. *Buffalo Evening News*, "Murdered Man Identified by Startled Wife," 2-5-1923, 1.

582. *Buffalo Evening News*, "Man Murdered by Unknown Terrorist," 4-6-1925, 2.

583. *Buffalo Evening News*, "Two Theories in Murder of John Gambino," 7-14-1925, 3.

584. *Buffalo Evening News*, "Gunmen Shoot Down Soft Drinkery Owner," 8-14-1926, 1.

585. Ibid.

586. *Courier-Express*, "Sequel to Long Feud," 2-28-1929, 1.

587. Critchley, *Origin of Organized Crime*, 225.

588. [Rochester] *Democrat and Chronicle*, "Think Liquor War Behind Killing of Erie Cafe Owner," 1-28-1928, 1.

589. *Courier-Express*, "Local Vendetta Claims Life of Another Victim," 2-28-1929, 1.

590. Ibid.

591. Ibid.

592. Critchley, *Origin of Organized Crime*, 224.

593. Onewal.com, "The Good Killers, www.onewal.com.

594. *Buffalo Evening News*, "Mystery of Shooting of Luigi Lozzi Bears Marks of Feud," 5-7-1928, 3.

595. *Buffalo Evening News*, "Niagara Street Man Shot Down Returning from Cousin's Bier. Boarder Held," 5-8-1928, 3.

596. [Rochester] *Democrat and Chronicle*, "Think Liquor War Behind Killing of Erie Cafe Owner," 1-28-1928, 1.

597. *Niagara Falls Gazette*, "Solution of Murders Centers in Buffalo, Detective Declares," 1-28-1928, 1.

598. *Courier-Express*, "Local Vendetta Claims Life of Another Victim," 2-28-1929, 1.

599. *Randolph* [NY] *Register*, "Old Times in Randolph," 7-23-1928, 14.

600. *Buffalo Evening News*, "2 Aides Hunted in Palmisano Racket Killing," 2-20-1934, 1.

601. *Buffalo Evening News*, "Mafia's Hand Traced in Palmisano Death," 2-21-1934, 1, 4.

602. *Niagara Falls Gazette*, "Few Clues Revealed in Effort to Solve Death of Rome Man," 10-3-1930, 1.

603. Ibid.

604. *Niagara Falls Gazette*, "Follow Many Angles in Search for Clues to Slaying at Falls," 10-28-1930, 13.

605. Ibid.

606. *Niagara Falls Gazette*, "Arrest Four in Alleged Attempt to Extort Money from Falls Man," 9-8-1931, 26.

607. *Niagara Falls Gazette*, "Marcello Ventrigo Falls Before Volley of Gangland Bullets," 9-5-1931, 1.

608. *Courier-Express*, "Killers Speed Away, Leaving Body in Road," 9-5-1931.
609. *Buffalo Evening News*, "Brothers Put On Spot Near Their Saloon," 8-26-1933, 1.
610. *Courier-Express*, "Gunmen Kill Two Men in Connecticut Street; Man and Girl Wounded," 8-26-1933, 10.
611. *Niagara Falls Gazette*, "Buffalo Politician Is Held for Murder of Angello Porello," 1-14-1933, 1.
612. *Buffalo Evening News*, "Brothers Put On Spot."
613. Ibid.
614. *Courier-Express*, "Gunmen Kill Two Men in Connecticut Street; Man and Girl Wounded," 8-26-1933, 10.
615. Ibid.
616. Ibid,
617. *Courier-Express*, "Uncover Still in Police Raid at Jamestown," 8-30-1933, 1.
618. *Niagara Falls Gazette*, "Release Three Held in Buffalo Double Murder," 9-13-1933, 1.
619. *Buffalo Evening News*, "Buffalo Man, Gun Unfired, Found Slain," 9-5-1933, 1.
620. *Buffalo Evening News*, "Car Bombing Stirs Dual Murder Hunt," 9-28-1933, 1.
621. *Niagara Falls Gazette*, "Police Say Killer Imported for Gang Slaying in Buffalo," 4-30-1934, 1.
622. [Rochester, NY] *Democrat and Chronicle*, "Mobman Slain at Car Wheel," 8-19-1935, 7.
623. Ibid.
624. *Buffalo Evening News*, "Probe by Jurors in Gang Slaying Met by Silence," 4-7-1938, 1.
625. *Niagara Falls Gazette*, "Hold Five More Men for Questioning in Slaying of Barbera," 4-13-1938, 6.

A LESSON FROM THE MOB

626. FBI files, "Stefano Magaddino, 9-19-1963.
627. *Niagara Falls Gazette*, "Magaddino Ruled 'Domain,'" 12-16-1968, 11.
628. *Courier-Express*, "Victim of Gang Slaying Trailed by U.S. Agents," 6-9-1944, 20.
629. *Niagara Falls Gazette*, "Magaddino Ruled."
630. *Tonawanda* [NY] *Evening News*, "Sewer Searched for Gambling Figure's Body," 12-8-1949, 1.

631. *Niagara Falls Gazette*, "'The Baron Is Dead' Mysterious Caller Tells Police Chief," 8-22-1953, 1.

632. *Tonawanda News*, "Police Net Out for Brink's Holdup Man," 8-4-1955, 1.

633. *Buffalo Evening News*, "Cleveland 'Hood' Believed Slayer of Escaped Convict," 3-14-1957, 1.

634. *Niagara Falls Gazette*, "Mother of Two Aquinos Has Ideas on Murders," 3-15-1959, 6D.

635. FBI files, "Fred Randaccio."

636. *Courier-Express*, "Aquino Slaying Tied to Bookmaking Feud," 9-15-1958, 1.

637. *Niagara Falls Gazette*, "Two Men Held in Gun-Whipping of Buffalo Pair," 10-22-1952, 44.

638. *Niagara Falls Gazette*, "Magaddino Ruled 'Domain,'" 12-16-1968, 11.

639. *Niagara Falls Gazette*, "Mother of Two."

640. *Niagara Falls Gazette*, "Slain Man's Brother Is Sought," 9-16-1958, 6.

641. *Courier-Express*, "Gambling Probed as Gang Murder Clue," 9-13-1958.

642. *Courier-Express*, "Disfigured Body Is Found in Field," 9-18-1958.

643. Ibid.

644. *Niagara Falls Gazette*, "Phone List Found on One of Victims of Buffalo Mobsters," 9-21-1958, 4-A.

645. *Tonawanda* [NY] *News*, "3 Slayings Turn Spotlight on Organized Crime in Area," 10-20-1958, 14.

646. *Niagara Falls Gazette*, "Mother of Two."

647. *Tonawanda* [NY] *News*, "Falls Man Is Found Slain in Car," 10-14-1958, 1.

648. *Niagara Falls Gazette*, "New Clue Sought Linking DeLuca to Slain Aquinos," 10-16-1958, 1.

649. *Tonawanda* [NY] *News*, "Police Link DeLuca Murder and Shakedown of Taverns," 10-17-1958, 12.

650. *Niagara Falls Gazette*, "Man Quizzed in Three Gang Deaths Missing," 3-8-1959.

651. Ibid.

652. *Courier-Express*, "Slain Man's Appointment List Checked," 9-24-1965, 1.

653. *Buffalo Evening News*, "2 Buffalo Men Found Slain," 8-12-1961.

654. *Courier-Express*, "Solution of Gang Killings Hampered by Code of Silence," 6-20-1976, 21.

655. *Buffalo Evening News*, "Friend of Slain Pair Reappears; Had Been Missing for 6 days," 8-14-1961.

656. *Buffalo Evening News*, "Three Key Figures Being Re-Questioned in Gang Murder Probe," 8-17-1961.

657. *Titusville* [PA] *Herald*, "Victim Is Indicted in Buffalo Assault," 9-11-1962, 1.

658. *Tonawanda* [NY] *News*, "Assault Trial of Santangelo Starts Monday," 3-2-1963, 10.

659. *Buffalo Evening News*, "Politano Found Guilty of One Perjury Count," 9-18-1965.

660. *Tonawanda* [NY] *News*, "Location of Gangland Slaying Being Probed in Investigation," 9-24-1965, 1.

661. *Courier-Express*, "Body Brutally Beaten, Bound," 9-23-1965, 1.

662. Buffalo Police Then and Now, "Richard Battaglia," www.bpdthenandnow.com/richardbattaglia.html.

663. *Courier-Express*, "2 Sought; 2 More Deny Charges in Mob Killings," 4-29-1977, 1.

664. *Courier-Express*, "Admissible Data for Indictments," 6-9-1977, 1.

665. *Tonawanda* [NY] *News*, "Police Seeking Car Involved in Murder," 2-11-1972, 8.

666. *Courier-Express*, "3 Said Responsible for 2nd Mob 'Hit,'" 11-24-1977, 1.

667. *Courier-Express*, "'Gangland Slaying' Victim Identified," 2-19-1976, 1.

668. *Buffalo News*, "Cheektowaga Man Tied to 2 Murders; Suspect Awaits Trial in Drug Case," 10-29-1994, C1.

669. Ibid.

670. *Tonawanda* [NY] *News*, "Police Arrest Suspect in Old Murder Case," 7-3-1975, 8.

671. *Courier-Express*, "Details of Mob-Style Killings Revealed," 1-5-1979, 1.

672. *Courier-Express*, "Solution of Gang Killings Hampered by Code of Silence," 6-20-1976, 21.

673. *Courier-Express*, "Reingold's Body Found in Auto; Tied, Shot in Head," 5-30-1976, 1.

674. *Niagara Falls Gazette*, "3 Youths Questioned in Breakin," 2-28-1964, 1.

675. *Buffalo Evening News*, "Motive in Piccolo Slaying Eludes Longtime Partner," 4-21-1979, B1.

676. Ibid.

677. *Buffalo News*, "15 Deaths, 1 Disappearance Linked to Mob Since 1974; Arrests Were Made in Only 1 Case," 5-7-1989, A17.

678. *Buffalo News*, "Two Brothers Charged with Tax Evasion—Accused of Concealing Earnings in Marketing Hair-Growth Product," 4-24-1990, B5.

679. *Buffalo News*, "Police Believe Monaco Ran Afoul of Mob," 4-21-1981, B1.

680. *Buffalo News*, "Man Slain by Gunman Was Held in '77 Sting," 2-3-1985, 1.

681. *Buffalo News*, "Drug War Indicated in Slaying," 2-4-1985, C5.

682. Ibid.

683. *Buffalo News*, "Did Drug Wars Cost Life of Man Who Lived in Fast Lane?" 10-5-1986, B1.

WHERE TO FIND EVERYTHING

684. FBI files, "Stefano Magaddino," 92-61; *Criminal Intelligence Digest*, March 4, 1964.

685. Cuban Information Archives, "Gangsters with Florida Addresses:"Top One Hundred," 1959. Cuban-exile.com/doc_326-350/doc347.html.

686. Ibid.

687. Hunt and Tona, "Men of Montedoro," 32.

688. Ibid.

689. [Tonawanda] *Evening News*, "Speeder Leaves Pair of 'Comps' for Policemen," 4-28-1923, 1.

690. Hunt and Tona, "Men of Montedoro," 32.

SELECTED BIBLIOGRAPHY

691. JFK Exhibit F-629, FBI surveillance of Stefano Magaddino, May 23, 1963.

SELECTED BIBLIOGRAPHY

We are in a bad situation in Cosa Nostra. When Profaci died, the Borgata [family] *broke up.*[691]
—*Stefano Magaddino*

Bonanno, Bill. *Bound by Honor: A Mafioso's Story.* New York: St. Martin's Paperback, 2000.
———. *The Last Testament of Bill Bonanno: The Final Secrets of a Life in the Mafia.* New York: HarperCollins, 2011.
Bonanno, Joseph. *A Man of Honor.* New York: Simon and Schuster, 1983.
Capeci, Jerry. *The Complete Idiot's Guide to the Mafia.* 2nd ed. New York: Alpha Books, 2004.
Chiocca, Olindo Romeo. *Mobsters and Thugs: Quotes from the Underworld.* N.p.: Guernica, 2000.
Critchley, David. *The Origin of Organized Crime in America: The New York City Mafia, 1891–1931.* New York: Routledge, 2009.
Dash, Mike. *The First Family: Terror, Extortion, Revenge, Murder and the Birth of the American Mafia.* New York: Random House, 2009.
Demaris, Ovid. *The Last Mafioso.* New York: Times Books, 1981.
Dubro, James. *Mob Rule: Inside the Canadian Mafia.* Ontario: Totem Books, 1986.
Dubro, James, and Robin Rowland. *King of the Mob: Rocco Perri and the Women Who Ran His Rackets.* Canada: Viking, 1987.
Earley, Pete, and Gerald Shur. *Witsec: Inside the Federal Witness Protection Program.* New York: Bantam, 2002.
Edwards, Peter, and Antonio Nicaso. *Deadly Silence: Canadian Mafia Murders.* Toronto: Macmillan, 1993.

Ferrara, Eric. *Manhattan Mafia Guide.* Charleston, SC: The History Press, 2011.

Griffin, Joe. *Mob Nemesis: How the FBI Crippled Organized Crime.* Amherst, NY: Prometheus Books, 2002.

Humphreys, Adrian. *The Enforcer: Johnny Pops Papalia, a Life and Death in the Mafia.* Toronto: HarperCollins, 2002.

Kurek, Albert S. *The Troopers Are Coming: New York State Troopers 1917–1943.* New York: Rooftop Publishing, 2007.

Lait, Jack, and Lee Mortimer. *Chicago Confidential.* New York: Crown, 1951.

Lay, Shawn. *Hooded Knights on the Niagara: The Ku Klux Klan in Buffalo, New York.* New York: New York University Press, 1995.

Mafia: The Government's Secret File on Organized Crime. New York: HarperCollins, 2007.

Mass, Peter. *Underboss.* New York: HarperCollins, 1997.

———. *The Valachi Papers.* New York: Bantam, 1972.

McShane, Thomas, with Dary Matera. *Stolen Masterpiece Tracker.* Fort Lee, NJ: Barricade Books, 2006.

Mollenhoff, Clark R. *Strike Force: Organized Crime and the Government.* Upper Saddle River, NJ: Prentice-Hall, 1972.

Morello, Celeste A. *Before Bruno: Book 1—1880–1931.* N.p., 1999.

Mottram, James. *Public Enemies: The Gangster Movie A–Z.* London: B.T. Batsford, 1999.

Nicasio, Antonio. *Rocco Perri: The Story of Canada's Most Notorious Bootlegger.* Ontario: Wiley, 2004.

Pistone, Joseph D., with Richard Woodley. *Donnie Brasco: My Undercover Life, I: The Mafia.* New York: New American Library, 1987.

Porello, Rick. *To Kill the Irishman.* Novelty, OH: Next Hat Press, 2006.

Poulsen, Ellen. *Don't Call Us Molls: Women of the John Dillinger Gang.* Oakland Gardens, NY: Clinton Cook Publishing Corp., 2002.

Raab, Selwyn. *Five Families: The Rise, Decline & Resurgence of America's Most Powerful Mafia Empire.* New York: St. Martins Press, 2005.

Reid, Ed. *The Grim Reapers.* New York: Bantam, 1970.

Rizzo, Michael F. *They Call Me Korney.* Createspace, 2009

———. *Through the Mayors' Eyes.* Raleigh, NC: Lulu, 2005.

Sifakis, Carl. *The Mafia Encyclopedia.* 2nd ed. New York: Checkmark Books, 1999.

Talese, Gay. *Honor Thy Father.* New York: Ivy Books, 1992.

Waller, Leslie. *Hide in Plain Sight.* New York: Dell, 1976.

Yans-McLaughlin, Virginia. *Family and Community: Italian Immigrants in Buffalo, 1880–1930.* Chicago: University of Illinois Press, 1982.

INDEX

ABOUT THE AUTHOR

Michael Rizzo was born and raised in the suburbs of Buffalo. History was not his first love, but after purchasing an 1893 house in Buffalo, a light bulb went off in his head. He released his first book in 2005 and has not stopped since.

Other books by this author:
Buffalo's Legacy of Power and Might
They Call Me Korney: The True Story of Buffalo's Korney Gang
Nine Nine Eight: The Glory Days of Buffalo Shopping
Through the Mayors' Eyes

Visit NakedBuffalo.com for history tours in the Buffalo area and MichaelFRizzo.com for an exclusive e-book of "lost" chapters.

CPSIA information can be obtained
at www.ICGtesting.com
Printed in the USA
BVOW08*0905050318

509717BV00011B/922/P